発音できれば聞き取れる！

リスニング×スピーキングの トレーニング 演習編

Spiral Training in Listening and Speaking

高山芳樹 監修
問題執筆・英文校閲 Adam Ezard

はじめに

　『発音できれば聞き取れる！リスニング×スピーキングのトレーニング』にようこそ！　このシリーズでは，みなさんの英語の発音を「通じる英語」に改良することで，リスニング力の向上と，相手に負担感なく理解してもらえるスピーキング力の獲得を目指します。

　みなさんは英語のリスニング力を鍛えるためにどのような学習をされてきましたか。「大学入試や民間の資格・検定試験のリスニング問題集を解きまくる！」とか「英語をひたすら聞く！」という学習をされてきた方が少なくないと思います。私の身の回りでも，受験予定の大学のリスニングの過去問や資格・検定試験のリスニングの予想問題集の音声をひたすら聞いて勉強している人が少なくありません。また，現在ではオンラインで，いわゆる「生の英語」を常時聞くことができますから，そういった英語のシャワーを浴びることでリスニング力を鍛えているという人もいるかと思います。確かにリスニング力をつけるには大量の英語音声インプットに触れることが不可欠です。しかしながら，音声をただやみくもにひたすら浴びるだけでは，リスニング力を効果的に伸ばすことはできないのです。

　英語が聞き取れるようになるためには，リスニングの入り口の段階で，英語の音を正確に，かつ，すばやくキャッチできないといけません。しかし，体の中に英語の正しい音声データベースが構築されていないと，その音が英語の音声だと認識できず，キャッチし損ねるのです。そして，英語の音声データのスムーズな蓄積の障害となっているもの，それは実は私たちの母語である日本語です。自分の体に染み込んでいる日本語の影響を受けた音声の処理の仕方によって，私たちは日本語の特徴をそのまま持ち込んだゆがんだ英語発音をしてしまい，また，英語音声をそのままスムーズに体に取り込むことが難しくなってしまうのです。

　本書は，日本人にありがちなゆがんだ英語発音の原因と特徴を理解したうえで，そのゆがみを矯正するためのさまざまなトレーニングに取り組むことで，英語を正しく聞き取れる耳と，相手にとって通じやすい英語を話す口の獲得を目指します。日本語の影響を受けた発音のゆがみをなくし，リスニング力を飛躍的に向上させ，取り込んだ大量のインプットをベースに，スピーキング力の向上につなげていきましょう。道のりは長いですが，本書で紹介するリスニングとスピーキングのトレーニングをひとつひとつ丁寧にこなしていけば，飛躍的な伸びを体感できるはずです。

　本書の作成にあたってはＺ会編集部の浅野藍さん，向後祥子さん，小林ゆみ子さんに大変お世話になりました。この場を借りて御礼申し上げます。

　本書を手に取ってくださる方すべてに，本書が役に立つことを願っています。

2020 年 1 月　高山　芳樹

CONTENTS

■ 本書の構成と利用法

問題

【Lesson 1 ～ 16】

❶ Goal!
レッスンの目標を確認しましょう。

短い情報の聞き取り1（短文選択）

解答冊子 p.2／
音声はこちらから▶

Goal!
□ 短い発話を聞き、話者の意図が
きる

❷ 2次元コード
音声は，ページ上
部の2次元コード
から聞けます。

❹ Tips for Listening*
音声のスクリプトと解答を確認し
たら，解説で理解を深めましょう。

（答えとスクリ
スクリプト
The theater will be closed on Friday. ／ 映画館は金曜日はお休みだよ。その翌日に映画
Why don't we go to see the movie the ／ を見に行かない？
next day?

選択肢訳
① 話し手は映画を見に行かないだろう。
② 話し手は金曜日に映画を見た。
③ 話し手は土曜日に映画を見るだろう。
④ 話し手は木曜日に映画を見た。

【答え】③

Step1
練習問題
聞こえてくる英文の内容に最も近い意味の

❸ Step 1 練習問題*
練習問題を解きましょう。

Tips for Listening 短い情報の聞き取り1（短文選択）

　金曜日は映画館が休みだと言ったあと，その翌日（the next day）つまり土曜
日に映画を見に行こうと誘っている。Why don't we ...? は「…しましょう」と相
手を誘う表現。Let's ... で言い換えることもできる。
　短い情報の聞き取りでは、中心を
えばこの問題では、中心を
着目すればよいことを
過さないよう注意し

③ The speaker will see the movie on Saturday.

④ The speaker saw the movie on Thursday.

Training
♪音声を聞いて，空
□(1) The theater
□(2) Why don't we g

♪音声に続けて，英文
クボックス □ にチ

❺ Training*
聞き取りや発音のトレーニングをし
ましょう。
🎧 聞き取りのトレーニング
🗣 発音のトレーニング
各トレーニングのポイントは，解答
解説に掲載しています。

Step2
実戦問題
■ それぞれの問いについて，聞こえてくる英文の内容に最も近い意味のものを，
四つの選択肢（①～④）のうちから一つずつ選びなさい。
(1)

❻ Step 2 実戦問題
練習問題と同じ形式のリスニング
問題にチャレンジします。実戦問
題は大学入学共通テストや民間の
英語資格・検定試験で出題される
形式の問題を出題しています。

Training
♪音声を聞いて，空所に入る語を書きましょう。
□(1) _____ _____ the window?
□(2) I _____ any clouds.
□(3) What happened to _____ _____, Ken?
□(4) So, _____ do I press?

❼ Training*
しょう。発音できたら，チェッ

Step3
Let's Speak!
■ カッコ内の語句を並べ替えて文を完成させましょう。
□(1) (close / could / you) the window? I can't hear the TV.
□(2) The forecast in the morning was for rain, but I (any / can't / see) clouds.
□(3) What happened to ① (new / smartphone / your), Ken? ② (broken / is / screen /
the).

(3)
① The speaker got a new smartphone.
② The smartphone is old and damaged.
③ The old smartphone has a new screen.
④ Ken's new smartphone is already damaged.

the). Smile! So,

❽ Step 3 Let's Speak! *
1：整序英作文問題で **Step 2
Training** で聞いた音声を復習し
ます。2：完成させた英文を聞
いて，自分でも声に出してスピー
キング練習をしましょう。

てみましょう。発音
しょう。

(4)
① The speaker is operating an elevator.
② The speaker is taking a photo of someone.
③ The speaker is sending an email.
④ The speaker is choosing a button.

【Lesson 17 ～ 20】まとめの問題

各回4～5問構成で，**Lesson 16** までに取り組んださまざまな形式の問題を組み合
わせた問題で力をはかります。※ **Lesson 16** までの*部分はありません。

解答解説

② 2次元コード
ここから音声にアクセスして聞き直してみましょう。

① Training
Step1 Training の答えと発音のポイントを確認しましょう。●や⌒で音の強弱やイントネーションを表しています。

⑤ Training
Step2 Training の答えと発音のポイントを確認しましょう。

③ 音声ポイント
各問題の音声ポイントを確認しましょう。

⑥ Step3 Let's Speak! の答え。

④ スクリプト，和訳，解説
スクリプト内で「音声ポイント」に関連する箇所を青マーカー，解答につながる箇所を青下線で示しています。

⑦ Words & Expressions
まとめて覚えたい語を掲載しています。

■音声について

本書には，問題演習およびトレーニング用の音声が付属しています。映像および音声は，それぞれ専用 web ページよりご利用ください。

音声：左記の2次元コード，または下記 URL よりご利用ください。

https://service.zkai.co.jp/books/zbooks_data/dlstream?c=2668

Sound Focus のまとめ

　ここからは，本書の姉妹本『リスニング×スピーキングのトレーニング　基礎編』で紹介されている，リスニング，スピーキングに効く15の音声ポイント（Sound Focus）を解説します。基礎編に取り組んだことがない人は，Lesson 1 からの問題に取り組む前に，下記の15のポイントをぜひ確認しておきましょう。各ポイントに発音トレーニング映像が付属していますので，映像を見ながらポイントを確認し，発音練習をしてみましょう。映像は，各ポイントの2次元コード，または下記のURLからアクセスできます。

https://www.zkai.co.jp/books/lstraining_v

1. 音のかたまりの数に注意！

映像

　英語と日本語では，音のかたまりの数が異なります。日本語の「サラダ」は「サ・ラ・ダ」と3つのかたまりとして発音されますが，英語の salad は sal-ad と2つのかたまりとして発音されるのです。このように，日本語と英語では多くの場合，音のかたまりの数が異なるので，注意が必要です。指を1本，2本と順に立てながら sal-ad と発音したり，ペンで机を2回叩くのに合わせて sal-ad と発音するなど，各単語の「音のかたまりの数」を，体を使って覚えていきましょう。

2. 音の強弱に注意！

映像

　日本語と英語の違いは，音のかたまりの数だけではありません。英語には，「強く・高く・長く・はっきりと」発音するところ（●で表します）と，「弱く・低く・短く・あいまいに」発音するところ（•で表します）があり，このようなメリハリをつけた発音の仕方が身についていないと，聞き取りも難しくなります。また，VOL-ley-ball（●••）や BAS-ket-ball（●••）のように，中程度の強さを持つ音のかたまり（●）を含む単語もあります。日本人は弱い発音が特に苦手なので，一番小さな•のところは十分に口元の筋肉をゆるめて，力を抜いて発音できるように練習しましょう。

3. 強弱の位置に注意！

　bananaも potatoも，音のかたまりの数は日本語・英語ともに３つで同じですが，発音は大きく異なります。英語では，ba-NAN-a（●●●），po-TA-to（●●●）のように，２つ目の音のかたまりを「強く・高く・長く・はっきりと」発音します。同様に，hotelは ho-TEL（●●），violinは vi-o-LIN（●●●）のように発音するので，やはりカタカナの発音とかなり異なります。

4. 余分な音に注意！

　日本語の「かきくけこ」をローマ字で見ると ka, ki, ku, ke, koと「子音k+母音あいうえお」の組み合わせになっています。このように，日本語はほとんどが「子音＋母音」の組み合わせから成っているため，bagや coatのように英単語の語尾が子音で終わっていても，「bagう」「coatお」のように，余分な「う」や「お」を入れてしまいがちなので，注意しましょう。

5. 子音のかたまりに注意！

　英語には，dress, train, streetのように，子音が連続して並ぶ「子音結合」を持つ単語がたくさんあります。「dお ress」「tお rain」「sうtお reet」のような発音にならないよう，dr, tr, strといった子音結合のところは，１つの音のように一気に発音してみるとよいでしょう。

6. つながる音に注意！

　take outという表現は，takeの語末の子音 /k/ が，outの最初の /au/（アウ）という母音と自然にくっついて /kau/（カウ）と発音されます。同様に，Can itも canの語末の子音 /n/ と itの最初の母音 /ɪ/ がつながって /nɪ/（ニ）となり，全体で「キャニット」のように発音されます。英文を音読する時は，音のつながりを意識して練習するようにしましょう。

7. 変身する音に注意！

　didのように子音 /d/ で終わる単語の直後に youの冒頭の子音 /j/ が出会うと，２つの音が影響し合い，/d/ ＋ /j/（ドゥ＋ユ）が /dʒ/（ヂュ）という音に変身するということがよくあります。「はじめまして」のNice to meet you. の meet you（ミートゥユー）で「ミーチュー」のように音が変身するのも，同様の現象です。

8. 脱落する音に注意！

映像

英語には next door の /t/ と /d/ のように，お互いに似た音が隣り合わせになると，1 つ目の音を落として発音する「音の脱落」という現象が起こることがあります。例えば，next door や a hot day は，/t/ の音を脱落して nex(t) door, a ho(t) day のように発音されます。また，hot tea や a good day のように同じ子音が隣り合わせになる場合も，いちいち同じ音を繰り返さずに省エネで発音するため「音の脱落」が起こり，ho(t) tea, a goo(d) day のようになります。

9. 文の強弱リズムに注意！

映像

Do you live in a house or an apartment? の文中の単語は，目で見ると簡単なものばかりですが，live, house, apartment が「強く・高く・長く・はっきりと」発音されるのに対し，Do, you, in, a, or, an は「弱く・低く・短く・あいまいに」発音されるので，文全体が聞き取れなかった人もいるかと思います。一般的に，名詞，動詞（be 動詞は除く），形容詞，副詞，what, when, where, which, why, how のような疑問詞，「これ」「それ」を意味する代名詞の this や that，否定を表す not のような語は強く発音しますが，be 動詞や助動詞，冠詞，前置詞，接続詞などの語は弱く発音します。

10. 文のイントネーションに注意！

映像

You play soccer. と You play soccer? を聞き比べるとはっきりわかると思いますが，前者が文の最後で音程が下がる「下げ調子」で発音されるのに対し，後者は「上げ調子」で発音されます。You play soccer. のような普通の文や Play soccer. のような命令文は下げ調子のイントネーションとなります。一方，Do you play soccer? のような Yes / No 疑問文は上げ調子ですが，what や when などの疑問詞を使った疑問文は，アメリカ英語では，通常は下げ調子のイントネーションとなるので要注意です。

11. 「ウ」に聞こえる L の音に注意！

映像

　カタカナでよく見かける「ミラクル」ですが，英語の miracle の cle は「クル」ではなく「コゥ」のように発音されます。同様に bottle についても，tle は「トォゥ」のような発音になります。実は，英語のLには，New Zealand, play のような「明るいL」と，miracle, final のように「暗いL」の2種類の発音があるのです。暗いL は「ゥ」のような発音になり，日本語のラ行とは異なるので注意が必要です。

12. ラ行に聞こえる T の音に注意！

映像

　better や water の /t/ は「ベラー」「ゥワラー」のように，日本語のラ行に近い音に変化する場合があります。これは，アメリカ英語でよく起こる現象です。Get on the bus. の get on の部分が「ゲロン」，Not at all. が「ナラローゥ」と発音されるのも，同じ現象です。

13. 母音のかたまりに注意！

映像

　bowl の ow の部分は「オ」を強く長めに発音し，すぐに口を丸めて，なめらかに小さい「ゥ」を添えて発音してみましょう。ball の a の部分の「オー」のようにやや長めに発音する音とは異なるので，注意する必要があります。つづりは違いますが，goal や coat, home や only もこの「オゥ」の音です。同様に，game や make の a は「エー」ではなく「エィ」のような母音のかたまりです。

14. 紛らわしい子音に注意！

映像

　英語の sheet も seat もカタカナでは「シート」と表記されますが，英語発音では冒頭の子音 sh と s の音がまったく異なります。sea を発音しようとして she と発音する人も多いのですが，これらは別の単語なので，しっかりと区別して発音することが重要です。「sh と s」のように日本人にとって紛らわしい子音のペアとしては，他にも「v と b」や「th と s」があります。vote（投票する）を boat（ボート），think（考える）を sink（沈む）のように発音しないように注意しましょう。また，英語の「l」や「r」の音が日本語のラ行音にならないようにも気をつけましょう。lock（鍵）と rock（岩），collect（集める）と correct（正す）のペアを正確に発音できるようになれば，これらの子音の聞き分けも楽になります。

紛らわしい子音の大まかな発音方法は以下の通りです。実際の発音をよく聞き，何度も真似してみることが重要です。

- seat：舌先を上の歯茎に近づけ，その隙間から空気を出す。
- sheet：唇を丸め，舌全体を上あごに近づけて「シュー」と空気を出す。
- think：舌先を上の前歯の裏に軽く当て，その隙間から空気を出す。

- breeze：seat と同様に，舌先を上の歯茎に近づけ，その隙間から空気を出しながら，声を出す。
- breathe：think と同様に，舌先を上の前歯の裏に軽く当て，その隙間から空気を出しながら，声を出す。

- vote：上の前歯に下唇を軽く当て，その隙間から空気を出しながら，声を出す。
- boat：「バ行」の子音に近いが，唇をしっかり閉じて発音する。

- lock：舌先を尖らせて上の歯の付け根につけ，舌の両側から声を出す。
- rock：舌先を口の中で浮かせて声を出す。唇を少し丸めるとよい。

15. 紛らわしい母音に注意！

映像

　特に日本人に難しいのは，duck の /ʌ/ と dog の /ɑː/ という日本語の「あ」の音に似た母音の聞き分けです。/ʌ/ は口を大きく開けすぎず，何かに驚いたように，のどの奥で短めに「アッ」と発音します。一方，/ɑː/ は口を大きく縦に開いて，口の奥から発する「ア」です。「あ」の音に似た母音としてはもう1つ angry の /æ/ もありますが，この音は口元を横に引いて「エァ」のように発音します。同様に，bath と birth や，sit と seat の区別にも注意が必要です。これらの紛らわしい母音を区別して発音し分けられると，聞き分けもできるようになるので，発音練習を十分に行いましょう。

MEMO

Lesson 1
短い情報の聞き取り1（短文選択）

解答冊子 p.2 ／
音声はこちらから➡

Goal!
□ 短い発話を聞き，話者の意図や状況を把握することがで
きる

Step1
練習問題

聞こえてくる英文の内容に最も近い意味のものを，四つの選択肢（①～④）のうちか
ら一つ選びなさい。

① The speaker is not going to see a movie.

② The speaker saw the movie on Friday.

③ The speaker will see the movie on Saturday.

④ The speaker saw the movie on Thursday.

答えとスクリプト

スクリプト	和訳
The theater will be closed on Friday. Why don't we go to see the movie the next day?	映画館は金曜日はお休みだよ。その翌日に映画を見に行かない？

選択肢訳

① 話し手は映画を見に行かないだろう。

② 話し手は金曜日に映画を見た。

③ 話し手は土曜日に映画を見るだろう。

④ 話し手は木曜日に映画を見た。

答え ③

🔊 Tips for Listening 短い情報の聞き取り1 （短文選択）

　金曜日は映画館が休みだと言ったあと，その翌日（the next day）つまり土曜日に映画を見に行こうと誘っている。Why don't we ...? は「…しましょう」と相手を誘う表現。Let's ... で言い換えることもできる。

　短い情報の聞き取りでは，内容を事前に予測できると聞き取りが楽になる。例えばこの問題では，選択肢から映画を「見ない／見るだろう／見た」，「曜日」に着目すればよいことがわかる。英文の時制，曜日などポイントとなる情報を聞き逃さないよう注意しよう。

Training

🎧 音声を聞いて，空所に入る語を書きましょう。

☐ (1) The theater ＿＿＿＿＿ ＿＿＿＿＿ ＿＿＿＿＿ on Friday.

☐ (2) Why don't we go to see the movie ＿＿＿＿＿ ＿＿＿＿＿ ＿＿＿＿＿ ?

🔊 音声に続けて，英文を2回ずつ声に出して読みましょう。発音できたら，チェックボックス（☐）にチェック（✓）を入れましょう。

Step2 実戦問題

1 それぞれの問いについて，聞こえてくる英文の内容に最も近い意味のものを，四つの選択肢 (①~④) のうちから一つずつ選びなさい。

(1)

① There is a loud noise outside.

② The room is getting cold.

③ The TV is not working.

④ The windows are all closed.

(2)

① The forecast was wrong.

② The speaker thinks it will rain.

③ It was cloudy this morning.

④ The sky is getting dark.

(3)

① The speaker got a new smartphone.

② The smartphone is old and damaged.

③ The old smartphone has a new screen.

④ Ken's new smartphone is already damaged.

(4)

① The speaker is operating an elevator.

② The speaker is taking a photo of someone.

③ The speaker is sending an email.

④ The speaker is choosing a button.

Training

🎧 音声を聞いて，空所に入る語を書きましょう。

☐ (1) _____ _____ _____ the window?

☐ (2) I _____ _____ any clouds.

☐ (3) What happened to _____ _____ _____, Ken?

☐ (4) So, _____ _____ do I press?

🗣 音声に続けて，英文を2回ずつ声に出して読みましょう。発音できたら，チェックボックス（☐）にチェック（✓）を入れましょう。

Step 3
Let's Speak!

1 カッコ内の語句を並べ替えて文を完成させましょう。

☐ (1) (close / could / you) the window? I can't hear the TV.

☐ (2) The forecast in the morning was for rain, but I (any / can't / see) clouds.

☐ (3) What happened to ① (new / smartphone / your), Ken? ② (broken / is / screen / the).

☐ (4) OK. You look perfect ① (front / in / monument / of / the). Smile! So, ② (button / which) do I press?

2 音声を聞いて，発話者になったつもりで**1**の全文を音読してみましょう。発音できたら，チェックボックス（☐）にチェック（✓）を入れましょう。

Lesson 2
短い情報の聞き取り2（ビジュアル）

解答冊子 p.5／
音声はこちらから➡

Goal!

☐ 短い発話を聞き，身の回りの事柄についての状況を把握
　することができる

Step1
練習問題

聞こえてくる英文の内容に最も近い絵を，四つの選択肢（①〜④）のうちから一つ選
びなさい。

①

| | | library | post office | |

②

| | | post office | library | |

③

| | | post office |
| | library | |

④

| | post office | |
| | library | |

答えとスクリプト

スクリプト	和訳
If you take the second left, the post office is across from the library.	2番目の角を左に曲がれば，郵便局は図書館の向かいです。

答え ④

🔊 Tips for Listening　短い情報の聞き取り2（ビジュアル）

2番目の角を左折し，図書館の向かいに目的地がある地図を選択する。④が正解。

放送が流れる前に，地図の中で目印になる建物の位置を確認し，放送中は，曲がる交差点の位置，進行方向，各建物の位置関係を聞き逃さないようにしよう。

take the second left は turn left at the second corner と同意。単に「左折する」は take a left。

Training

🎧 音声を聞いて，空所に入る語を書きましょう。

□(1) If you take the _____ _____ , the post office is _____ _____ the library.

🗣 音声に続けて，英文を2回ずつ声に出して読みましょう。発音できたら，チェックボックス（□）にチェック（✓）を入れましょう。

実戦問題

1 それぞれの問いについて，聞こえてくる英文の内容に最も近い絵を，四つの選択肢（①〜④）のうちから一つずつ選びなさい。

(1)

①

```
                                    ×
  ┌─────────────────────────┐
  │ FILE40.17               │
  └─────────────────────────┘

                         OK   Cancel
```

②

```
                                    ×
  ┌─────────────────────────┐
  │ File40.17               │
  └─────────────────────────┘

                         OK   Cancel
```

③

```
                                    ×
  ┌─────────────────────────┐
  │ File14.70               │
  └─────────────────────────┘

                         OK   Cancel
```

④

```
                                    ×
  ┌─────────────────────────┐
  │ FILE14.70               │
  └─────────────────────────┘

                         OK   Cancel
```

(2)

①

②

③

④

(3)

①

②

③

④

(4)

①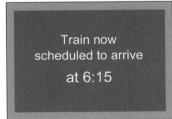

Train now
scheduled to arrive
at 6:15

②

Train now
scheduled to arrive
at 6:05

③

Train now
scheduled to arrive
at 6:10

④

Train now
scheduled to arrive
at 6:25

Training

🎧 音声を聞いて，空所に入る語を書きましょう。

☐(1) The password is capital F, then i, l and e in small letters, _____

_____ _____.

☐(2) It's not raining _____ but the weather forecast says it may start

_____ _____.

☐(3) I introduced John to Lisa for the first time and _____ _____ _____.

☐(4) The train _____ _____ has been updated. The 6:15 express has

been delayed by ten minutes.

🔊 音声に続けて，英文を2回ずつ声に出して読みましょう。発音できたら，チェックボックス（☐）にチェック（✓）を入れましょう。

*Step*3

Let's Speak!

1 カッコ内の語句を並べ替えて文を完成させましょう。

☐(1) The password is capital F, (and / e / i / in / letters / small / then / l /,), 40 dot 17.

☐(2) It's not raining now but the weather forecast says (it / later / may / on / start).

☐(3) I introduced John to Lisa for the first time and (hands / shook / they).

☐(4) The train ① (been / has / information / status / updated). The 6:15 express

has been ② (by / delayed / minutes / ten).

2 音声を聞いて，**1**の全文を音読してみましょう。発音できたら，チェックボックス（☐）にチェック（✓）を入れましょう。

Lesson 3
短い対話の聞き取り1（短文選択）

解答冊子 p.8 ／
音声はこちらから➡

Goal!
☐ 短い対話を聞き，身の回りの事柄についての概要や要点
を把握することができる

Step1
練習問題

対話を聞き，問いの答えとして最も適切なものを，四つの選択肢（①〜④）のうちか
ら一つ選びなさい。（問いの英文は書かれています。）

女性に誘われた男性が，予定について話しています。

What day is it today?
① Wednesday
② Thursday
③ Friday
④ Saturday

スクリプト	和訳
W: Do you want to go for coffee?	女性：コーヒーを飲みに行きたくない？
M: I'd love to, but I have to go to the library. My books should be returned by Friday.	男性：そうしたいけど，図書館へ行かなきゃならないんだ。本を金曜日までに返さないといけないから。
W: You still have two days. Why don't you take them tomorrow?	女性：まだ 2 日あるじゃない。明日持って行ったら？
M: I'm practicing for Saturday's game tomorrow and the day after.	男性：明日と明後日は土曜日の試合の練習をするんだ。

設問訳　選択肢訳

今日は何曜日か。

① 水曜日
② 木曜日
③ 金曜日
④ 土曜日

答え　①

🔊 Tips for Listening　短い対話の聞き取り 1 （短文選択）

　選択肢から曜日が問われることがわかるので，曜日や日に関する表現に特に注意して聞こう。「金曜日までに本を返す」，「まだ 2 日ある」という情報から，「今日」は金曜日の 2 日前，つまり水曜日であると判断できる。正解は①。明日，明後日（木，金）は土曜日の試合のために練習するという発言とも矛盾しない。

　短い対話の聞き取りでは，やり取りの中から必要な情報を過不足なく聞き取ることが求められる。必ず放送前に選択肢に目を通し，注目すべき情報を意識して聞くよう心がけよう。

Training

🎧 音声を聞いて，空所に入る語を書きましょう。

☐ (1) You still have ＿＿＿＿ ＿＿＿＿ .
☐ (2) I'm practicing for Saturday's game tomorrow and ＿＿＿＿ ＿＿＿＿ ＿＿＿＿ .

🔊 音声に続けて，英文を 2 回ずつ声に出して読みましょう。発音できたら，チェックボックス（☐）にチェック（✓）を入れましょう。

実戦問題

1 それぞれの問いについて，対話を聞き，問いの答えとして最も適切なものを，四つの選択肢（①～④）のうちから一つずつ選びなさい。（問いの英文は書かれています。）

(1) 土曜日の予定について相談しています。

What is the woman going to do on Saturday?

① Go to a concert and a restaurant.

② Go to the movies and a restaurant.

③ Go to the movies only.

④ Go to a restaurant only.

(2) 遊園地での予定について話しています。

What will they do on the first day at the Holiday Park?

① Take a rest and then go swimming.

② Go to the pool, then have a rest before dinner.

③ Rest until dinner, then go to the café.

④ Walk through the forest and rest later.

(3) 明日のテストの準備について話しています。

What will the man study tonight?

① History and science

② History only

③ Science only

④ History and math

(4) お店で昼食の注文をしています。

What is the woman's final order?

① Coffee and carrot cake

② Coffee, a sandwich and carrot cake

③ Coffee and a sandwich

④ Just coffee

Training

🎧 音声を聞いて，空所に入る語を書きましょう。

☐ (1) Didn't you hear? The singer _____ _____ .

☐ (2) Okay, let's go _____ _____ _____ and then go swimming.

☐ (3) I'm just going to prepare _____ _____ _____ .

☐ (4) I'm afraid it's not _____ _____ _____ for the lunch set.

🔊 音声に続けて，英文を 2 回ずつ声に出して読みましょう。発音できたら，チェックボックス（☐）にチェック（✓）を入れましょう。

Step3 Let's Speak!

1 カッコ内の語句を並べ替えて文を完成させましょう。

☐ (1)　Man：Are you still going to that concert on Saturday?

　　Woman：Didn't you hear? ① (got / sick / singer / the).

　　Man：Really? Well, are you free on that day, then? Would you like to come to the movies with us?

　　Woman：I don't feel like seeing a movie, but I'll ② (dinner / for / meet / you) after.

☐ (2)　Man：Well, how about ① (a / café / at / taking / the / rest)? We can enjoy the beautiful scenery from there.

　　Woman：Really? We can see the beautiful forest, can't we? Okay, let's go to the café and ② (go / swimming / then).

☐ (3) Woman：① (have / history / the / test / we) next week. This week is math and science.

　　Man：Those are my strongest subjects. ② (going / just / I'm / prepare / to) for next week, then go to bed early.

☐ (4) Woman：A tuna sandwich and a coffee, please.

　　Man：For just 50 cents more, you can add a dessert.

　　Woman：Okay. I'll have the carrot cake, please.

　　Man：I'm afraid it's not on the list ① (lunch / for / set / the).

　　Woman：Okay. Then, ② (extra / I'll / pay).

2　音声を聞いて，対話の登場人物になったつもりで**1**の全文を音読してみましょう。発音できたら，チェックボックス（☐）にチェック（✓）を入れましょう。

Lesson 4
短い対話の聞き取り2（ビジュアル）

解答冊子 p.12 ／
音声はこちらから➡

Goal!

□ 短い対話を聞き，正しいイラストを選ぶことができる

Step1
練習問題

対話とそれについての問いを聞き，その答えとして最も適切なものを，四つの選択肢
（①〜④）のうちから一つ選びなさい。

Where will they place the benchs?

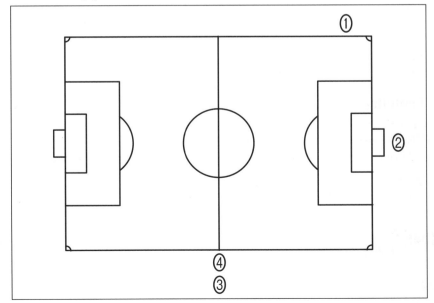

スクリプト	和訳
W: Where should we put the benches for the parents to sit?	女性：親御さんたちが座るベンチはどこに置いたらいいかな。
M: Not there. The goal is in the way. Try somewhere near the center.	男性：そこじゃないな。ゴールが邪魔だよ。中央近くのどこかを試してみよう。
W: Sure, but this is a little dangerous.	女性：そうね、でもここはちょっと危険ね。
M: You're right, let's move them back from the field a little.	男性：そうだね。ベンチをフィールドから少し後ろに移そう。

問　彼らはどこにベンチを置くか。

答え　③

🔊 Tips for Listening　短い対話の聞き取り２（ビジュアル）

　女性が最初に提案したのはゴール近くの場所で，男性はそれに反対し，中央付近を提案している。最終的には男性が最初に提案した場所から少し後ろに下がった位置に移しているから，図の③が該当する。

　短い対話の聞き取りでは，やり取りの結論や話者の主張が問われることが多い。対話の展開に沿って，相手の発言に同意しているのか，別の情報を追加しているのか，などを区別しながら聞こう。事前に選択肢に目を通し，テーマや聞き取りの要素を推測するのは鉄則。

Training

🎧 音声を聞いて，空所に入る語を書きましょう。

☐ (1) The goal is in the way. Try somewhere _____ _____ _____.

☐ (2) You're right, let's _____ _____ _____ from the field a little.

🔊 音声に続けて，英文を２回ずつ声に出して読みましょう。発音できたら，チェックボックス（☐）にチェック（✓）を入れましょう。

Step2　実戦問題

1　それぞれの問いについて，対話とそれについての問いを聞き，その答えとして最も適切なものを，四つの選択肢（①〜④）のうちから一つずつ選びなさい。

(1) When will the man drive?

| | | | ① | ② | ③ | ④ |
M	T	W	T	F	S	S
1	2	3	4	5	6	7
8	9	10	⑪	⑫	⑬	⑭
15	16	17	18	19	20	21
22	23	24	25	26	27	28
29	30	31				

Lesson 4

(2) Which bag will they buy?

(3) How much will they spend on the shopping?

MILK $3

$4

JAM $6

① $13.00　　② $14.40　　③ $15.40　　④ $16.00

(4) Where will they meet?

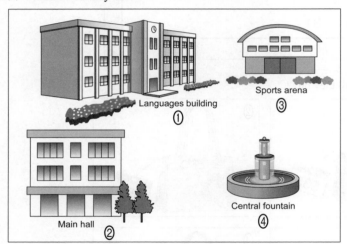

Training

🎧 音声を聞いて，空所に入る語を書きましょう。

☐ (1) _____ _____ be tired after work?

☐ (2) Which handbag do you think Mom _____ _____ ?

☐ (3) Oh, we need _____ _____ _____ milk.

☐ (4) If you come to _____ _____ , I'll walk with you to the cafeteria in the main hall.

🎵 音声に続けて，英文を2回ずつ声に出して読みましょう。発音できたら，チェックボックス（☐）にチェック（✓）を入れましょう。

Step 3 Let's Speak!

1 カッコ内の語句を並べ替えて文を完成させましょう。

☐(1) Man : I'm thinking of driving to your house on Friday.

Woman : ① (be / tired / you / won't) after work? Why not come on Saturday or Sunday?

Man : You're right, but traffic on Saturday is terrible, and Sunday is too late. ② (a / day / I'd / off / take / rather) on Friday and drive.

Woman : That sounds good.

☐(2) Woman : Which handbag ① (do / like / Mom / think / would / you)?

Man : It's Mother's Day, so let's get something nice. Those ones with a ribbon look nice.

Woman : Yeah, but the ones ② (handles / long / the / with) are over our budget.

Man : Those two with a pocket are out of fashion. Why don't we get this and give her some flowers, too?

☐(3) Man : Right! We've got bread, jam, milk, one of each. That's everything! How much will that cost?

Woman : Let's see. Oh, we need ① (milk / bottles / two / of).

Man : I almost forgot. And use this coupon. You can ② (get / off / percent / ten).

Woman : Great. Oh, no. It's expired.

☐(4) Man : Sounds good, but why don't we have lunch before?

Woman : Okay. You're in the sports arena in the morning, right? Meet me at the central fountain.

Man : ① (gets / it / busy / pretty) there after class. ② (arena / come / if / the / to / you), I'll walk with you to the cafeteria in the main hall. We can get something and eat in the student center.

2 音声を聞いて，対話の登場人物になったつもりで**1**の全文を音読してみましょう。発音できたら，チェックボックス（☐）にチェック（✓）を入れましょう。

Lesson 4

Lesson 5
短い対話の聞き取り3（複数枝問）

解答冊子 p.16／
音声はこちらから➡

Goal!
□ 短い対話を聞き，内容を理解したうえで，情報を整理することができる

Step1
練習問題

Listen to the teacher talking to a student about activities.
What activity will each person take part in?
Write one or two letters (A-D) next to each person.

People

1: Richard		
2: Joanne		
3: Meg		
4: Max		
5: Susan		
6: Nicholas		
7: A female student		

Activities

A Campfire building
B Cooking
C Mountain biking
D Kayaking

答えとスクリプト

スクリプト

M: Good morning. Well, this is our first day of summer camp. Has everyone decided which activities they want to take part in today?

W: Yes, I have a list here. Mountain biking seems to be the most popular activity today. Richard, Joanne, Max and I would like to join this ride.

M: Cool! But is it okay for Joanne? Didn't she hurt her leg yesterday?

W: That's right, but she says she will be fine. Meg, Susan and Nicholas will do the campfire building.

M: Great. That is just a morning activity. Do they have a plan for after lunch?

W: Nicholas wants to relax but the other two are doing kayaking.

M: It sounds like everyone is ready to go. Isn't there anyone for the cooking?

W: Meg was interested, but she chose to do it tomorrow so that she could get two activities in today.

M: That's no problem. Let's get everybody together first.

和訳

男性：おはよう。さあ，今日はサマーキャンプの初日です。今日参加したい活動を全員決めたかな。

女性：はい。ここに一覧表があります。マウンテンバイクが今日の一番人気みたいです。リチャードとジョアン，マックスと私がマウンテンバイクに参加したいです。

男性：いいね。でもジョアンは大丈夫かな。昨日足をけがしてなかったかい？

女性：そのとおりですが，ジョアンは大丈夫だって言っています。メグとスーザンとニコラスは火起こしをします。

男性：素晴らしい。火起こしは午前中だけの活動だね。彼らは昼食後の計画はあるの？

女性：ニコラスはのんびりしたがっていて，あとの2人はカヤックに参加します。

男性：みんな準備ができているようだね。料理に参加する人はいないの？

女性：メグは興味があったのですが，今日2つの活動ができるように，料理は明日やることにしました。

男性：それで問題なしだ。まずみんなを集めよう。

設問訳 選択肢訳

先生が1人の生徒に活動について話しているのを聞きなさい。それぞれの生徒はどの活動に参加しますか。A〜Dのうち1つまたは2つを名前の横に書きなさい。

A　火起こし
B　料理
C　マウンテンバイク
D　カヤック

🔊 Tips for Listening　短い対話の聞き取り３（複数枝問）

　次々と名前と活動名が出てくるので，放送を聞きながら表を埋めていこう。マウンテンバイクはリチャード，ジョアン，マックスと話し手の女性，メグとスーザンとニコラスは火起こしに参加する。ニコラス以外の２人（メグとスーザン）は午後はカヤックに参加する。料理に参加する人は今日はいない，というのが対話からわかる参加状況である。

　本問のように単純な情報を聞き取って整理する問題では，次々と与えられる情報を聞きながら的確にメモする能力が問われる。慣れが必要なので，苦手な人は類問で練習しておこう。

Training

🎧 音声を聞いて，空所に入る語を書きましょう。

☐(1) Mountain biking seems to be the most popular activity today. Richard, Joanne, Max and I would _____ _____ _____ this ride.

☐(2) Nicholas wants to relax but _____ _____ _____ are doing kayaking.

🔊 音声に続けて，英文を２回ずつ声に出して読みましょう。発音できたら，チェックボックス（☐）にチェック（✓）を入れましょう。

Step2
実戦問題

1　Look at the four sentences for this part. You will hear a man and a woman talking about households. Decide if each sentence is correct or incorrect.

(1) Jack sometimes helps out in the garden.

　　Yes / No

(2) They need to water the garden first.

　　Yes / No

(3) They will take some fruit today.

Yes / No

(4) Broccoli should be collected before flowers appear.

Yes / No

2 You will hear an interview with an author and documentary maker Ellen Wright. For each question, choose the best answer.

(1) How did Ellen become interested in nature?

① Her parents were scientists.

② She had holidays at a farm.

③ She loved learning about animals at school.

(2) Who first taught Ellen all about nature?

① The university

② The TV show

③ Her grandfather

(3) How did she first become a TV presenter?

① Another presenter got sick.

② She wrote a book about nature.

③ She began a TV show at her university.

(4) What is she doing now?

① She is working on her farm.

② She is making a new episode of the Wild World Show.

③ She is teaching people to save the Earth on TV.

Training

🎧 音声を聞いて，空所に入る語を書きましょう。

☐ (1) What _____ _____ _____ ?
☐ (2) It's best to pick broccoli _____ _____ _____ the flowers.
☐ (3) My grandparents lived on a farm and I _____ _____ spend every
summer holiday there, playing in the fields and the local river.
☐ (4) It was _____ _____ _____ taught me the names of all the
plants and animals.

🗣 音声に続けて，英文を2回ずつ声に出して読みましょう。発音できたら，チェックボックス (☐) にチェック (✓) を入れましょう。

Step3 Let's Speak!

1 カッコ内の語句を並べ替えて文を完成させましょう。

☐(1)　Man : Oh, I remember you telling me that you liked gardening. Sure, I'd love
to help. But, ① (new / I'm / this / to). What do we have to do?

Woman : I think we have two main jobs. First of all, we need to tidy up around
the plants and flowers. We've had quite a bit of rain, so there's no need
to water anything. But there are a lot of weeds.

Man : ② (do / mean / what / you)?

☐(2) Woman :We also need to check the broccoli to see if there are any flowers.

Man : Are flowers good?

Woman : ① (for / not / us). It's best to pick broccoli ② (see / before / the /
flowers / you). Actually, let's check that first.

Man : Fantastic. Lead the way.

☐(3)　Man : Now, we'll cover your latest TV series in a moment. But let me just
ask, what was it that really began your interest in nature?

Woman : Well, I guess I've always been fascinated by wildlife, ever since I was a
little girl. My grandparents lived on a farm and I ① (every / holiday /
spend / summer / to / used) there, playing in the fields and local river.
② (grandfather / it / my / was) who taught me the names of all the
plants and animals.

□ (4) Woman : Then the producer said to me one day that one of the hosts ① (become / had / sick). He asked me to appear on the show for a couple of episodes, and I guess they liked me.

Man : I'd say they liked you very much, as you went on to host the Wild World Show until 2010. Now, tell us a little about the new show.

Woman : It's called Our Planet. It tells the tale of how we are slowly destroying nature. We are trying to show people how they can ② (become / healthy / help / the / to / planet) again.

Lesson 5

2 音声を聞いて，対話の登場人物になったつもりで**1**の全文を音読してみましょう。発音できたら，チェックボックス（□）にチェック（✓）を入れましょう。

Lesson 6
比較・整理1（ビジュアル）

解答冊子 p.23 ／
音声はこちらから➡

Goal!

☐ 必要な情報を聞き，図表を完成させたり並べ替えること
で話し手の意図を把握することができる

Step1 練習問題

女の子が昨日の出来事について話しています。話を聞き，その内容を表したイラスト（①〜④）を，聞こえてくる順番に並べなさい。

①

②

③

④

音声

答えとスクリプト

スクリプト

Yesterday, I had a very busy morning even before the first class began. I usually walk to school, but I left my house a little late, so I decided to go by bicycle. On the way, I stopped at the store to buy a sandwich for lunch. Outside the store, I met a friend of mine and he asked me about our math homework. I looked in my bag, but it wasn't there, so I went back home quickly to get it. Luckily my father was leaving for work by car, so he dropped me off at school just in time.

和訳

昨日，私は1時間目が始まる前からとても忙しい朝を過ごしました。いつもは歩いて学校へ行きますが，家を出るのが少し遅かったので自転車で行くことにしました。途中で昼食用のサンドウィッチを買おうと店に立ち寄りました。店の外で友人に会い，彼が数学の宿題についてたずねてきました。私はカバンの中を見ましたが宿題はそこにありませんでした。だから急いで家に取りに帰りました。運よく父が車で仕事に出るところだったので，ぎりぎり間に合う時間に学校まで車で送ってくれました。

答え ②→④→①→③

🔊 Tips for Listening 比較・整理1（ビジュアル）

放送が流れる前にイラストを一通り見て出来事を確認しておくこと。エピソードが時系列で語られるので，イラストの場面が放送されるたびにイラストに番号を振っていこう。

自転車で学校へ向かう（②）→（昼食を買うために店に寄る）→店の前で友人に会う（④）→（宿題の話をする）→カバンの中の宿題を探す（①）→（家に取りに帰る）→父親に車で送ってもらう（③），という流れである。

Training

🎧音声を聞いて，空所に入る語を書きましょう。

□(1) I usually walk to school, but I left my house a little late, so I decided to go ＿＿＿＿ ＿＿＿＿ .

□(2) Luckily my father was leaving for work by car, so he ＿＿＿＿ ＿＿＿＿ ＿＿＿＿ at school just in time.

🔊音声に続けて，英文を2回ずつ声に出して読みましょう。発音できたら，チェックボックス（□）にチェック（✓）を入れましょう。

Step2
実戦問題

1 男の子が家で起こった出来事について話しています。話を聞き，その内容を表したイラスト（①～④）を，聞こえてくる順番に並べなさい。

①

②

③

④

2 遊覧船の料金についての説明を聞き，下の空欄 a ～ d にあてはめるのに最も適切なものを，選択肢のうちから一つずつ選びなさい。選択肢は 2 回以上使ってもかまいません。

	One way	Round-trip	Day Pass
Lower Deck	$25	a	b
Top Deck	c	$45	d

38

① $20　② $35　③ $45　④ $50

3 語学研修についての説明を聞き，下の空欄 a ～ c にあてはめるのに最も適切な
ものを，選択肢のうちから一つずつ選びなさい。選択肢は 2 回以上使ってもかま
いません。d にはあてはまる数字を入れなさい。

	Duration	Hours/day	Self-study time/day	Fees (early application)
Standard Course	3 weeks	b hours	an hour	$ d
Premium Course	a weeks	6 hours	c hours +	$1,350

① 2　② 3　③ 4　④ 6

Training

🎧 音声を聞いて，空所に入る語を書きましょう。

☐ (1) On Saturday, my little brother Ben and his friend Mike asked me to play a game of _____ .

☐ (2) In addition, we offer a day pass for $50 that allows you to sit anywhere on the boat and to _____ _____ _____ _____ at any of our six stops between the bridge and the park, between 9 a.m. and 6 p.m.

☐ (3) Both courses run for the _____ _____ _____ of August.

☐ (4) Standard course students are _____ _____ _____ cover the writing homework.

🔊 音声に続けて，英文を 2 回ずつ声に出して読みましょう。発音できたら，チェッ
クボックス（☐）にチェック（✓）を入れましょう。

Step 3 Let's Speak!

1 カッコ内の語句を並べ替えて文を完成させましょう。

☐ (1) On Saturday, my little brother Ben and his friend Mike asked me to ① (a / hide-and-seek / game / of / play). As I was the oldest, I decided to count first. After counting to fifty, I heard a sound in the living room. I quickly opened the living room curtains and found Mike standing there. ② (and / I / seek / started / to / Mike) Ben, but we couldn't find him anywhere. The two of us looked all over and after an hour my parents joined us. We started to get worried. I sat on my bed and thought about where he could be. Suddenly something moved and I ③ (him / found / asleep / blanket / the / under).

☐ (2) Welcome to the Royal River Cruise, the best way to visit the city. We have seats on the lower deck ① (a / for / from / journey / starting / $25 / one-way) from City Bridge to Docklands Park, or $35 round-trip. We recommend the open top deck for a better sightseeing experience, at ② (more / just / $10) than the lower deck. In addition, we offer a day pass for $50 that allows you to sit anywhere on the boat and to ③ (and / get / off / on) at any of our six stops between the bridge and the park, between 9 a.m. and 6 p.m.

☐ (3) ① (courses / run / both) for the first three weeks of August. The premium course has six hours of classes per day, split into three-hour blocks in the morning and afternoon. Students on the standard course attend the ② (sessions / morning / only). As afternoon sessions include presentation classes, students will be expected to prepare for a minimum of two hours each evening, ③ (around / including / hour / one) for the daily writing task. Standard course students are only expected to cover the writing homework.

2 音声を聞いて，説明の話者になったつもりで**1**の全文を音読してみましょう。発音できたら，チェックボックス（☐）にチェック（✓）を入れましょう。

Lesson 7
比較・整理2（複数話者）

解答冊子 p.28 ／
音声はこちらから➡

Goal!

□ 複数の情報を聞き，状況・条件に基づいて比較して適切
な候補を選ぶことができる

Step1
練習問題

四人の説明を聞き，下の条件に最も合うものを，選択肢のうちから選びなさい。

状況

あなたはスマートフォンに入れる新しいコミュニケーションのアプリを探して
います。あなたが考えている条件は以下のとおりです。

条件

A　世界中のほとんどの国で使える。

B　ビデオ通話が無料で使える。

C　少なくとも同時に4人に接続できる。

	A. Used in most countries	B. Free video calls	C. Connect with at least four people
① Message Me			
② Go Friend			
③ Talk Pal			
④ Instant			

① Message Me　　　　　　　② Go Friend

③ Talk Pal　　　　　　　　④ Instant

スクリプト

①：Message Me allows you to stay in touch instantly. This app supports video calling for groups of up to eight free of charge, as well as sending text messages. Available in Japan, Korea and Taiwan.

②：We want nothing less than to connect the world with the Go Friend service. Our trial service allows text messaging and video calling between you and another user. Upgrade to the fee-based service and create groups of ten friends.

③：Connect to friends anywhere on Earth with Talk Pal. We have been the number one free service for two years running. This app can support groups of six on one screen with incredibly clear sound and images.

④：When simple is best, Instant is the right application for users of all ages. All the functions of this easy application can be used free of charge. Our simple text-based service can be used at the touch of a button. The easiest application ever created.

和訳

①：メッセージ・ミーを使うとすぐに連絡を取り合うことができます。このアプリでは，テキストメッセージはもちろん，無料で最大8名までグループでのビデオ通話ができます。日本，韓国，台湾でご利用いただけます。

②：我々はゴー・フレンドのサービスを使って，まさに世界を結びたいと思っています。お試し版ではあなたともう1人の間でテキストメッセージとビデオ通話をお使いいただけます。有料版にアップグレードすれば10人のグループを作ることができます。

③：トーク・パルで世界中のどこでも友達とつながりましょう。我々は2年連続で無料サービスのNo.1です。このアプリでは素晴らしく明瞭な音と画像で1つの画面上で6名のグループにお使いいただけます。

④：シンプルが一番ならば，インスタントはあらゆる年齢の方にぴったりのアプリです。この易しいアプリのすべての機能が無料でお使いいただけます。我々のシンプルな文字ベースのサービスはボタンをタッチするだけで使うことができます。今まで作られた中で最も簡単なアプリです。

選択肢訳

① メッセージ・ミー　　　② ゴー・フレンド
③ トーク・パル　　　　　④ インスタント

答え ③

		A. ほとんどの国で使える	B. 無料のビデオ通話	C. 少なくとも４人がつながる
①	Message Me	×（３カ国）	○	○（８人まで）
②	Go Friend	○	△（２人まで無料）	×（無料は２人）
③	Talk Pal	○	○	○（６人まで）
④	Instant	不明	×（文字のみ）	不明

🔊 Tips for Listening　比較・整理２（複数話者）

　身近な話題に関する説明を聞いて，必要な情報を聞き取り，複数の情報を比較して条件に合うものを選ぶことが求められている。表が用意されているので，条件に関する内容はその場でメモをとること。

　本問では，有料のサービスと無料のサービスを聞き分けることも求められる。トーク・パルは anywhere on Earth（世界のどこでも），groups of six（６人グループ），free service（無料サービス），clear sound and images（鮮明な音と画像）というキーワードから条件を３つとも満たしている。

Training

🎧 音声を聞いて，空所に入る語を書きましょう。

☐ (1) Connect to friends _____ _____ _____ with Talk Pal.

☐ (2) This app can support groups of six on one screen with incredibly clear _____ _____ _____.

🔊 音声に続けて，英文を２回ずつ声に出して読みましょう。発音できたら，チェックボックス（☐）にチェック（✓）を入れましょう。

Step2　実戦問題

1　四人の説明を聞き，下の条件に最も合うものを，選択肢のうちから選びなさい。

状況

あなたは６人で夕食を食べに行くためのレストランを選んでいます。あなたが考えている条件は以下のとおりです。

条件

A　料理3品と飲み物がついて1人30ドル未満である。

B　メンバーの2人のために，ベジタリアンのための選択肢がある。

C　シーフードアレルギーに対応している。

	A. Price	B. Vegetarian option	C. Seafood allergy
① Stanley's Natural Food Deli			
② Simon's Barbecue			
③ Maria's Italian			
④ Fish Shack			

① Stanley's Natural Food Deli　　　　② Simon's Barbecue

③ Maria's Italian　　　　④ Fish Shack

2　四人の説明を聞き，下の条件に最も合うものを，選択肢のうちから選びなさい。

状況

あなたは6人で1泊の卒業旅行を計画しています。宿泊先に関して，あなたが考えている条件は以下のとおりです。

条件

A　予算は合計600ドル未満である。

B　グループ専用の浴室がある。

C　朝食がプランに含まれている。

	A. Total budget	B. Private bathroom	C. Breakfast
① Woodland Apartments			
② Woodland Executive			
③ Garden Chalets			
④ Garden Lakeside Apartments			

① Woodland Apartments   ② Woodland Executive
③ Garden Chalets   ④ Garden Lakeside Apartments

3 四人の説明を聞き，下の条件に最も合うものを，選択肢のうちから選びなさい。

状況
あなたは大学で入部する部活動について考えています。4つのクラブに興味が
ありますが，あなたが考えている条件は以下のとおりです。
条件
A　日曜日はアルバイトをしているので活動できない。
B　道具や部費に 100 ドル以上使いたくない。
C　1 年生のうちから試合に出たい。

	A. Free on Sunday	B. Equipment and fees	C. Taking part in games and competitions
① basketball club			
② soccer club			
③ karate club			
④ softball club			

① basketball club   ② soccer club
③ karate club   ④ softball club

Training

🎧 音声を聞いて，空所に入る語を書きましょう。

☐ (1) Simon's _____ _____ a vegetarian and a non-vegetarian course, each including drinks.

☐ (2) Starting with a choice of salad, we have the best range of _____ and _____ with a wonderful homemade ice cream dessert.

☐ (3) The Woodland Executive _____ _____ those who wish to have a relaxing time.

☐ (4) We hold competitions most weekends, so if you are available _____ Saturday _____ Sunday, this is the club for you.

Step3 Let's Speak!

1 カッコ内の語句を並べ替えて文を完成させましょう。

□(1) Simon's ① (a / and / Barbecue / offers / vegetarian) a non-vegetarian course, each including drinks. Either course costs $30 and includes our special pumpkin starter. You can choose steak or vegetarian curry for the main course. Desserts can be added for ② (an / $4.50 / extra / person / per).

□(2) At Maria's Italian we take pride in our traditional $28 Mediterranean course. Starting with a choice of salad, we have ① (best / range / of / pizza / the) and pasta with a wonderful homemade ice cream dessert. Drinks can be added for an extra $7 per head. Please feel free to ② (course / order / vegetarian / the), of course!

□(3) The Woodland Executive ① (those / wish / who / suite / suits) to have a relaxing time. Situated in the forest, these suites each contain a private bathroom and accommodate two to three guests. Rooms start ② (breakfast / from / night / including / $350 / per /,).

□(4) Join our new soccer club. We hold competitions most weekends, so if ① (are / available / you / either / or / Saturday / Sunday), this is the club for you. We believe in active training, so ② (all / in / matches / members / new / participate) from early on. The university covers our court costs; students just need to cover transport to away games.

2 音声を聞いて，説明する人になったつもりで**1**の全文を音読してみましょう。発音できたら，チェックボックス（□）にチェック（✓）を入れましょう。

46

Goal!

□ 対話や案内放送を聞き，必要な情報をまとめ，書くこと
ができる

Step1

練習問題

You will hear a woman asking for information about performances.

Listen and fill in the missing information in the blanks (1) - (5).

(1) Day of the performance：〔   〕
(2) Number of performances on that day：〔   〕
(3) This group will see the performance at _____.
(4) The rows they will sit in：〔   〕
(5) Total cost of the tickets, including booking fees：〔   〕

M：Hello. This is the Rose Theater, how may I help you?

W：Hi. I'd like to book four tickets for Saturday the 12th, please. Could you tell me the performance times?

M：Sure. We have an afternoon performance at one thirty, an early evening performance at five and a late performance from seven thirty, which has already sold out.

W：That's fine. We'd like tickets for the early evening show, please.

M：Sure. There are only a few seats left, so I'm afraid I can't seat you all together. Are there any children in the party?

W：Yes, two.

M：Okay, I can find you two seats together in row C and two in row E. Children are $12 and adults $20. Would you like to pay by credit card?

W：Yes, please.

M：Please be aware that there is a booking fee of $1 per ticket. Also, please be aware that there is a cancellation charge of 50% of the price of the tickets. Do you wish me to go ahead?

W：Yes, that's fine.

M：Thank you. May I have your credit card number, please?

男性：こんにちは。こちらはローズ劇場です。ご用件をどうぞ。

女性：こんにちは。12日土曜日のチケットを4枚予約したいのですが。公演時間を教えてくれますか。

男性：もちろんです。午後の公演は1時半，夜の早い部は5時，遅い部は7時半からです。7時半の公演はすでに売り切れです。

女性：よかった。夜の早い部のチケットをお願いします。

男性：かしこまりました。お席の残りがわずかなため，申し訳ありませんがまとまったお席がありません。ご同伴の方にお子様はいらっしゃいますか。

女性：ええ，2名です。

男性：わかりました。C列に2席，E列に2席ご用意できます。お子様は12ドル，大人は20ドルです。クレジットカードでのお支払いですか。

女性：ええ，お願いします。

男性：チケットごとに1ドルの手数料がかかることをご承知おきください。また，キャンセル料はチケット代の50％かかることもご承知おきください。このまま進めてよろしいですか。

女性：ええ，けっこうです。

男性：ありがとうございます。では，クレジットカード番号をお伺いしてよろしいですか。

設問訳 女性が公演の情報をたずねる音声が流れます。
聞いて，抜けている情報(1)〜(5)を記入しなさい。

(1) 公演の曜日 〔　　　　〕

(2) その日の公演数 〔　　　　〕

(3) このグループは＿＿＿＿＿＿＿＿の公演を見るだろう。

(4) 彼らが座る席の列 〔　　　　〕

(5) 予約手数料も含めたチケット代の合計 〔　　　　〕

答え (1) Saturday　(2) three　(3) five (o'clock)　(4) C and E　(5) $ 68

📣 Tips for Listening　書き取り1（メモ空所補充）

　day は「曜日」を表すのがふつう。「日付」は date。公演数は午後に1回，夜は早い部，遅い部の2回だから1日では計3回。女性は夜の早い部のチケットを求めており，その開始時間は直前の男性の説明から5時である。座席はC列とE列に2席ずつである。チケット代は子ども12ドル×2枚，大人20ドル×2枚，手数料1ドル×4枚で，合計68ドルになる。

　短い対話を聞き，メモの空所を書き取る問題では，あらかじめメモに目を通し，聞き取るべき情報を聞き逃さないよう注意すること。そのまま語句を書き取ればよいものと，公演数やチケット代など情報を整理したり計算したりする必要があるものがある。

Lesson 8

Training

🎧 音声を聞いて，空所に入る語を書きましょう。

☐ (1) We'd like tickets for the ＿＿＿＿＿＿ ＿＿＿＿＿＿ show, please.

☐ (2) Please be aware that there is a ＿＿＿＿＿＿ ＿＿＿＿＿＿ of ＿＿＿＿＿ per
ticket.

👄 音声に続けて，英文を2回ずつ声に出して読みましょう。発音できたら，チェックボックス（☐）にチェック（✓）を入れましょう。

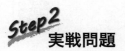
実戦問題

1 You will hear a woman making a reservation for a hotel.
Listen and fill in the missing information in the blanks (1) - (6).

(1) The date they will begin their stay：〔   〕
(2) Day they will arrive：〔   〕
(3) Number of nights they will stay：〔   〕
(4) The kind of rooms they will reserve：〔   〕
(5) The total charge：〔   〕
(6) They will check out before _____.

2 You will hear some information about a Reed College.
Listen and fill in the missing information in the blanks (1) - (5).

(1) Visit the college office to find out _____.
(2) When science buildings were built：〔   〕
(3) Where the coffee shop is：〔on the   of the student center〕
(4) The number of books the library has：〔over   〕
(5) They will meet in thirty minutes at the _____.

3 You will hear some information about an activity.
Listen and fill in the missing information in the blanks (1) - (5).

(1) The visitors must _____ at all times.
(2) Height from the start point of the treetop walk：〔   〕
(3) What you should do if you feel sick：〔   〕
(4) Should move within 〔   〕 after the rope slide
(5) Varieties of helmet size：〔   〕

Training

🎧 音声を聞いて，空所に入る語を書きましょう。

☐ (1) We can add _____ _____ _____ _____ per head for each day.

☐ (2) _____ _____ _____, thank you. We need to catch the train at 10:30 on the Sunday.

☐ (3) Please feel free to look through the library and meet me back in the student center _____ _____ _____.

☐ (4) If you _____ _____ at any time, please raise your hand and a guide will come to assist you.

🔊 音声に続けて，英文を2回ずつ声に出して読みましょう。発音できたら，チェックボックス（☐）にチェック（✓）を入れましょう。

$Step^3$ Let's Speak!

1 カッコ内の語句を並べ替えて文を完成させましょう。

☐ (1) Woman : That's perfect for us. ① (and / arriving / leaving / Friday / Sunday / we're).

Man : Great. For those dates, we only have one single room left. Would you be okay with a single and a double? The single is ② (and / double / night / per / the / $30 / $40).

☐ (2) To the right ① (are / buildings / science / the / three). These are pretty new; they were built just five years ago, and we are lucky to have such modern facilities.

Moving on, you can see the student center. It is set ② (and / the campus / has / in / five floors / very / middle / the / of), as well as a concert hall in the basement. There is a restaurant on the first floor ③ (a / at / coffee shop / and / the / top), which has a great view over the whole college.

☐ (3) Try to ① (of / move / the / out / 10 seconds / way / within) so that the next person can come down smoothly. Again, if you have any problems, our guides will help you. Okay, we are ready with the helmets now. Please choose small, medium, large ② (extra / from / large / the box / over / or / here).

2 音声に合わせて，話者になったつもりで**1**の全文を音読してみましょう。発音できたら，チェックボックス（☐）にチェック（✓）を入れましょう。

Lesson 9
書き取り２（短文空所補充）

解答冊子 p.41 ／
音声はこちらから➡

Goal!

□ 案内放送を聞き，必要な情報をまとめ，書くことができ
る

Step1
練習問題

You will hear an announcement about a closing-down sale.

For each question, fill in the missing information in the blanks.

SMITHWOOD'S CLOSING-DOWN SALE

(1) The duration of the sale: 〔   〕

(2) The price of a 50-inch TV: 〔   〕

(3) _____ comes with a $400 desktop computer.

(4) The tablets are so cheap because _____.

(5) When to buy a cheap camera : 〔   〕

(6) Closing time on Saturday : 〔   〕

答えとスクリプト

スクリプト

Smithwood's closing-down sale has more bargains than you can imagine. Starting from Tuesday, for five days only we are offering a huge range of electronic devices at great discounts.

Our TV and video section has 42-inch TVs for $200 and 50-inch for $300, a $100 discount off the original prices.

Find amazing prices on our PC floor, where you can buy a desktop computer with a printer for only $400. We also have a huge range of tablets, including some old models only for $50.

In our camera area you can find the latest models with up to twenty-five percent off the regular price. Make sure you come early as we have a feeling that these will be gone by the end of the first day.

Hurry! We open each day at 9 a.m. and close our doors at 6 p.m. on Saturday for the last time. Don't be disappointed, come as soon as you can to Smithwood's final ever sale!

和訳

スミスウッドの閉店セールは，あなたの想像を超えるバーゲンが満載です。火曜日から始まり，5日間だけ広範に渡る電化製品を大きく割引してご提供します。

テレビ・ビデオコーナーでは42インチテレビが200ドル，50インチテレビが300ドルで，当初の価格より100ドルお安くなっています。

パソコンフロアでは，驚きの価格を目にしてください。プリンター付きのデスクトップコンピューターがたったの400ドルで購入できます。たったの50ドルの旧式タブレットを含め，幅広い種類のタブレットも取り揃えております。

カメラコーナーでは最新モデルが通常価格の最大25%オフです。これらは初日終了までには売れてしまうと思われますので，必ず早くお越しください。

急いで！ 毎日午前9時に開店し，最終的に土曜日の午後6時に店のドアを閉めます。がっかりすることのないように，スミスウッドの最終セールにできるだけ早くお越しください。

Lesson 9

設問訳 閉店セールに関するアナウンスが流れます。
各質問の空所に抜けている情報を記入しなさい。

○スミスウッド閉店セール

(1) セールが続く期間：〔　　　〕

(2) 50インチのテレビの値段：〔　　　〕

(3) ＿＿＿＿が400ドルのデスクトップパソコンについてくる。

(4) タブレットは＿＿＿＿なのでそんなに安い。

(5) 安いカメラを買いに行くべき時：〔　　　〕

(6) 土曜日の閉店時間：〔　　　〕

🔊 Tips for Listening　書き取り2（短文空所補充）

　閉店セールのお知らせである。a huge range of, great, amazing などおおげさな表現に交じって，セール期間やそれぞれの商品の価格など，宣伝のポイントとなる語句は強くはっきりと発音されるので，強調されている語句を聞き取ればよい。

　質問に先に目を通し，アナウンスの内容をある程度予測しておくこと。選択肢式の問題と違い，語句を補充する問題では正確に単語を聞き取り，正しいつづりで書く必要がある。日ごろからディクテーション（聞き書き）の練習をしておくとよい。

Training

🎧 音声を聞いて，空所に入る語を書きましょう。

☐ (1) Starting from Tuesday, _____ _____ _____ only we are
offering a huge range of electronic devices at great discounts.

☐ (2) Find amazing prices on our PC floor, where you can buy a desktop computer
_____ _____ _____ for only $400.

🔊 音声に続けて，英文を2回ずつ声に出して読みましょう。発音できたら，チェックボックス（☐）にチェック（✓）を入れましょう。

Step 2 実戦問題

1 You will hear a weather forecast on Sunday.
For each question, fill in the missing information in the blanks.

WEATHER FORECAST

(1) This forecast runs until 〔   〕.
・southwest (2)— It's going to be 〔   〕.
・southeast (3)— It will rain on 〔   and   〕.
・central regions
   (4)— The temperature will drop to 〔   〕 by Friday.
・northwest (5)— It will rain especially 〔   〕.
・northeast (6)— The sky will be 〔   〕.

2 You will hear an announcement about a high school festival.
For each question, fill in the missing information in the blanks.

SAKURA HIGH SCHOOL FESTIVAL

○ Main Hall
(1) The school orchestra features 〔   〕 in each concert.
(2) Dance event will be held from 〔   〕.
○ Main Sports Field
・Soccer team will play games.
   (3)— The soccer club won the city competition in 〔   〕.
○ By the entrance
(4) First-year students are collecting money for 〔   〕.
○ Themed presentations —(5) You can get a drink in 〔   〕.
○ Gymnasium —(6) You can see 〔   〕.

3 You will hear guidance for the students from a foreign country.
For each question, fill in the missing information in the blanks.

SCHOOL INTRODUCTION

○ Before the class

(1) The principal will give his speech in 〔   〕.

   Start a tour of our school after the speech.

○ At 9:30

   You will join the English class.

(2) Students will 〔   〕 first.

○ In the Gymnasium

(3) Students will play indoor sports because 〔   〕.

○ At 12:30

(4) Students will 〔   〕.

○ In the afternoon

   Group A takes math first.

(5) Group B takes 〔   〕 first.

○ After school / the following week

   A welcome party will be held.

(6) Students will meet again on 〔   〕.

Training

🎧 音声を聞いて，空所に入る語を書きましょう。

☐ (1) Starting in the southwest, it's going to be a _____ _____
   _____ week.

☐ (2) They have been practicing very hard, so help to give them _____
   _____ by clapping for them.

☐ (3) Each classroom will hold a _____ _____ .

☐ (4) Group A will do math first, then science. Group B will do the

   _____ _____ _____ .

🔊 音声に続けて，英文を2回ずつ声に出して読みましょう。発音できたら，チェックボックス（☐）にチェック（✓）を入れましょう。

$Step^3$ Let's Speak!

1 カッコ内の語句を並べ替えて文を完成させましょう。

☐ (1) It's 7:55 on this warm Sunday evening, so now let's take a look at the weather ① (country / from / Friday / Monday / over / to / the / whole). Starting in the southwest, it's going to be a warm and sunny week. The warm weather will continue throughout the south of the country, but the southeast will also experience some rain ② (first / days / of / over / two / the / the week).

☐ (2) Each classroom will ① (a / hold / presentation / themed). As every room is different, we ask you to visit each one. There is so much to enjoy, including a haunted house, a game center and a cake shop. In ② (cake shop /, / enjoy / the / can / you) hot tea, coffee, or orange juice.

☐ (3) After we have lunch you will join our regular classes for the two afternoon lessons. We have a math class and a science class. ① (do / group A / first / math / will), then science. Group B will do the other way around.

After school there will be a welcome reception in the meeting room. We will have some snacks and drinks and you will meet your host families. Please ② (days / enjoy / over / the / the / two / weekend) with your family and we will ③ (at / back / Monday / on / school / see / you).

2 音声を聞いて，話者になったつもりで**1**の全文を音読してみましょう。発音できたら，チェックボックス（☐）にチェック（✓）を入れましょう。

Lesson 10
比較・整理3（講義）

解答冊子 p.48 ／
音声はこちらから➡

Goal!

☐ 講義文を聞き，情報を比較・整理することができる

Step1
練習問題

Part A

大学ランキングに関する経済学の講義を聞き，それぞれの問いの答えとして最も適切なものを選択肢のうちから一つずつ選びなさい。

○ワークシート

University rankings

Organizations producing rankings	→	**A** Governments Websites

Citations:

Universities that teach in English	a)
Universities which focus on the arts	b)
Universities which focus on the sciences	c)
Smaller universities	d)

(1) ワークシートの空所 ___A___ にあてはめるのに最も適切なものを，選択肢のうちから選びなさい。

① TV news

② Print media

③ Universities in China and the UK

④ Global organizations

(2) ワークシートの空欄 a) ～ d) にあてはめるのに最も適切なものを，選択肢のうちから選びなさい。

選択肢は 2 回以上使ってもかまいません。

① Relatively higher reputation

② Relatively lower reputation

(3) 講義の内容と一致するものはどれか。最も適切なものを，選択肢のうちから選びなさい。

① University rankings help to promote higher standards around the world.

② English is becoming less important as universities in non-English-speaking countries improve.

③ University ranking may not be focusing on student experiences.

④ A larger number of research papers indicates a better university.

| Part B |

講義の続きを聞き，下のグラフから読み取れる情報と講義全体の内容から，どのようなことが言えるか，最も適切なものを，選択肢のうちから一つ選びなさい。

Graph A

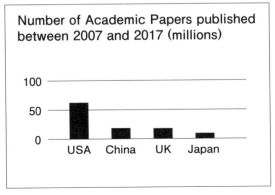

Number of Academic Papers published between 2007 and 2017 (millions)

Lesson 10

Graph B

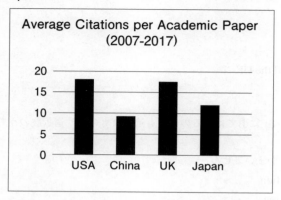

Average Citations per Academic Paper
(2007-2017)

① The universities in the United States are of a higher quality than universities in the other countries shown here.

② The number of citations is directly linked to the number of papers produced.

③ Research in Asia is influenced by the research methods of North America and Europe.

④ Language may be a greater influence than volume on the number of citations.

音声

答えとスクリプト

Part A

スクリプト

One aspect of globalization in the area of education that has been focused on a lot recently is that of university and college rankings. Global rankings are produced by a range of organizations including newspapers, magazines, governmental departments and online websites, with the top three most highly regarded ranking organizations located in the United Kingdom and China.

Each ranking organization uses a different method, but most focus on easily measured criteria, such as research output or student-to-teacher ratio. These seem logical at first, but may not accurately measure some aspects that are most important to new students. For example, some methods do not consider the size of a university, namely the number of students and teachers. If we measure research output, it is natural for a larger university to outrank a smaller one just because a larger number of graduate students will on average produce more research papers. A ranking system that compares number of research papers per student may more accurately reflect research output. Another problem with ranking research is the bias towards natural sciences, particularly medical and industrial research. Researchers in sciences in general produce more research papers than those in the arts, so universities with large science faculties

和訳

教育分野のグローバル化で最も注目される側面の1つは大学ランキングに関するものです。国際的なランキングは新聞，雑誌，政府機関，インターネットサイトなどのさまざまな組織によって出され，最も高い評価を得ている上位3位までのランキング組織はイギリスと中国にあります。

それぞれのランキング組織は異なる手法を用いますが，ほとんどは，研究の発表数や教員と生徒の割合など測定しやすい基準に重点を置いています。これらは初めは論理的であると思われますが，新入生にとって最も大切な側面を正確には測っていないかもしれません。例えば，いくつかの手法では大学の規模，すなわち生徒数や教員数を考慮していません。研究の発表数を測定するなら，より大勢の大学院生がいれば平均してより多くの研究論文を発表するでしょうから，より大きな大学の方が小さな大学よりもランクが上になるのは当然です。学生1人あたりの研究論文の数を比較するランキング方法なら，研究の発表数をもっと正確に反映するかもしれません。研究論文のランキングのもう1つの問題は，自然科学，特に医学的な研究や工業的研究への偏りです。一般的に，理系の研究者は人文科学系の研究者よりも多くの研究を発表するので，大規模な理系学部のある大学はより高くランキングされる傾向にあります。言語もランキングに影響を与えます。多くの組織は大学のランキングを行う道具として，引用数を用います。これは，1つの研究が別の研究を引用したり，考えや情報を別の論文から利用する過程です。英語で発表された論文は，幅広く

Lesson 10

61

will tend to be ranked higher. Language also has an influence on ranking. Many organizations use number of citations as a tool to rank universities. This is the process in which one research paper refers to, or takes ideas and information from, another paper. Universities teaching in English tend to experience a positive bias as papers published in English receive a wider global readership and therefore a greater number of citations.

Critics of university ranking say there are aspects of university education that may be more important to students than research output or a university's reputation. These aspects include facilities, contact between staff and students and the kinds of jobs students can expect to find after graduation. While there are some ranking organizations that focus on student welfare and experiences, many of the larger organizations pay less attention to these matters.

University ranking is set to be with us for some time. Whether this will reflect different aspects of the university experience remains to be seen.

世界中の読者に読まれるため，より多く引用されることになり，英語で教える大学はプラスの偏りを経験する傾向にあります。

大学ランキングを批判する人々は学生にとって研究の発表数や大学の評判よりももっと大切であろう大学教育の側面があると言っています。これらの側面には，設備や学生と大学職員との間のやり取り，卒業後に期待できる職業の種類などが含まれます。学生福祉や学生の経験に重点を置いたランキング組織もありますが，大きな組織の多くはこれらの事柄にはそれほど注目していません。

大学ランキングはしばらくの間，我々とともにあることになりそうです。これが大学の経験のさまざまな側面を反映するかどうかは，今後の課題です。

選択肢訳

(1) ① テレビニュース
   ② 活字メディア
   ③ 中国とイギリスの大学
   ④ 世界的組織

(2) ① 比較的高評価
   ② 比較的低評価

(3) ① 大学ランキングは世界中でより高い水準を促進するのに役立つ。

② 非英語圏の大学が伸びるにつれて，英語はあまり重要ではなくなってきている。

③ 大学ランキングは学生の経験には重点が置かれていないかもしれない。

④ 研究論文が多数あることが良い大学であることを示している。

答え (1) ② (2) a) ① b) ② c) ① d) ② (3) ③

○ワークシート

大学ランキング

ランキングを発表する組織	A
	政府
	インターネットのサイト
引用：	
英語で授業を行う大学	a)
人文科学系大学	b)
理系大学	c)
小規模大学	d)

Lesson 10

Part B

スクリプト	和訳
If we look at the number of scientific papers produced over a recent ten-year period in graph A, we can compare countries in terms of their total output (with these papers mainly coming from domestic universities). It is also possible to compare the average citations per paper for the countries in graph B.	グラフ A の，最近 10 年間に発表された科学論文の数を見ると，論文の合計発表数という観点から国を比較することができます（これらの論文は主に国内大学からのもの）。グラフ B では，国ごとの論文あたりの引用数の平均を比較することもできます。

グラフ A：2007 年から 2017 年に発表された学術論文の数（100 万単位）
グラフ B：学術論文ごとの平均引用数（2007 年から 2017 年）

選択肢訳

① アメリカの大学はここに示されている他の国の大学よりも質が高い。

② 引用数は発表された論文数と直接関連がある。

③ アジアにおける研究は北アメリカとヨーロッパの研究手法に影響されている。

④ (論文の) 量よりも言語が，論文の引用数に影響し得る。

🔊 Tips for Listening　比較・整理3（講義）

Part A (1), (2)では放送を聞きながらメモを取る要領で解答しよう。(1)は本文で newspapers, magazines と言われていたものを print media に置き換える。(2)については，本文では「英語で書かれている」，「科学系論文」，「大規模な大学」が数の上でランキングに有利だと述べている。(3) ③が最後から2番目の段落の最終文の内容と一致する。Part B グラフBから中国と日本が平均引用数が比較的少ないことがわかる。グラフAの論文数と比較するとイギリスが中国に逆転し，日本にも差をつけており，引用数には論文の数よりも言語が英語かどうかが影響していると考えられる。④が正解となる。

　本問では講義を聞き，ポイントをメモすること，概要・要点をつかむこと，講義の内容とグラフから読み取れる情報を組み合わせて判断することが求められる。

Training

🎧 音声を聞いて，空所に入る語を書きましょう。

☐ (1) Many organizations use ＿＿＿＿＿ ＿＿＿＿＿ ＿＿＿＿＿ as a tool to rank universities.

☐ (2) While there are some ranking organizations that focus on student welfare and experiences, many of the larger organizations ＿＿＿＿＿ ＿＿＿＿＿ ＿＿＿＿＿ to these matters.

🔊 音声に続けて，英文を2回ずつ声に出して読みましょう。発音できたら，チェックボックス（☐）にチェック（✓）を入れましょう。

Step2 実戦問題

1 カーボンオフセットという考え方についての講義を聞き，それぞれの問いの答えとして最も適切なものを選択肢のうちから一つずつ選びなさい。

Part A

○ワークシート

Driving 3,000 miles by car takes	A		times as long as a flight.		
Take back the CO₂ produced by the flight	① indirectly or ② directly			③ renewable energy etc. or ④ tree planting
The most common way	a)	Pay money to the airline		c)
Another way	b)	Invest money into a fund		d)

(1) ワークシートの空所 A にあてはめるのに最も適切なものを，選択肢のうちから選びなさい。

① 6 　　② 10 　　③ 12 　　④ 20

(2) ワークシートの空欄 a) 〜 d) にあてはめるのに最も適切なものを，選択肢のうちから選びなさい。選択肢は 2 回以上使ってもかまいません。

① indirectly 　　② directly 　　③ renewable energy 　　④ tree planting

Part B

講義の続きを聞き，下のグラフから読み取れる情報と講義全体の内容から，どのようなことが言えるか，最も適切なものを，選択肢のうちから一つ選びなさい。

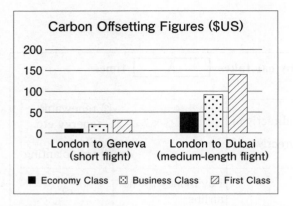

① Planes produce more CO$_2$ per passenger on shorter flights.

② Traveling business class uses less CO$_2$ than economy or first class.

③ More expensive classes produce more CO$_2$ per passenger.

④ A plane with only economy class seats would produce more CO$_2$ per passenger.

2 ユーラシア・アカリス（Eurasian red squirrel）の個体数の減少とそれに影響を
与えるトウブハイイロリス（eastern grey squirrel）に関する講義を聞き，それぞ
れの問いの答えとして最も適切なものを選択肢のうちから一つずつ選びなさい。

Part A

○ワークシート

○**Population of red squirrels in UK**
before crash＝3.5 million
after crash＝150,000 (most in Scotland)
(population in England＝ [**A**])

		Red Squirrel	Grey Squirrel
① **native** or ② **introduced**		a)	b)
③ **relatively strong against** or ④ **relatively weak against**	High levels of tannin	c)	d)
	High population density	e)	f)
	Presence of pine martens	g)	h)

Lesson 10

(1) ワークシートの空所 [A] にあてはめるのに最も適切なものを，選択肢のうちから選びなさい。

① 1.5 million　　② 350,000　　③ 100,000
④ 35,000　　　　⑤ 15,000　　　⑥ 10,000

(2) ワークシートの空欄 a) ～ h) にあてはめるのに最も適切なものを，選択肢のうちから選びなさい。選択肢は 2 回以上使ってもかまいません。

① native　　　　　　　　　　② introduced
③ relatively strong against　　④ relatively weak against

(3) 講義の内容と一致するものはどれか。最も適切なものを，選択肢のうちから選びなさい。

① Red squirrel populations had been in decline for some time before the arrival of the grey squirrel.

② Red squirrels are unable to take food from the grey squirrels due to their smaller size.

③ Grey squirrels do not tend to be affected by the squirrel pox virus.

④ Pine martens have declined in number due to the action of the grey squirrels.

講義の続きを聞き，下のグラフから読み取れる情報と講義全体の内容から，どのようなことが言えるか，最も適切なものを，選択肢のうちから一つ選びなさい。

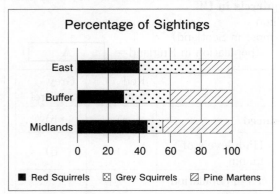

① High populations of red squirrels tend to keep the grey squirrel populations down.

② Larger pine marten population helps to keep down the number of grey squirrels.

③ Fewer grey squirrels mean less food and therefore results in fewer pine martens.

④ Grey squirrels are more successful when there are fewer red squirrels around.

Training

🎧 音声を聞いて，空所に入る語を書きましょう。

☐ (1) Although airplanes account ＿＿＿＿＿＿ ＿＿＿＿＿＿ 2.5% of global CO_2 emissions, it has been hard for customers in the past to imagine the actual pollution of a flight.

☐ (2) Many websites offer to invest money ＿＿＿＿＿ ＿＿＿＿＿ ＿＿＿＿＿ which looks at renewable energy and other green technology.

☐ (3) The remaining squirrels survive mostly in Scotland, with the population in England only around 10% ＿＿＿＿＿ ＿＿＿＿＿ ＿＿＿＿＿ .

☐ (4) The grey squirrel has a ＿＿＿＿＿＿ ＿＿＿＿＿＿ ＿＿＿＿＿＿ red squirrel populations in a variety of ways.

🗣 音声に続けて，英文を2回ずつ声に出して読みましょう。発音できたら，チェックボックス（☐）にチェック（✓）を入れましょう。

Step 3 Let's Speak!

1 カッコ内の語句を並べ替えて文を完成させましょう。

☐ (1) However, ① (drive / if / one / the / to / 3,000 miles / were) from New York to Los Angeles in a car, at an average speed of 50mph, the journey ② (around / complete / 60 hours / take / to / would). The driver would certainly notice how much fuel they had used. But making the same journey by plane ③ (five / only / hours / takes), which makes it difficult for the passenger to feel how much fuel the journey uses.

☐ (2) The new trees are able to take CO_2 out of the atmosphere, and people can calculate how much they should pay to offset the carbon they use by calculating the cost of planting trees. ① (can / done / be / indirectly / using / this / websites) which provide the calculations, and also, increasingly, is done ② (a / as / by / airlines / directly / service / the), which offer you the chance to pay the extra to plant trees when you buy your ticket.

☐ (3) However, perhaps the most damaging impact the grey squirrels have is as carriers of the squirrel pox virus. ① (being / disease / immune / to / the), grey squirrels carry the virus everywhere, infecting red squirrels, which do not have immunity. Whole populations of red squirrels ② (be / can / by / destroyed) this disease.

☐ (4) One method employed is indirect action involving the reintroduction of the pine marten to areas of England and Wales. The pine marten ① (effectively / hunts / grey squirrels / more) than red squirrels as they spend more time on the ground and are more easily caught, and it is this behavior that is thought to be one reason for ② (numbers / greater / the / of) red squirrels in Scotland, where many pine martens live.

2 音声に合わせて，講義者になったつもりで**1**の英文を音読してみましょう。発音できたら，チェックボックス（☐）にチェック（✓）を入れましょう。

Lesson 11
比較・整理4（対話）

解答冊子 p.56 ／
音声はこちらから➡

Goal!

☐ 対話を聞き，発言者の主張を把握し，比較することができ
る

練習問題

Part A

対話を聞き，それぞれの問いの答えとして最も適切なものを四つの選択肢のうちから
一つずつ選びなさい。

(1) What is Yuta's main point?

① It is okay to eat animals because it is natural.

② People should eat more fish because it is good for our health.

③ We should all try to be vegetarian in the future.

④ People should eat both meat and vegetables.

(2) What is the main reason that Olivia became vegetarian?

① She didn't think it was right for humans to kill animals.

② She thought that a vegetarian diet was the healthiest one.

③ She liked the taste of vegetarian food more.

④ Raising animals for meat is bad for the environment.

音声

Part B

テレビの討論で，肉を食べることに関するメリットとデメリットが議論されています。
聞き手と 3 人のゲスト，Martina，Paulo，Michael が発言します。

(1) 4 人のうち，肉を食べることに反対の立場なのは誰か，四つの選択肢のうちから一つ選びなさい。

① Martina and Interviewer
② Paulo and Michael
③ Michael and Martina
④ Paulo and Interviewer

(2) Paulo の意見を支持するグラフを，四つの選択肢のうちから一つ選びなさい。

①

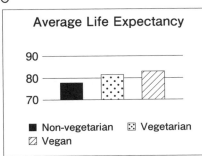

②

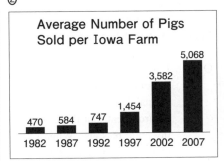

③

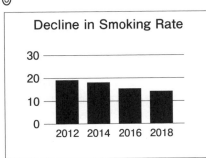

④

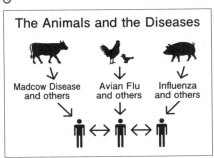

Lesson 11

71

Part A

| 和訳
---|---

スクリプト

Yuta : Hi, Olivia.　　Would you like to try some karaage?　It's like Japanese fried chicken.

Olivia : Oh, no thank you, Yuta.　I'm actually a vegetarian.

Yuta : Oh, right.　So you don't eat any meat at all?

Olivia : That's right!　I don't eat fish, either.　I stopped eating meat when I was nine.

Yuta : Was that because you wanted to be healthy?

Olivia : I think it is healthier to be vegetarian and also, raising animals for meat is bad for the environment, but these weren't my main reasons.　When I was nine, I was more worried about the ethical side of eating meat.

Yuta : I'm not sure I understand.

Olivia : Oh, I just mean that I thought, well I still think, that killing animals for meat is wrong.

Yuta : But don't you think it is better for humans to keep a balance between plants and animals for food?　Especially with fish, there are so many good things for our bodies, like vitamins and some oils.

Olivia : I guess everybody feels differently about what they eat, but if you eat a well-balanced vegetarian diet, you can be very

和訳

ユウタ : やあ，オリヴィア。唐揚げを食べてみたくない？　日本のフライドチキンのようなものだよ。

オリヴィア : いいえ，いらないわ，ありがとうユウタ。わたし実はベジタリアンなの。

ユウタ : ああ，そうなの。じゃあ肉は全然食べないの？

オリヴィア : そのとおり！　魚も食べないよ。9歳の時に肉を食べるのを止めたの。

ユウタ : それは，健康的になりたかったのが理由なの？

オリヴィア : ベジタリアンであることはより健康的だし，それに肉のために動物を飼育するのは環境によくないとも思うけど，そういうのが主な理由じゃないの。9歳の時，肉を食べることの倫理面がもっと気になってしまって。

ユウタ : よくわからないな。

オリヴィア : まあ，肉のために動物を殺すのは間違っていると思ったという意味よ。今でもそう思っているよ。

ユウタ : でも食べ物として植物と動物のバランスを保つ方が人間にとっていいと思わない？　特に魚はビタミンとかある種の油とか体にいいものがたくさんあるよ。

オリヴィア : 誰もが，自分が何を食べるかについてそれぞれの感じ方があると思うけど，バランスのとれたベジタリアン食を食べたら，とても健康

72

healthy. Here, try some of this vegetarian pizza! It's great!	的になるわよ。ほら，このベジタリアン用のピザを食べてみて！おいしいから！

設問訳 選択肢訳

(1) ユウタの発言の要点は何か。

① 動物を食べることは自然なことだから問題ない。

② 魚は健康によいので，人々はもっと魚を食べるべきだ。

③ 私たちはみんな，将来はベジタリアンになろうとするべきだ。

④ 人々は肉と野菜の両方を食べるべきだ。

(2) オリヴィアがベジタリアンになった主な理由は何か。

① 人が動物を殺すのは正しくないと思ったから。

② ベジタリアンの食事が最も健康的なものだと考えたから。

③ ベジタリアンの食べ物の味の方が好きだったから。

④ 肉用の動物を飼育することは環境によくないから。

答え　(1) ④　(2) ①

Part B

スクリプト	和訳
Interviewer：Welcome back to the show. We are joined by some guests here. First of all, Martina, what message would you like to give to our viewers?	聞き手：今回も番組にようこそ。ゲストが何人かいらしています。初めにマルティナ，視聴者の皆さんにどんなメッセージを伝えたいですか。
Martina：Thank you. Basically, I think that the health aspects of being vegetarian have been over-emphasized. As long as you have a healthy diet, exercise and don't smoke, there is no reason why eating some meat is a problem.	マルティナ：ありがとう。基本的に，ベジタリアンであることの健康面が強調され過ぎていると思います。健康的な食事をして，運動をして，喫煙しないでいる限り，肉を食べることが問題だという理由がありません。
Interviewer：Paulo, do you disagree with this point?	聞き手：パウロ，この点には反対ですか？
Paulo：No, I don't disagree. I understand it's possible for people to eat meat to have a healthy and balanced	パウロ：いえ，反対しません。肉を食べても，人々が健康でバランスのとれた生活をすることが可能だってことは理解しています。僕に

lifestyle. For me, I'm worried more about another point. The meat industry has grown from small farms to huge factories, and I don't feel that it is right to keep animals in these conditions.

Martina : So, you don't think it is wrong to eat meat?

Paulo : All things considered, I think it's the wrong idea. It is certainly wrong to eat the meat of animals that have been raised inside factories, where they live inside a cage inside a building. You are vegetarian for the same reason, aren't you?

Interviewer : Yes, it is true that I haven't eaten meat for several years. Michael, what do you say to this?

Michael : I'm not sure that the conditions of the animals are so bad these days. There are good safety standards in this country and so most animals are raised appropriately. I'm happy enough to buy what is available in the supermarket.

Interviewer : So, you don't feel any problem with what you have heard from our other guests?

Michael : I understand their point of view, but I think most people in the country see things the same way that I do.

とっては，別の点がもっと気になります。食肉産業は小さな農場から巨大な工場に成長してきました。こんな状況に動物を置いておくのは正しくないと感じています。

マルティナ：では，肉を食べることは間違っているとは思わないんですね。

パウロ：全体を考えると，それは間違った考えだと思います。工場の中で飼育された動物の肉を食べるのは確かに間違っています。工場では動物は建物の中のおりの中で生活しているんです。あなたは同じ理由でベジタリアンなんですよね？

聞き手：ええ，何年も肉を食べていないのは本当です。マイケル，これに対してあなたの意見はどうですか。

マイケル：近頃は，動物の状況がそれほど悪いという確信はありません。この国にはよい安全基準があるから，ほとんどの動物は適切なやり方で飼育されています。僕は喜んでスーパーで手に入るものを買いますよ。

聞き手：では，他のゲストから今まで聞いたことには問題がないと思いますか。

マイケル：彼らの見解は理解できるけど，この国のほとんどの人は僕と同じように見ていると思います。

選択肢訳

(1) ① マルティナと聞き手

② パウロとマイケル

③ マイケルとマルティナ

④ パウロと聞き手

グラフ

(2) ① 平均余命 非菜食・菜食・ヴィーガン（卵・チーズ・牛乳・はちみつなどもとらない完全菜食）

② アイオワの農場当たりの豚の平均販売数 ③ 喫煙率の低下 ④ 動物と病気

(牛から) 狂牛病など

(鳥から) 鳥インフルエンザなど

(豚から) インフルエンザなど

答え (1) ④ (2) ②

🔊 Tips for Listening 比較・整理4 (対話)

Part A では2人の会話を聞き，全体を通しての発話の要点を把握する。ユウタは主にオリヴィアに質問する立場だが，最後の発言で「植物と動物のバランスのとれた食生活がよい」と自分の意見を述べている。(2)についてはいくつか理由を挙げていたが，一番の理由はオリヴィアの最後から2番目の発言にある。Part B では複数の人の意見を比較検討し，肉を食べることに賛成・反対のどちらの立場で意見を言っているかを整理する。(2)では発言者のうちの1人の主張を把握し，その裏付けとなるグラフを選択する。図表を読み取る力も試される。②は「食肉産業は小さな農場から巨大な工場に成長してきた」という主張を支持するグラフである。

Lesson 11

Training

🎧 音声を聞いて，空所に入る語を書きましょう。

☐ (1) Oh, I just mean that I thought, well I still think, that _____ _____ _____ meat is wrong.

☐ (2) It is certainly wrong to eat the meat of animals that have been raised inside factories, where they live _____ _____ _____ inside a building.

🔊 音声に続けて，英文を2回ずつ声に出して読みましょう。発音できたら，チェックボックス (☐) にチェック (✓) を入れましょう。

実戦問題

1

Part A

対話を聞き，それぞれの問いの答えとして最も適切なものを四つの選択肢のうちから一つずつ選びなさい。

(1) What is Brian's main point?

① Using smartphones is better than no technology.

② Tablets are not good for the classroom as some people play games.

③ Technology is useful in the classroom.

④ Teachers should hold more classes in a computer room.

(2) What is Emi's main point?

① Smartphones should be banned from school.

② It is best to have some classes without technology.

③ Students should start bringing laptops or tablets to school.

④ Students would do more homework if they could do it on the Internet.

Part B

先生と生徒が，教室でデジタル機器を使用することについて話し合っています。

教室でデジタル機器を使用することを支持しているのは誰か，四つの選択肢のうちから一つ選びなさい。

① Moderator (Mike) and Roy

② Roy and Mary

③ Mary and Jane

④ Jane and Moderator (Mike)

2

Part A

対話を聞き，それぞれの問いの答えとして最も適切なものを四つの選択肢のうちから一つずつ選びなさい。

(1) How does Martha feel about apartments?

① She feels that buying an apartment gives more freedom to decorate.

② She thinks that buying an apartment is a lot more expensive than renting.

③ She worries that renting an apartment is unstable.

④ She hopes to live in her apartment for as long as possible.

(2) How does Takashi feel about renting an apartment?

① It is much cheaper than buying an apartment.

② Renting a new apartment makes life more comfortable.

③ He can decorate a rented apartment any way he likes.

④ He can choose where he lives more easily.

Part B

住居に関するテレビの短い討論を聞いて，以下の質問に答えなさい。

(1) 4人のうち，若いうちに家を購入することに反対しているのは誰か，四つの選択肢のうちから一つ選びなさい。

① Male presenter (Paul) and Mark

② Female presenter and Nicole

③ Male presenter (Paul) and Nicole

④ Nicole and Mark

Lesson 11

(2) マークの意見を支持するグラフを，四つの選択肢のうちから一つ選びなさい

①

②

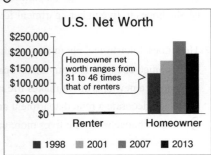

③

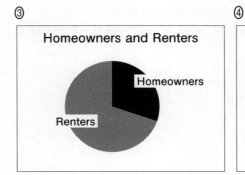

④

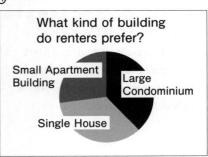

Training

🎧 音声を聞いて，空所に入る語を書きましょう。

☐ (1) _____ _____ use technology in your classes at school?

☐ (2) They can be useful, but to be honest, they have _____ _____
_____ .

☐ (3) But I prefer _____ _____ _____ .

☐ (4) But if you start to buy somewhere now, _____ _____ _____
so much to pay in the future.

🔊 音声に続けて，英文を2回ずつ声に出して読みましょう。発音できたら，チェックボックス（☐）にチェック（✓）を入れましょう。

Step3 Let's Speak!

1 カッコ内の語句を並べ替えて文を完成させましょう。

☐ (1) Brian : But I think that if the teacher is careful, ① (can / help / it / learn / more / to / us) in class if we have access to the Internet.

Emi : I'm not sure. I think there is a place for technology, but in some classes we should ② (away / devices / keep / our) and think by ourselves. We have to keep our smartphones in our lockers and I also think that is a good thing. I prefer our system here.

☐ (2) Moderator : I've got to say, ① (agree / I / you / with). But in what way?

Roy : Well, there are some lessons where we need those devices. For example, looking up different opinions or using certain programs that go with the class. But in most classes, ② (are / necessary / not / they). The teachers should probably use technology more, though.

☐ (3) Takashi : Yes, renting is very expensive. But I prefer to be flexible. If I change my job, I can ① (a / and / leave / new / place / rent). I'm afraid that apartments in some areas are difficult to sell.

Martha : But another thing about having your own apartment is that you ② (can / decorate / however / it / want / you). In a rented apartment this is difficult.

☐ (4) Nicole : Well, for me, that's kind of where I am now. I'm just starting work, and I don't know if I'll stay here or move in the future. ① (a / bought / couple / have / friends / my / of / recently), but for me, you know, I just don't want to save up money now. I mean, I don't really earn that much, yet.

Mark : But ② (exactly / that's / why) you should do it!

2 音声に合わせて，対話の登場人物になったつもりで**1**の英文を音読してみましょう。発音できたら，チェックボックス（☐）にチェック（✓）を入れましょう。

Lesson 12
長めの聞き取り（対話）

解答冊子 p.66 ／
音声はこちらから➡

Goal!

☐ 長めの対話を聞き，状況を理解し，内容を把握すること
ができる

Step1

練習問題

対話を聞き，次の質問の答えとして最も適切なものを四つの選択肢のうちから一つず
つ選びなさい。

(1) What is the main topic of this conversation?

① How to sign up for a college sports club.

② Becoming a member of the college sports center.

③ Booking a swimming session in the university pool.

④ How to transfer membership from the previous campus.

(2) Why is the student a little unhappy about the introductory safety course?

① He feels he is at a more advanced level.

② He is not available at the times that the course is being held.

③ He has already taken a safety course in the past.

④ The health and safety procedures appear too strict.

(3) Which of the following is true about swimming time for regular swimmers?

① There are lanes open when the aqua aerobics class is held.

② There are no swimming lanes open until 9 am.

③ There may be lane restrictions for regular swimmers in the afternoon.

④ Aqua aerobics classes are open to female swimmers only.

答えとスクリプト

スクリプト

M：Hi, I'd like to sign up to use the college sports center. I think I need to register for the year.

W：Sure, let me just get the form.

M：Do you need to see my student card?

W：No, you should be registered in the system when you entered the college. Can I just get your student ID number?

M：It's PY200451. Do you know if I can start using the facilities from today?

W：Just a moment ... Okay, I've found you. You're free to join any sports clubs from today and to use the pool, but you'll need to go through the safety course before you can use the weights room.

M：Is that necessary? I already took the course last year.

W：I know what you mean, but it's part of our health and safety policy. During the first week of term, they hold the introductory sessions every morning from 9. It should take about an hour.

M：Okay, I guess I have no choice then. Can you put me down for Wednesday?

W：There's no need to sign up. Just show up around 9. Here, I'll hand you a guide to the facilities. You can see the pool down there and the male changing rooms are on

和訳

男性：こんにちは。僕は届けを出して大学スポーツセンターを使いたいです。今年の登録をする必要があります。

女性：はい。申込書をいただけますか。

男性：学生証を見ますか？

女性：いいえ，大学入学時にシステムに登録されているはずです。学生番号を教えてもらえますか。

男性：PY200451 です。今日から施設を使えるかどうかご存知ですか。

女性：少々お待ちください。はい，確認できました。今日から自由にどの運動部にも参加でき，プールも利用できます。ただし，ウェイトトレーニング室を使う前に安全講習を受ける必要があります。

男性：必要ですか？ 去年，すでに受けましたけど。

女性：おっしゃることはわかりますが，これはここの健康と安全策の一環なのです。学期の最初の週は毎朝9時から入門講習があります。1時間ほどかかります。

男性：わかりました。選択の余地はないということですね。水曜日に予約できますか？

女性：予約の必要はありません。9時頃いらっしゃるだけで大丈夫です。施設の案内書をお渡しします。プールはその下に見えます。男性の更衣室は右側です。階段を進むと競技場とウェイトトレーニング室

Lesson 12

81

| the right. The stairs will take you to the arena and weights room. | に行けます。 |

M：What time is the pool open from?

男性：プールは何時からですか。

W：If you look here on the back, there is a weekly schedule. Basically, it opens from 8, but you need to be careful as there are quite a lot of private sessions during the week.

女性：ここの後ろに週間スケジュールがあります。基本的にプールは 8 時に開きますが週の間にかなり個人授業があるので注意する必要があります。

M：Okay, so it says here "aqua aerobics" each day from 8 till 9. Does that mean the pool is closed to swimmers?

男性：わかりました。スケジュールを見るとアクア・エアロビクスが毎朝 8 時から 9 時までありますね。泳ぐ人はプールに入れないということですか。

W：No, as long as you are okay with lane swimming. Two lanes are open during the aerobics session. The only time the pool is completely booked is during the ladies' time, from 9 to 11 on Mondays and Thursdays. Other than that, you are free to swim until closing at 9 p.m.

女性：いいえ，レーンに沿って泳ぐのでかまわないなら大丈夫です。エアロビクスの授業の間は 2 つのレーンが開いています。プールが完全に予約されているのは，月曜日と木曜日の 9 時から 11 時の女性専用タイムの間だけです。それ以外は午後 9 時の閉館時間まで自由に泳ぐことができます。

M：Okay, thanks. I think I'm okay for now.

男性：わかりました。ありがとう。もう大丈夫だと思います。

W：No problem! Have a nice day!

女性：問題ありません。よい 1 日を。

設問訳 選択肢訳

(1) この会話の中心となる話題は何か。

① 大学の運動部への加入の仕方。

② 大学のスポーツセンターの会員になること。

③ 大学プールの水泳の授業を予約すること。

④ 以前のキャンパスから会員権を移す方法。

(2) なぜ学生は入門安全講習について少し不満なのか。

① 自分がもっと進んだレベルだと思っている。

② 講習が行われている時間の都合が悪い。

③ 過去に安全講習をすでに受けたことがある。

④ 健康と安全の手続きが厳しすぎるように思える。

(3) 次のうち，普通に泳ぐ人の水泳時間について正しいのはどれか。

① アクア・エアロビクスの授業が行われているとき，開いているレーンがある。

② 午前9時まで水泳用のレーンは開いていない。

③ 午後に普通に泳ぐ人にはレーンの制限があるかもしれない。

④ アクア・エアロビクスの授業は女性泳者だけに開かれている。

答え (1) ② (2) ③ (3) ①

🔊 Tips for Listening 長めの聞き取り（対話）

　ある程度長い対話を聞き，複数の問いに答える問題である。対話の場面，話者の立場や目的などを早い段階で把握することが大切である。

　本問では両者の初めの発言から男性は学生で，スポーツセンターに入会したいこと，女性はセンターの担当者であると推測できる。主に男性の希望や疑問点を女性が説明する形で対話が進んでいく。語句レベルの理解だけでなく，発言を通して話者の意図は何かをつかみとる力が試される。

Training

🎧 音声を聞いて，空所に入る語を書きましょう。

☐ (1) Hi, I'd like to sign up to use the college sports center. I think I need to _____ _____ the year.

☐ (2) Is that necessary? I _____ _____ the course last year.

🔊 音声に続けて，英文を2回ずつ声に出して読みましょう。発音できたら，チェックボックス（☐）にチェック（✓）を入れましょう。

Step2 実戦問題

1 対話を聞き，次の質問の答えとして最も適切なものを四つの選択肢のうちから一つずつ選びなさい。

(1) Why has the woman come to the help desk?

① She wants to register an account with the library.

② She can't access her account online.

③ She needs help to access certain areas of her account.

④ She missed the deadline for setting up an account in the first week.

(2) How does the printing service work at this institution?

① You have several printing options available after you open an account.

② IT services will charge you for any printing you do after you pick up the documents.

③ You can't access printing services if you don't have a credit card.

④ You need to put some money in the account before you can print.

(3) What is the most likely reason for not receiving emails from the study group?

① Permission needs to be given before study group emails are accepted.

② Not entering $5 into the printing account.

③ The email server is blocking some addresses from the inbox.

④ There are too many emails in the inbox already.

2 対話を聞き，次の質問の答えとして最も適切なものを四つの選択肢のうちから一つずつ選びなさい。

(1) What is the woman going to do?

① Make a reservation for a room at this dormitory.

② Check into her room for the year.

③ Change her room to a single until October.

④ Find someone to carry her bags to her room.

(2) What does the man at the desk mention about the life in the Hall?

① Students must clean the bathroom every day.

② The woman will share the room with another student before October.

③ Breakfast is served on the second floor of the Derwent Hall.

④ Students who go out must return by 11.

(3) What does the man at the desk imply about the laundry room?

① The room is only available while the desk is open.

② Students need to arrive early as there are not many washers and dryers.

③ Preparing coins in advance may be a good idea.

④ There is no elevator so carrying washing will be difficult.

音声

Training

🎧 音声を聞いて，空所に入る語を書きましょう。

☐(1) I actually registered online before the opening week, but I'm having a
_____ _____ some areas of my account.

☐(2) If you click it, you should get an _____ _____ _____ .

☐(3) Other than that, students here must come back to the Hall _____ _____ .

☐(4) They're open twenty-four seven, but you _____ _____ _____ ,
so make sure to get some change beforehand.

🗣 音声に続けて，英文を2回ずつ声に出して読みましょう。発音できたら，チェックボックス（☐）にチェック（✓）を入れましょう。

Step 3
Let's Speak!

1 カッコ内の語句を並べ替えて文を完成させましょう。

☐(1) Woman : Hi, can I speak to someone on the IT help desk?

Man : Actually, IT and library services are combined so we can all assist you.
① (a / are / account / new / registering / you)?

Woman : No. I actually registered online before the opening week, but ② (a / accessing / areas / having / I'm / problem / some) of my account.

☐(2) Man : Okay, so you signed up, but it looks like you haven't set up your account. See, ① (money / some / put / should / you) into the account before using the printing service.

Woman : Oh, so I have to prepay before I can print.

Man : You need a minimum of $5 in your account ② (access / before / can / options / printing / you). You can pay by credit card or use one of our prepaid cards, which you can get from the machine over there.

☐(3) Man : You're in the right place. Sit down here for a moment. ① (are / here / register / stay / to / you / your)?

Woman : Yes, I'm transferring from Japan for this academic year. I should ② (a / here / for / have / room / the / year).

Man : Let's see..., Ms. Yamaguchi, is that right?

Woman : Yes. I think I'm in room 205.

Lesson 12

85

☐ (4) Man : There are bathroom areas at each end of the floor, with shared showers
             and toilets. These are cleaned each week, but we do ask you to ① (as /
             as / after / clean / much / possible / up / yourself).

       Woman : Right..., sure, that's no problem.

       Man : Other than that, students here must   ② (back / before / come / 11 /
             the Hall / to). If you need to stay out past this time, you need to get
             permission from Mrs. Wilson, the supervisor of the Hall.

2 音声を聞いて，対話の登場人物になったつもりで**1**の全文を音読してみましょ
       う。発音できたら，チェックボックス（☐）にチェック（✓）を入れましょう。

Lesson 13
長めの聞き取り（講義）

解答冊子 p.73／
音声はこちらから➡

Goal!

□ 講義を聞き，内容に合った答えを選ぶことができる

Step 1
練習問題

生物学の講義を聞き，次の質問の答えとして最も適切なものを四つの選択肢のうちから一つずつ選びなさい。

(1) What is this lecture mainly about?

① Which vaccine to use against different diseases.

② Categorizing different types of vaccine.

③ Understanding why boosters are necessary.

④ The history of vaccines in the fight against disease.

(2) According to the professor, why do some vaccines need to be given several times?

① Some vaccines are too dangerous to be given in large amounts.

② It is important to use several different types of vaccine on one disease.

③ The body doesn't have a long-term response to some vaccines.

④ Many people's immune systems become weaker when they get sick.

One topic we need to be familiar with when researching disease is the development of vaccines. As you are aware, different diseases are caused by different types of organism, including bacteria, viruses, protists and fungi, and these billions of tiny organisms require us to produce a large range of vaccines.

While there are, of course, many vaccines being developed or already in use, most fall into one of four main categories. The first is what we call live-attenuated, or weakened vaccines. This vaccine contains a weak or damaged version of the disease, and so the body can give a strong immune response, which can last a lifetime. Such vaccines are used in the MMR vaccine, and also against smallpox and yellow fever. One downside to using a live vaccine is that it can be hard to give them to people with weak immune systems, I mean, to people who are already sick.

Inactivated vaccines are the next category and usually involve introducing dead viruses, which can't grow in the body. The influenza vaccine is an example, and these vaccines tend not to give life-long immunity due to the weaker immune response. Booster shots are often required several times to maintain immunity to the disease.

The next step down from using a killed virus is developing a subunit vaccine, created from just a part of the

病気を研究する際に熟知しておくべきテーマはワクチンの開発である。お気づきのとおり、さまざまな病気は、バクテリア、ウイルス、原生生物、真菌類などを含むさまざまな種類の有機体によって引き起こされ、これらの何十億もの小さな有機体のために、我々は幅広い種類のワクチンを作り出す必要がある。

もちろん、開発中であったりすでに使用されたりしているワクチンが多くあるが、それらのほとんどは4つのカテゴリーの1つに分類される。1つ目はいわゆる弱毒生ワクチン、つまり弱めたワクチンである。このワクチンは、病原性が弱いもの、または抑えられたものを含んでいるので、体が強い免疫反応を示すことができ、この免疫反応は生涯続くことがある。このようなワクチンは新三種混合ワクチンで使われており、天然痘や黄熱病も防ぐ。生ワクチンを使うことの1つのマイナス面は、免疫システムが弱っている人、つまりすでに病気の人に与えるのは難しいということだ。

不活化ワクチンが次のカテゴリーで、通常、不活化ワクチンは体の中で増えることができない死んだウイルスを取り入れることになる。インフルエンザワクチンが1つの例で、これらのワクチンは免疫反応が弱いので、生涯にわたる免疫を得ることはできない傾向にある。病気に対する免疫を維持するためには、追加接種を何度もする必要があることが多い。

死んだウイルスを利用する次の段階は、サブユニットワクチンの開発であり、これらはたんぱく質のような、病気の原因となる有機体の一

disease-causing organism, such as a protein. As these also give a weaker immune response, they can be given to almost any patient. But, as we saw with inactivated vaccines, subunits don't usually give a lifelong immunity and boosters will be needed to maintain protection. Subunit vaccines are used against HPV and hepatitis B, as examples.

Finally, toxoid vaccines involve using a substance created by the virus that is poisonous or dangerous to the body. The immune response develops against that poison, rather than against the virus itself. Again, boosters are required, mainly when exposed to the virus, and examples are vaccines against tetanus and diphtheria.

部だけから作られる。これらも免疫反応が弱いので，ほとんどどんな患者にも与えることができる。しかし，不活化ワクチンで見たとおり，サブユニットワクチンは普通は生涯にわたる免疫は付かないので，予防効果を維持するためには追加接種が必要となる。サブユニットワクチンは，例としてヒトパピローマウイルス，B型肝炎などに対して使われている。

最後に，トキソイドワクチンは体に毒であったり危険であったりするウイルスから作られた物質を使用することを必要とする。免疫反応はウイルスそのものに対するものではなく，その毒に対して生じる。この場合も主にウイルスにさらされた時に追加接種が必要である。例として破傷風やジフテリアに対するワクチンが挙げられる。

設問訳 選択肢訳

(1) この講義の主な話題は何か。
① さまざまな病気に対してどのワクチンを使うべきか。
② さまざまな型のワクチンの分類。
③ ブースター（追加の予防接種）の必要性を理解すること。
④ 病気と戦ってきたワクチンの歴史。

(2) 教授によると，なぜいくつかのワクチンは何度も投与される必要があるのか。
① いくつかのワクチンは危険で大量に与えることができない。
② 1つの病気に数種類のワクチンを使うことが大切だ。
③ いくつかのワクチンに対して人体は長期間の反応をしない。
④ 多くの人々の免疫システムは病気の時は弱くなる。

Lesson 13

答え (1)② (2)③

🔊 Tips for Listening　長めの聞き取り（講義）

　聞き慣れない単語の連続に戸惑った人も多いだろう。病気の名前など専門用語が多用されるが，それぞれの日本語訳を正確に知っている必要はなく，何か病名を表す単語だろうと見当がつけばよい。難しい語は or のあとに日常的な語で言い直している場合もある。落ち着いて概要を聞き取ろう。

　全体では，ワクチンの4つのカテゴリーを1つずつ紹介しているから，(1)は②が正解。何度か打つ必要があるワクチンは1つめの生ワクチン以外の3つのワクチンで，それぞれ3，4，5段落の最後の方で追加接種が必要であることが述べられる。理由は得られる免疫が弱いからだから，(2)の正解は③である。

Training

🎧 音声を聞いて，空所に入る語を書きましょう。

☐ (1) The first is what we call live-attenuated, _____ _____ vaccines.

☐ (2) The influenza vaccine is an example, and these vaccines _____ _____ _____ _____ life-long immunity due to the weaker immune response.

🔊 音声に続けて，英文を2回ずつ声に出して読みましょう。発音できたら，チェックボックス（☐）にチェック（✓）を入れましょう。

音声

Step 2 実戦問題

1 川の変化過程に関する地学の講義を聞き，次の質問の答えとして最も適切なものを四つの選択肢のうちから一つずつ選びなさい。

(1) What is the main topic of this lecture?
① There are many kinds of river throughout the world.
② How rivers affect the land.
③ Rivers create valleys high up in the hills.
④ Rivers go through different stages as they flow to the sea.

(2) Why does the lecturer contrast fast and slow-moving water?
① The river flows faster at its source than it does further down.
② Different speeds create different effects on the surrounding land.
③ He is interested in the energy created by water flowing over rocks.
④ Rocks move more slowly when the water slows down.

(3) Why does the lecturer say, "You can see now what is going to happen"?
① He has described a scenario which the students can picture.
② He is asking the students to look at a diagram.
③ He thinks the students studied this point in the past.
④ He wants the students to pay close attention.

2 英文学の授業での講義を聞き，次の質問の答えとして最も適切なものを四つの選択肢のうちから一つずつ選びなさい。

(1) What is this talk mainly about?
① The differences between some of the plays written by Shakespeare.
② The importance of maintaining characters across a tetralogy.
③ An introduction to the two tetralogies of Shakespeare.
④ The importance of historical plays in English literature.

Lesson 13

bar

bogus

(2) In what way does Alvin Kernan praise the second Henriad?

① There is a grander, more epic story over the four works.

② It was written later, when Shakespeare was writing at his peak.

③ It shows us history more accurately from a Tudor perspective.

④ It gives us the background to the War of the Roses.

(3) According to the professor, why did some critics feel the Henriad plays had a political nature?

① They were written about an important dynasty of kings.

② They show us a human side to some of the great characters.

③ They avoid criticizing the Tudor dynasty.

④ They contrast problems in the past with relative internal calm in Shakespeare's time.

Training

🎧 音声を聞いて，空所に入る語を書きましょう。

☐ (1) This is where I'd like to turn our attention today, as the river flows wider and more slowly over _____ _____ on its journey to the coast.

☐ (2) This creates a _____ _____ in the river.

☐ (3) _____ , the human aspect of the characters, many of which appear many times throughout the tetralogy, are perhaps what makes this series of plays a _____ _____ _____ .

☐ (4) Critics in the past have sought to place a _____ _____ behind the Henriad.

🐦 音声に続けて，英文を2回ずつ声に出して読みましょう。発音できたら，チェックボックス（☐）にチェック（✓）を入れましょう。

Step 3 Let's Speak!

1 カッコ内の語句を並べ替えて文を完成させましょう。

☐ (1) The process is called erosion. Due to the process of erosion by the water,
① (becomes / deeper / the / valley), and when ice around the river melts, the
rocks from the sides of the valley fall into the river and eventually are carried
to the coast. This is where ② (attention / I'd / like / our / to / turn) today, as the
river flows wider and more slowly over flatter land on its journey to the coast.

☐ (2) This creates ① (a / bend / in / river / sharper / the). On the other bank, the slow-
moving water on the inside drops sand and mud, leading to the formation of a
beach or slope. These two processes, fast water on the outside and slow-moving
water inside cause the river ② (and / bend / more / more / to) over the flatter
low-lying land.

☐ (3) While the first Henriad contains one of Shakespeare's better-known works,
namely *Richard III*, it is the second Henriad that critics ① (a / as / masterpiece /
regard / true). Kernan cites the "large scale heroic action" of the plays. However,
the human aspect of the characters, many of which appear many times throughout
the tetralogy, are perhaps ② (makes / of / plays / series / this / what) a truly great
work.

☐ (4) Shakespeare, writing in the time of Tudor queen Elizabeth I, certainly provides
a narrative of historical chaos, which ends ① (and / in / modernity / of / order /
rise / the) as the Tudor dynasty begins. However, the two tetralogies, especially
the second Henriad, are so much more than just a political history. These
plays represent ② (English / literature / of / of / one / the / true / peaks) from a
playwright at the height of his powers.

2 音声に合わせて，講義者になったつもりで**1**の英文を音読してみましょう。発
音できたら，チェックボックス（☐）にチェック（✓）を入れましょう。

Lesson 14
技能融合 1 (Listening → Speaking)
(短文での応答)

解答冊子 p.80 ／
音声はこちらから➡

Goal!

□ 質問文を聞いて，自分の意見や考えを述べることができる

Step1

練習問題

放送される質問を聞き，あなた自身の答えを述べましょう。

【答えとスクリプト】

スクリプト	和訳
Do you often go to the library in your town, and why?	あなたは町の図書館へよく行きますか。それはなぜですか。

【解答例】

Yes, I do. I go to the library when I have tests at school. It is very quiet, so I can study there, and I can also find books to help me study.

【解答例の和訳】

はい，行きます。学校でテストがある時に図書館へ行きます。とても静かなのでそこで勉強することができ，勉強の助けとなる本も見つけることができます。

🔊 Tips for Speaking 技能融合1（Listening → Speaking）（短文での応答）

　質問の意図をくみ取り，的確に答えよう。ここでは地元の図書館へ行くかどうかと，その理由・目的が問われている。Do you ... で始まる質問にはまず Yes / No で答えるのが基本。そのあとに Yes または No に応じた理由や目的を述べよう。

　疑問詞で始まる疑問文では，疑問詞で問われている内容に確実に答えることが必須。また A or B などで答えの選択肢が決まっている問題では，その範囲で答えよう。自分の答えがその範囲から逸脱する場合は，その理由もきちんと述べること。

Training

🎧 音声を聞いて，空所に入る語を書きましょう。

☐(1) ＿＿＿＿＿ ＿＿＿＿＿ often go to the library in your town, and ＿＿＿＿＿?

🗣 音声に続けて，英文を2回ずつ声に出して読みましょう。発音できたら，チェックボックス（☐）にチェック（✓）を入れましょう。

実戦問題

1 放送される質問を聞き，あなた自身の答えを述べましょう。

(1)

(2)

(3)

(4)

Training

🎧 音声を聞いて，空所に入る語を書きましょう。

☐ (1) ＿＿＿＿＿ ＿＿＿＿＿ ＿＿＿＿＿ like to travel in the future, and why?
☐ (2) ＿＿＿＿＿ ＿＿＿＿＿ at your school did you enjoy the most?
☐ (3) Which season ＿＿＿＿＿ ＿＿＿＿＿ ＿＿＿＿＿ do you like best and why?
☐ (4) Do you prefer to go to the ＿＿＿＿＿ ＿＿＿＿＿ ＿＿＿＿＿ ＿＿＿＿＿ in the summer?

🗣 音声に続けて，英文を2回ずつ声に出して読みましょう。発音できたら，チェックボックス（☐）にチェック（✓）を入れましょう。

Let's Speak!

1 カッコ内の語句を並べ替えて文を完成させましょう。

☐ (1) (like / to / travel / where / would / you) in the future, and why?
☐ (2) What event at your school (enjoy / did / most / the / you)?
☐ (3) Which season (best / do / of / like / the / year / you) and why?
☐ (4) Do you (go / prefer / to / to) the beach or the mountains in the summer?

2 音声に合わせて，相手に質問するつもりで**1**の英文を音読してみましょう。発音できたら，チェックボックス（☐）にチェック（✓）を入れましょう。

Lesson 15
技能融合 2 （Reading → Listening （対話） → Speaking）

解答冊子 p.84 ／
音声はこちらから➡

Goal!
□ 英文を読んで，関連する対話を聞き，話者の意見をまとめて話すことができる

Step 1
練習問題

この問題では，短い文章を読み，同じ話題についての会話を聞きます。その上で音声で流れる質問に答えなさい。

The library has posted rules about lending limitations during the exam period. Give yourself 100 seconds to read the notice about the special limitations.

Special Measures during the Examination Period

All students should note that the library will operate certain special measures over the examination period. These measures and restrictions will begin from 8 a.m. on May 25 and end at 5 p.m. on June 25.

Library office hours will be extended until 10 p.m. each day (except Sundays) and several study areas will be open 24 hours a day (check the map below for the study areas included).

Please note that, with certain exceptions, no books may be removed from the library during the examination period. This is in order to ensure that all students have access to books for study purposes in exam month. All books must be returned to the front desk after use to allow for smooth and accurate replacing of books in the correct places.

The library is expected to be busy during this period, so we ask all students to

---

keep the noise to a minimum and to make space for others if possible.
Thank you for your attention to this matter.

University Library

英文訳

図書館に試験期間中の貸し出し制限に関するきまりが掲示されました。100 秒間で，この特別な制限に関する掲示に目を通しなさい。

試験期間中の特別措置

　試験期間中は図書館が特別措置を始めることを全学生は承知しておくこと。これらの措置と制限は 5 月 25 日午前 8 時に始まり，6 月 25 日午後 5 時に終了します。

　図書館事務室の業務時間は毎日（日曜を除く）午後 10 時まで延長され，いくつかの学習エリアは 24 時間使用可能となります（該当する学習エリアについては下の地図を確認のこと）。

　次のことに注意してください。例外を除き，この試験期間の本の貸し出しは中止します。これはすべての学生が試験月間に勉強のための本を確実に利用できるようにするためです。円滑かつ正確に正しい場所に本を戻すために，すべての本は使用後は受付に返却してください。

　この期間中，図書館は混雑が予想されますので，できるだけ物音をたてず，できれば他の人と場所を譲り合ってください。
本件への関心を感謝します。

大学図書館

答えとスクリプト

スクリプト	和訳
Now listen to two students discussing the notice.	では，2 人の学生がこの掲示について話し合うのを聞いてください。
W：Did you see the notice on the door of the library as we came in?	女性：入ってくる時に図書館のドアの掲示を見た？
M：Yeah, we also received the same info by email last week. Didn't you check it? They do the same every year.	男性：うん。先週，同じ情報をメールでも受け取ったよ。確認しなかったの？ 毎年同じだよ。
W：I didn't know that. I'm kind of worried about this as I'm in the	女性：知らなかった。今，私はレポートの途中で，来週借り出したい本が何冊かあるか

middle of my report and there are several books that I wanted to take out next week. It doesn't seem fair to stop people borrowing books for such a long time.

M : I guess the exams go on for that whole month. But you can still access the books you need, right?

W : I guess so. But I would need to visit the library every day to do that. I think a better system would be to allow you to take books out, but limit the length of time you can take the books out. You know, from the usual three weeks to one week, or something like that. Or even just overnight would be better than having to spend all the time in the library.

M : That seems to be the point, though. To stop people from taking the books out so that everyone can use them.

W : You know what would really make sense. Imagine if the majority of textbooks, or at least the books recommended by tutors, were available online. We can do this with journals and research papers, so it must be time soon for books to be more widely available online.

M : You're probably right. I think it is starting to happen more and more, but I don't think many of my core course books are online yet.

W : It's definitely the way to go for the future. Oh well, looks like I'll be back in the library again tomorrow.

らちょっと心配だな。こんなに長い間貸し出しに制限があるなんて，おかしいと思うな。

男性：試験は1カ月まるまる続くだろうからね。でも必要な本を使うことはできるよね。

女性：そうだろうけど，そうするためには毎日図書館へ来なければならないでしょ。貸し出しを許可するけど期間を制限するという方がいいと思うな。ほら，通常の3週間を1週間にするとか，そんなふうに。あるいは，1晩だけの貸し出しでもずっと図書館で過ごさなきゃならないよりはいいわ。

男性：だけど，そこがポイントなんじゃないかな。みんなが本を使えるように，本の持ち出しを禁止するんだよ。

女性：何が本当に意味があるのかわかっているのね。教科書の大部分，あるいは少なくとも教官が勧めた本はオンラインで見られるというのはどうかしら。雑誌や研究論文では，できるんだから，本もオンラインでもっと広範囲に見られるようになる時代がもうすぐくるにちがいないわ。

男性：おそらく君の言うとおりだよ。その手のことはどんどん起こり始めているんだろうけど，核となる授業の本はまだあまりオンラインにはないと思うよ。

女性：間違いなく将来に進むべき道ね。しかたない，私は明日もまた図書館へ来るようね。

Lesson 15

Give yourself 30 seconds to prepare your response to the following question. Then speak for 60 seconds.	次の質問に答えるための準備時間が 30 秒間あります。次に答えを 60 秒間で話してください。
The woman has some ideas and opinions regarding the notice from the library. State her opinions and the reasons she has for holding them.	女性は図書館の掲示に関して、いくつかのアイディアと意見を持っています。彼女の意見とそのような意見を持った理由を説明しなさい。

解答例

The woman is surprised that the library restricts book rentals over the examination period. For one month, students are not allowed to take books out of the library and the woman thinks this will cause her to come to the library every day to complete her report. She understands many students need to use the books, but suggests another system, such as shorter book rentals. However, her main idea is to have all the important books online so that anyone can access them from home.

解答例の和訳

女性は図書館が試験期間中の本の貸し出しを制限したことに驚いています。1 カ月間学生は本を図書館から持ち出すことができず、この女性はそのせいで自分のレポートを完成させるために毎日図書館へ来なければならないと思っています。彼女は多くの学生が本を利用する必要があることはわかっていますが、貸出期間を短くするなど他の方法を提案します。けれども彼女の一番の案は、誰でも家から利用できるように、重要な本はすべてオンライン上に置くということです。

◀€ Tips for Listening 技能融合２（R → L（対話）→ S）

　リーディング，リスニング，スピーキングの総合力が試される。リーディングでは掲示の要旨を素早くつかむこと。リスニングでは意見を主張する方の話者の論点を整理しながらメモしよう。スピーキングでは，自分自身の意見ではなく，リスニングパートの話者の１人の意見とその意見に至った理由が問われている。

　本問では，女性が貸し出し制限により，本を持ち出せなくなることに不満を持っており，試験期間中でも必要な本が図書館の外で使えるよう，①貸出期間を短くする，②オンラインで本を見られるようにする，という２つの案を出している。

Training

🎧 音声を聞いて，空所に入る語を書きましょう。

☐ (1) I think a better system would be to allow you to take books out, but ＿＿＿＿＿＿＿ ＿＿＿＿＿＿ ＿＿＿＿＿＿ ＿＿＿＿＿ you can take the books out.

☐ (2) Imagine if the majority of textbooks, or at least the books recommended by tutors, ＿＿＿＿＿ ＿＿＿＿＿ ＿＿＿＿＿ .

🔊 音声に続けて，英文を２回ずつ声に出して読みましょう。発音できたら，チェックボックス（☐）にチェック（✓）を入れましょう。

Step 2
実戦問題

1 この問題では，短い文章を読み，同じ話題についての会話を聞きます。その上で音声で流れる質問に答えなさい。

The college is changing the requirements for first-year students from next year. Give yourself 100 seconds to read the notice about the changes.

Second Language Classes to be Optional from Next Year

　Following the change in the number of students over the past few years, the college has decided to make changes regarding second language classes. Second language classes will continue to be offered to all students but students can decide whether they take those classes or not.

The college offers classes in French, Spanish and German, one of which is currently required by all first-year students. Due to the fact that more than half of our students are now entering the college from overseas, it was felt that the volume of language study should be reduced, especially for those students who do not speak English as a first language.

Elective classes in all three languages will remain available for any student wishing to study, although students should be prepared for classes to be slightly larger if many first-year students also elect to take a second language. This new system will be in place for a trial period over the next academic year as we research the demand for second language classes.

2 この問題では，短い文章を読み，同じ話題についての会話を聞きます。その上で音声で流れる質問に答えなさい。

There are some changes to the rules for student room applications next year. Read this article from the student newsletter. Give yourself 100 seconds to read the article.

University Accommodation to become a Lottery from the Second Year

Last week, the university accommodation board made an announcement. Students in their second year and above may need to enter a lottery to receive a guaranteed room in university halls, beginning this coming academic year. While many second years like to move out of university rooms and into shared houses with their friends, there are always a number of students who prefer to continue living on campus.

"Due to a higher-than-average number of first year students, we have only a few rooms left available", commented a member of the accommodation committee.

Although students with special needs will be considered separately, most students who wish to enter university accommodation for the second year will need to register with the lottery by July 3rd. While there has been no date set yet, decisions regarding who will and will not be accepted will be posted towards the end of August.

Training

🎧 音声を聞いて，空所に入る語を書きましょう。

☐ (1) Yeah, it was hard, but there were ＿＿＿＿＿＿ ＿＿＿＿＿＿ ＿＿＿＿＿＿
　　　　 ＿＿＿＿＿＿ , too.

☐ (2) As these classes are not related to your major, you ＿＿＿＿＿＿ ＿＿＿＿＿＿
　　　　 ＿＿＿＿＿＿ many students from various majors.

☐ (3) I just wish I'd ＿＿＿＿＿＿ ＿＿＿＿＿＿ ＿＿＿＿＿＿ earlier.

☐ (4) A little more information ＿＿＿＿＿＿ ＿＿＿＿＿＿ ＿＿＿＿＿＿ .

🔊 音声に続けて，英文を2回ずつ声に出して読みましょう。発音できたら，チェックボックス（☐）にチェック（✓）を入れましょう。

Step3
Let's Speak!

1 カッコ内の語句を並べ替えて文を完成させましょう。

☐ (1) Woman : What, you mean the second language classes? How come? To be
　　　　　　 honest, it was hard studying French in that first year.

　　　　 Man : Yeah, it was hard, but ① (a / positives / lot / there / of / were), too. I
　　　　　　 think a lot of students come here without having a strong view of the
　　　　　　 world. Even just learning a little of another language ② (can / more /
　　　　　　 give / of / understanding / you) the world.

☐ (2)　　 Man : But they could still benefit from learning another language. And there's
　　　　　　 another important point about these classes that goes beyond what you
　　　　　　 learn. As ① (are / classes / not / these / related / to) your major, you
　　　　　　 can communicate with many students from various majors.

　　　 Woman : I guess so. Like, ② (actually / did / meet / we) in that French class,
　　　　　　 now that you say it.

☐ (3) Woman : So, what are you going to do?

　　　　 Man : Well, I'll apply for a place, but I suppose I'll need ① (a / around /
　　　　　　 for / house / look / shared / to), not too far from the campus. I know
　　　　　　 they need to guarantee first-years' places, but if they are planning
　　　　　　 on taking more new first-years, you know, they should at least

② (accommodation / built / have / more) first.

□ (4) Woman : Maybe it's just a one-time event. Like, maybe the number of new students will go back down again next year.

Man : Who knows? At least, if they let us know just ① (available / how / many / places / were), we'd know what kind of chance we have of getting one of the rooms. It could be a hundred, it could be only ten. ② (a / information / little / more) would have helped. And sooner!

2 音声に合わせて，対話の登場人物になったつもりで**1**の英文を音読してみましょう。発音できたら，チェックボックス（□）にチェック（✓）を入れましょう。

Lesson 16

技能融合3（Reading → Listening（講義）→ Speaking）

解答冊子 p.91 ／
音声はこちらから➡

Goal!
□ 英文を読んで，関連する講義を聞き，講義の内容をまとめて話すことができる

Step1
練習問題

Read the following passage about hydrogen as a fuel. After reading the passage, you will listen to a lecture and you will then be asked a question. Begin reading now. (Reading time: 100 seconds)

In order to meet our energy requirements, while at the same time reducing environmental pollution, including harmful greenhouse gases such as carbon dioxide, many industries are looking to hydrogen as a cleaner alternative to the burning of fossil fuels. In fact, many of these emerging uses of hydrogen are already familiar to the public. For example, major car manufacturers are developing technology in which they use hydrogen to produce electricity to power the car. This technology is sold as clean energy, with the only by-product being water. However, there is one major problem with this concept. The production of hydrogen on a large scale is not yet at an environmentally-friendly level. Most of the world's hydrogen is still produced using fossil fuels, and so it is difficult to say when hydrogen will become a completely green fuel.

燃料としての水素に関する文章を読みなさい。文章を読んだあと，講義を聞き，続く質問に答えなさい。では，読み始めなさい。（制限時間：100秒）

二酸化炭素のような有害な温室効果ガスを含む環境汚染を減らすと同時に，我々のエネルギー需要を満たすために，多くの産業が化石燃料を燃やす代わりにもっとクリーンな代替エネルギーとして水素に注目しています。実際，こうした水素の新たな利用の多くはすでに広く知られています。例えば大手自動車メーカーは車を動かす電気を生み出すために水素を利用する技術を開発しています。この技術はクリーンエネルギーとして売られ，副産物は水だけです。けれども，この考え方には1つ大きな問題があります。大規模な水素の生産は，まだ環境に優しいレベルではありません。世界の水素のほとんどは，いまだ化石燃料を使って生産されており，そのため水素が完全に環境に優しい燃料になるのがいつであるかを言うことは難しいことです。

答えとスクリプト

スクリプト

Now listen to a part of a lecture on environmental science.

Let me take some time to outline the two major methods of hydrogen production. The first, steam reforming, accounts for the major share of current hydrogen production. In this method, a fossil fuel such as natural gas, oil or coal is mixed with steam at a high temperature and pressure. Natural gas is the most common fuel to be used and almost half the world's hydrogen is currently produced using steam reforming of natural gas. While this method produces large quantities of hydrogen, it also relies on a fossil fuel, and produces large amounts of carbon dioxide. Hydrogen produced in this manner cannot be said to be environmentally friendly.

和訳

では，環境科学の講義の一部を聞きなさい。

しばらく時間をとって，水素を製造する主な2つの方法の概要を説明します。1つ目は水蒸気改質という方法で，現在の水素製造の大部分を占めています。この製法では天然ガスや石油，石炭などの化石燃料が高温高圧で水蒸気と混ぜられます。天然ガスが最も一般的に使われる燃料で，現在，世界の水素のほぼ半分が天然ガスを使った水蒸気改質で生産されています。この製法では大量の水素を生産できますが，化石燃料に頼っており，大量の二酸化炭素も産み出します。この製法で作られた水素は環境に優しいと言うことはできません。

The second most common way to produce hydrogen is through electrolysis. This basically means using electricity to split water into hydrogen and oxygen, with no harmful by-products. Many people believe that by using renewable energy sources to produce electricity, such as solar or wind and wave energy, hydrogen could be produced cheaply and cleanly, becoming an eco-friendly source of energy. As of 2019, less than 5% of global hydrogen was produced in this way and there are many challenges to the spread of this method. However, the signs point towards a great deal of growth and investment in this area.

Give yourself 30 seconds to prepare your response to the following question. Then speak for 60 seconds.

Explain the concept of hydrogen as a clean fuel and how the lecture describes the current and possible future situation.

水素を生産するのに 2 番目によく用いられる方法は，電気分解によるものです。これは，基本的に水を水素と酸素に分解するのに電気を利用する方法で，有害な副産物は出ません。電気を作るのに太陽，風，波のエネルギーのような再生可能エネルギー源を使うことにより，水素はより安くよりクリーンに作り出せるようになり，エコフレンドリーなエネルギー源になり得ると，多くの人々が信じています。2019 年時点では，この方法で生産されたのは世界の水素の 5％未満であり，この方法が広まるにはさまざまな障害があります。けれども，この分野には大いなる成長と投資のきざしが見られます。

30 秒間で以下の質問への答えを準備してください。その後 60 秒間であなたの答えを話してください。

クリーン燃料としての水素の概念と，現在と将来起こり得る状況が講義ではどう述べられているかを説明しなさい。

解答例

Using hydrogen in a car, for example, is said to be clean as it produces only water as a by-product. It produces no harmful gases such as carbon dioxide. However, most hydrogen is produced using fossil fuels, which cannot be said to be environmentally friendly. The lecturer says the amount of hydrogen produced using renewable energy, such as solar energy, is less than 5% of global production, but the signs show a great deal of growth in the area.

Lesson 16

解答例の和訳

例えば，車で水素を利用することは副産物として水しか生じないのでクリーンだと言われています。二酸化炭素のような有害なガスは出ません。けれどもほとんどの水素は化石燃料を

使って生産され，環境に優しいとは言えません。講師は太陽エネルギーのような再生可能エネルギーを利用した水素の生産量は世界の生産量の５％未満だけれども，この分野での成長が見込まれると言っています。

🔊 Tips for Listening　技能融合３（R → L（講義）→ S）

テーマに基づいた読解資料を読み，それに関連する講義を聞き，それらの内容を整理して設問に答えることが求められている。

最初の指示文で，講義のテーマ（燃料としての水素）が示される。読解資料では概要や背景が示されることが多い。ここでは化石燃料よりもクリーンなエネルギーとして水素が紹介され，For example のあとに水素自動車の例，However のあとに問題点が述べられている。講義では読解資料の内容の詳細や発展事項が述べられることが多い。本問では水素生産の two major methods が紹介される。The first として紹介されるのは読解資料でも示されている化石燃料を利用した方法，The second で紹介されるのは再生可能エネルギーを利用した新しい方法である。

スピーチでは，燃料としての水素の概要は読解資料を参考に，水素利用の現在と将来については講義をもとにまとめよう。hydrogen（水素），fossil fuel（化石燃料），carbon dioxide（二酸化炭素）などキーワードとなる専門用語は，読解資料を参考にしよう。

Training

🎧 音声を聞いて，空所に入る語を書きましょう。

☐ (1) Hydrogen produced in this manner _____ _____ _____ to be environmentally friendly.

☐ (2) This basically means using electricity to split water into hydrogen and oxygen, _____ _____ _____ by-products.

🔊 音声に続けて，英文を２回ずつ声に出して読みましょう。発音できたら，チェックボックス（☐）にチェック（✓）を入れましょう。

Step 2 実戦問題

1 Now read a passage about peer-to-peer lending. After reading the passage, you will listen to a lecture and you will then be asked a question. Begin reading now. (Reading time: 45 seconds)

The online world has been shaping lending and borrowing more and more over the past few years, with peer-to-peer lending becoming a major source of investment. These peer-to-peer lending services are offered on a number of specialist websites. Investors and borrowers are matched through the websites, to the benefit of both. The investors, or lenders, are usually people who wish to make more money by lending it than they would in a traditional savings account. The borrowers may be companies or individuals who wish to pay less interest than a traditional bank loan. The peer-to-peer websites operate to bring these groups together, and as a concept, seem to make good business sense.

---

2 Now read a passage about the history of trees. After reading the passage, you will listen to a lecture and you will then be asked a question. Begin reading now. (Reading time: 45 seconds)

Until the relatively recent destruction brought about by human activity, our planet was a forest planet, covered in trees that spread almost all around the globe. And for many millions of years these trees were all gymnosperms; a word that means naked seeds. Then, around 200 million years ago, angiosperms, plants that produce flowers and fruits, began to develop. Today, there are hundreds of thousands of species of angiosperm, including many trees. On the other hand, there are thought to be only around 1,000 species of gymnosperm left throughout the globe.

Lesson 16

Training

- [ ] (1) Firstly, there is the chance of _____ _____ _____ by saving money in a bank.
- [ ] (2) The main one is, of course, the _____ _____ _____ money to people you don't know.
- [ ] (3) In contrast, angiosperms usually produce _____ _____ _____ .
- [ ] (4) Angiosperms are of far more importance to humans in terms of a _____ _____ .

🔊 音声に続けて，英文を2回ずつ声に出して読みましょう。発音できたら，チェックボックス（☐）にチェック（✓）を入れましょう。

Step3 Let's Speak!

1 カッコ内の語句を並べ替えて文を完成させましょう。

- [ ] (1) Firstly, there is the chance of earning more than by saving money in a bank. The interest rates are agreed in advance, so ① (be / income / should / steady / the). Peer-to-peer companies generally ② (background / check / borrowers / of / the / the), and lenders are able to control who they lend their money to in order to reduce some of the risk.

- [ ] (2) This means that ① (is / of / losing / possibility / the / there) some, or even all, of your investment if the borrowers do not repay the loan. Peer-to-peer websites ② (minimize / risk / this / to / work), but the risk is certainly higher than investing with a bank. Additionally, the websites do charge fees for these services——this is, after all, how they make their money——although a smart investor would ③ (account / fees / into / take / these) when planning to lend money in this way.

- [ ] (3) Another major difference is that most gymnosperms are evergreens, producing leaves in the shape of needles or scales, which ① (the / tree / on / remain) throughout the year. Angiosperms follow a seasonal lifecycle, ② (broad / flat / , / leaves / losing / often / their) in the autumn and re-growing them again in the spring.

110

☐(4) Both trees provide us with wood. Angiosperms produce hardwood, which grows slowly and is generally denser and ① (for / higher / products / quality / used). For most buildings and for cheaper furniture, the softwood timber of gymnosperms is used ② (because / grows / faster / it).

2 音声に合わせて，講義者になったつもりで**1**の英文を音読してみましょう。発音できたら，チェックボックス（☐）にチェック（✓）を入れましょう。

Lesson 17
まとめの問題 1

解答冊子 p.99 ／
音声はこちらから➡

実戦問題

1 対話とそれについての問いを聞き，その答えとして最も適切なものを，三つの選択肢（①～③）のうちから一つ選びなさい。

(1)

①

②

③

(2)

①

②

③

音声

2 You will hear a woman announcing a tour.
Listen and complete questions (1) - (7).

Second Part of the Trip: Tokyo
・Activities: Spend (1) _____ days in Japan's exciting capital city
・1st day
・Arrive by bullet train from (2) _____
・Enjoy lunch near the sumo (3) _____
・2nd day
・Spend time at a (4) _____ resort and relax in a (5) _____
・3rd day
・Walk around the (6) _____ before the river cruise
・Go to the airport by (7) _____

3

Part A

対話を聞き，それぞれの問いの答えとして最も適切なものを四つの選択肢 (①～④) のうちから一つずつ選びなさい。

(1) What is Sarah's main point?

① Tablets are more useful than phones.

② The school rules about phones were too strict.

③ She was unhappy when she didn't have a phone.

④ She didn't need a smartphone for her everyday life until recently.

(2) What is Kenta's main point?

① He thinks that people get phones when they are too young.

② He feels that young people need a phone for many reasons.

③ Phones are too expensive for young people to buy.

④ Young people spend too much time playing on their phones.

Part B

テレビの討論で，学校教育におけるテクノロジーの利用が議論されています。司会者と Carmichael 教授，2人のゲスト，John, Sandra が発言します。

Lesson 17

(1) 四人のうち，低年齢では教室でテクノロジーを使うことに反対の立場の人は誰か。

① The moderator and the professor

② The professor and John

③ The moderator and Sandra

④ John and Sandra

(2) 以下の中で，カーマイケル教授の発言の要点を支持する資料はどれか。

①

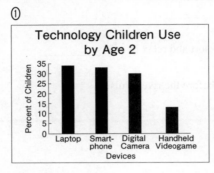

②

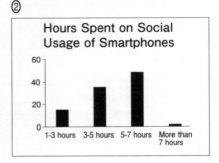

③

Wireless Technology in the Classroom

Do We Really Need it ?

➡ 3 out of 4 teachers say...

... apps are beneficial for teaching

➡ 86% of students say tablets help them study more efficiently

④

Problems With Technology in Classrooms

1 Pace of Change

2 Cost

3 Social Dynamics

4 Distraction

5 Purpose

4 放送される質問を聞き，あなた自身の答えを述べましょう。

(1)

(2)

(3)

(4)

5 この問題では，短い文章を読み，同じ話題についての会話を聞きます。その上で
音声で流れる質問に答えなさい。

The university is making some changes to its student services buildings. Read the
notice about the change. Give yourself 100 seconds to read the notice.

New Student Center to Open, October 1st.

As many of you are aware, the university began work last year on the new
Central Student Center, or CSC. For many years, we have felt that the university
lacked a "hub". We very much hope that the new center, which features the latest
technology, will be the very center of your active campus life.

The CSC will open on October 1st and will replace the four smaller centers that
are currently located in the department buildings. Two of these, in the language
department and the economics department are already closed. The small centers
in the science department and the library will remain open after the summer
vacation until the grand opening of the CSC, after which they will cease to
function as student centers and will be used mainly as meeting rooms and small
exhibition centers.

We hope you will all enjoy the CSC and we look forward to a new stage in the
development of the City University.

G Grant, Head of Student Services

Lesson 17

115

Lesson 18
まとめの問題 2

解答冊子 p.112 ／
音声はこちらから➡

実戦問題

1 対話を聞き，次の英文に続けるのに最も適切なものを三つの選択肢のうちから一つずつ選びなさい。

(1) Emma sent Tomoki some
　① postcards.
　② emails.
　③ pictures.

(2) In his free time, Tomoki
　① learned to swim.
　② tried to surf.
　③ took pictures of the beach.

(3) While he was in Australia, Tomoki
　① supported some international students.
　② helped an Australian to go to Japan.
　③ talked to a tutor every week.

(4) Tomoki stayed

① in a house for five people.

② in an international dormitory.

③ in an international house with two other students.

2 女の子が先週の出来事について話しています。話を聞き，その内容を表したイラスト（①〜④）を，聞こえてくる順番に並べなさい。

①

②

③

④

3 対話を聞き，次の質問の答えとして最も適切なものを四つの選択肢のうちから一つずつ選びなさい。

(1) Why does the student come to this office?

① She wants to rent a room at the university.

② She needs to pay her deposit.

③ She wishes to change rooms.

④ She is not sure how much to pay.

(2) What is the main problem that the student is experiencing?

① She can't study in the evening.

② She can't find good books in the library.

③ The library is a little far from these rooms.

④ There is too much noise at night.

(3) What reason does the office give for the current situation?

① There were not many rooms available.

② The room is close to many amenities.

③ The room is convenient and easy to get to.

④ This was the cheapest room in the college.

(4) What does the office imply about the double room?

① It is cheaper than the single room.

② Another student is staying there now, too.

③ The room is empty, but someone else could join at any time.

④ Even though it is a double, nobody else would use the room.

(5) What choice is the student most likely to make?

① Take the double room in the same building.

② Take the single room in another building.

③ Stay in the current cheaper room.

④ Wait for another cheap room to become available.

4 次のイラストについて放送される質問を聞き，英語で答えましょう。

(1)

(2)

(3)    (4)

5 Now read a passage about evolution. Begin reading now.
Reading time: 100 seconds

When talking about evolution, a change in environment can play an important part in aspects such as body size. While evolution can occur in many different ways, looking at the simple aspect of body size is very easy to visualize or imagine.

One common example is that of animals living on an island, where a small population has become isolated from the larger population on the mainland. This can happen if small numbers of animals manage to fly or swim to the island. However, among non-flying species, it is more common when land becomes separated due to rising sea levels.

If this occurs, body size can change in two ways, something that is called Foster's rule after the scientist J. Bristol Foster described this discovery in 1964.

Foster compared 116 species of animal. He found island dwarfism, where some animals on an island evolve to be smaller than those on the mainland. In contrast, he used the name island gigantism for when some species become larger than their mainland cousins.

Lesson 19
まとめの問題3

解答冊子 p.124 ／
音声はこちらから➡

実戦問題

1 対話を聞き，問いの答えとして最も適切なものを，四つの選択肢 (①～④) のうちから一つ選びなさい。（問いの英文は書かれています。）

(1) Which computer will the woman probably buy?

① The white one.

② The silver one.

③ The red one.

④ The blue one

(2) Where does the man finally suggest for their holiday?

① The Grand Hotel.

② The Hotel Superior.

③ The Beachside Hotel.

④ The Star Inn.

(3) What will the man try to do?

① Call some friends.

② Book a movie ticket.

③ Make a restaurant reservation.

④ Order some pizza.

(4) What will they try to do?
   ① Move the Christmas tree away from the window.
   ② Put the Christmas tree next to the TV.
   ③ Arrange the Christmas tree in the corner, away from the TV.
   ④ Put up two trees this year.

2   You will hear a woman talking about the National Stadium tour.
Listen and complete questions (1) - (5).

(1) Tomorrow: An international _____ game

(2) Changing rooms: home team on the _____, visiting team on the _____

(3) The lounge area is used by team _____ and coaching staff.

(4) Events held at the stadium: soccer games and _____.

(5) Entrance to the pitch: famous _____

3   講義を聞き，それぞれの問いの答えとして最も適切なものを四つの選択肢のうち
から一つずつ選びなさい。

○ワークシート

Moore's first law 　Began : _____ 　Ended : _____	Law held for : around	(A)	years

	① Moore's first law or ② Moore's second law		③ two years or ④ four years
Cost of individual processor	a)	Decreases every	b)
Number of transistors per circuit	c)	Doubles every	d)
Cost of processor / chip factory	e)		f)

(1) 次の数字の中で空所 (A) に合うものはどれか。

  ① 10 ② 35 ③ 47 ④ 60

(2) 6 カ所の空所に入れるのに，適切なものを次の中から選びなさい。

  ① Moore's first law ② Moore's second law ③ two years ④ four years

(3) 講義によれば，次の記述の中で正しいものはどれか。

  ① Moore's two laws have been advancing at the same rate since the 1960s.

  ② In the near future, it should be possible to produce transistors smaller than atoms.

  ③ What will be slower in the future is the rate at which processor speed increases.

  ④ The number of pixels in digital cameras will double every four years.

Part B

講義の続きを聞き，下の図から読み取れる情報と講義全体の内容から，どのようなことが言えるか，最も適切なものを，四つの選択肢のうちから一つ選びなさい。

Graph A

Graph B

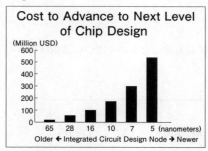

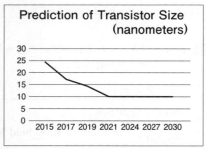

  ① Nanochips smaller than 5 nanometers cost more than double what 10 nanometer nanochips cost.

  ② Moore's law is likely to continue beyond 2023.

  ③ A 7nm technology node will be produced by 2020.

  ④ The time taken to advance smaller transistors to next level will increase more and more in the future.

4 放送される質問を聞き，あなた自身の答えを述べましょう。

(1)

(2)

(3)

(4)

5 この問題では，短い文章を読み，同じ話題についての会話を聞きます。その上で音声で流れる質問に答えなさい。

The university is making changes to the use of the student center. Read the notice about the changes. Give yourself 45 seconds to read the passage.

Changes to Use of the Student Center

As many students are already aware, the recent hurricane damaged the Robinson Building, which includes our dance studio and rehearsal rooms. The university is working to have the building repaired, but please be aware that this could take up to twelve months. For this reason, there will be a restriction on the use of the second floor of the student center, currently used for music and band rehearsals. Members of the dance and theater groups will be given use of the second floor on Saturdays and Sundays from 2 p.m. and will also be able to reserve sessions at other times. We realize the second floor is already in constant use and we ask for your understanding while we carry out the necessary repairs to the Robinson Building.

Lesson 19

Lesson 20
まとめの問題 4

解答冊子 p.137 ／
音声はこちらから➡

実戦問題

1 四人の説明を聞き，下の条件に最も合うものを，選択肢のうちから選びなさい。

状況
あなたは大学1年目にボランティア活動を行うことに興味があります。あなたが
考えている条件は以下のとおりです。

条件
a) 事前の登録なしで都合に合わせて参加できる。
b) 環境や保護を目的とした活動がよい。
c) 新しい友人ができるとよい。

---

	a) flexibility	b) environmental / conservation	c) make friends
① Companion Club			
② Our City			
③ Friends			
④ Green Earth			

2 哲学の講義の英文を聞き，次の質問の答えとして最も適切なものを四つの選択肢のうちから一つずつ選びなさい。

(1) What is this lecture mainly about?

① The greater importance of the classical philosophers over the pre-Socratic philosophers.

② How Aristotle learned from and developed the work of other philosophers.

③ An outline of the most important ideas and philosophers of the ancient period.

④ The influence of some of the ancient philosophers on modern society.

(2) According to the professor, which of the following sentences about the pre-Socratic philosophers is incorrect?

① They tried to understand the world without using stories of gods.

② They used religious beliefs to explain the natural world.

③ Early philosophers thought everything was made of one substance.

④ Some of them wondered how things could burn or ice melt.

(3) Which of the following is true about the influence of Socrates, according to the lecture?

① Socrates' work has influenced the science of matter and change.

② Later philosophers gained wisdom from reading the books of Socrates.

③ Socrates didn't understand how to decide right from wrong.

④ Socrates' method of questioning has helped society to develop.

(4) In the lecture, Plato's "Republic" is described as:

① A description of a city where there are three kinds of people.

② A guide for humans to achieve happiness.

③ A way of deciding people's roles in society.

④ A description of good versus evil.

(5) What might Aristotle's idea of happiness be, according to the professor?

① Aristotle showed that people need to reach conclusions based on truths.

② Aristotle recognized that people should try to find a middle path.

③ Plato thought that there were only three kinds of people.

④ Aristotle knew that humans must change their environment to be happy.

3 あなたは，インタビュー本番に備えてインタビューの練習をすることになりました。それぞれの設問で，まず，インタビューで質問する項目 A ～ C の条件に合う質問文を考えなさい。次に，練習用のインタビューの音声を聞き，それぞれの質問文への答えを日本語で簡潔に書きなさい。

(1) Ask questions about:

A) The books he/she prefers.

B) The book that has been important to him/her.

C) The book he/she will read in the future.

(2) Ask questions about:

A) The way he/she spends time off work.

B) The times he/she starts and leaves work.

C) How he/she eats during working hours.

(3) Ask questions about:

A) His/her first experience of technology.

B) The devices he/she regularly uses.

C) His/her view on negative effects of technology.

(4) Ask questions about:

A) The time he/she has worked in this job.

B) The job he/she would like most.

C) The best thing about his/her job.

4 Now read a passage about history and Christianity. Begin reading now.
Reading time: 100 seconds

One of the most important events in the history of Christianity was the Great Schism of 1054. A schism happens when a group of people split into two groups due to differences of opinion or belief. The Great Schism divided the Christian church into the Roman Catholic Church of Western Europe and the Eastern Orthodox Church, mainly in the East of Europe, Greece and Russia, and so is also known as the East-West Schism.

The origins of the schism lay in the growth and expansion of the Roman Empire many centuries earlier. In order to manage such a vast empire, in 245 AD the Roman Empire was split into the Western Roman Empire, centred on Rome, and the Eastern Roman Empire, or Byzantine Empire, centred on Byzantium, now in Turkey and known as Istanbul.

Christianity was adopted by the whole of the Roman Empire under Constantine the Great in the 4th century AD. However, in 395 the Roman Empire came to have two rulers, or emperors; one in Rome, where most people spoke Latin, and one in Byzantium (which was called Constantinople then), where Greek was the dominant language. This set the scene for tension between the two areas, and after several centuries led up to the Great Schism.

Lesson 20

〈 書籍のアンケートにご協力ください 〈

抽選で**図書カード**を
プレゼント！

Z会の「個人情報の取り扱いについて」はZ会
Webサイト（https://www.zkai.co.jp/poli/）
に掲載しておりますのでご覧ください。

発音できれば聞き取れる！
リスニング×スピーキングのトレーニング　演習編

初版第1刷発行 …………	2020年3月10日
初版第3刷発行 ………	2022年12月10日
監修 …………………………	高山芳樹
執筆協力・英文校閲 ……	Adam Ezard
執筆協力 …………………	渥美浩子
発行人 ……………………	藤井孝昭
発行 ………………………	Z会

〒411-0033　静岡県三島市文教町1-9-11
【販売部門：書籍の乱丁・落丁・返品・交換・注文】
TEL 055-976-9095
【書籍の内容に関するお問い合わせ】
https://www.zkai.co.jp/books/contact/
【ホームページ】
https://www.zkai.co.jp/books/

装丁 ……………………………	株式会社 ファームステッド
	阿部岳　木村梨穂
印刷・製本…………………	日経印刷株式会社
DTP …………………………	株式会社 デジタルプレス
音声録音・編集 …………	一般財団法人英語教育協議会（ELEC）

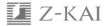

Z-KAI

発音できれば聞き取れる！

リスニング×スピーキングの
トレーニング　演習編

Spiral Training in Listening and Speaking

［解答解説］

CONTENTS

本書の音声は専用 web ページで聞くことができます。
右記の2次元コード，または下記 URL よりご利用ください。
https://service.zkai.co.jp/books/zbooks_data/dlstream?c=2668

Lesson 1
短い情報の聞き取り1（短文選択）

問題冊子 p.12／
音声はこちらから➡

Training

答え

(1) The theater will be closed on Friday. ↘

(2) Why don't we go to see the movie the next day? ↘

Step2
実戦問題

答え

■ (1)① (2)① (3)④ (4)②

解説

■ (1)①

◀€ Could you ...? は「…してくれませんか」と丁寧に依頼する言い方。「クジュー」のようにつながって聞こえるので注意しよう。

スクリプト	和訳
Could you close the window? I can't hear the TV.	窓を閉めてもらえますか。テレビが聞こえません。

選択肢訳

① 外でうるさい音がする。
② 部屋が寒くなってきている。
③ テレビが映らない。
④ 窓はすべて閉まっている。

　話し手は窓を閉めてほしいと頼んでいる。窓が開いているせいでテレビが聞こえないと不満を述べているので，外がうるさいのだと想像できる。答えは①。

(2)①

◀€ can't は単独では can と聞き分けづらいが文中では can't の方が強く長めに発音される。また文脈と but，any などの語からも否定文であると判断できる。

スクリプト	和訳
The forecast in the morning was for rain, but I <u>can't</u> see <u>any</u> clouds.	朝の天気予報では雨だったけど，雲１つ見えないよ。

選択肢訳

① 天気予報がはずれた。

② 話し手は雨が降ると思っている。

③ 今朝はくもりだった。

④ 空が暗くなってきている。

> not ... any ～は「１つも…ない」という強い否定。朝の天気予報は雨で，今は雲がまったくないのだから，答えは①。

(3) ④

スクリプト	和訳
What happened to <u>your new smartphone</u>, Ken? The screen <u>is broken</u>.	ケン，あなたの新しいスマートフォンはどうかしたの？ 画面が壊れているね。

選択肢訳

① 話し手は新しいスマートフォンを手に入れた。

② そのスマートフォンは古くて壊れている。

③ その古いスマートフォンには新しい画面がついている。

④ ケンの新しいスマートフォンはすでに壊れている。

> your new smartphone（あなたの新しいスマートフォン），is broken（壊れている）という発言から，④が正しい。「話し手のスマートフォン」，「古い」といった語句のある選択肢は不適切。「壊れている；故障している」を放送では broken，選択肢では damaged で表している。英語では smartphone を「スマホ」と短縮することはないので注意。

(4) ②

スクリプト	和訳
OK. <u>You look perfect</u> in front of the monument. <u>Smile!</u> So, which button do I press?	はい。記念碑の前でばっちりいい感じ。笑って！ それでどのボタンを押せばいいですか？

選択肢訳

① 話し手はエレベーターを操作している。

② 話し手は誰かの写真を撮っている。

3

③ 話し手はメールを送っている。
④ 話し手はボタンを選んでいる。

　どのような状況での発言かを考える。相手は記念碑の前におり，「笑って！」という発言もあることから，写真を撮っている場面だと推測できる。②が正解。buttonと「ボタン」，elevatorと「エレベーター」は，発音もアクセント位置も日本語とは違うので注意しよう。

注
◇ monument「記念碑〔塔，像〕；遺跡」

Training

答え

(1) Could you close the window? ↗

(2) I can't see any clouds. ↘

(3) What happened to your new smartphone ↘, Ken? ↗

(4) So, which button do I press? ↘

Step3 Let's Speak!

答え
1　(1) Could you close　　(2) can't see any
　　(3) ① your new smartphone　② The screen is broken
　　(4) ① in front of the monument　② which button

📖 Words & Expressions　天気

□ sun > sunny	名太陽 > 形晴れの
□ rain > rainy	名雨　動雨が降る > 形雨の
□ cloud > cloudy	名雲 > 形くもりの
□ snow > snowy	名雪 > 形雪の
□ wind > windy	名風 > 形風の強い
□ (weather) forecast	名（天気）予報
□ it gets dark	（日が落ちて）暗くなる

Lesson 2
短い情報の聞き取り 2 （ビジュアル）

問題冊子 p.16／
音声はこちらから➡

Training

答え

(1) If you take the second left, the post office is across from the library. ↘

Step2
実戦問題

答え

1 (1)② (2)② (3)① (4)④

解説

1 (1)②

🔊 forty (40) と fourteen (14)，seventy (70) と seventeen (17) の聞き分けがポイント。聞き間違いを避けるために "four zero dot one seven" のように1字ずつ発音することもある。

スクリプト	和訳
The password is capital F, then i, l and e in small letters, 40 dot 17.	パスワードは大文字の F，それから小文字の i, l, e，40，ドット (.)，17 です。

　capital は「大文字（の）」，in small letters は「小文字の」の意。dot はピリオドと同じ記号。パスワードは "File40.17" となる。②が正解。

---

(2)②

🔊 later の t は「レイラー」のように，ラ行音のように発音される。

スクリプト	和訳
It's not raining now but the weather forecast says it may start later on.	今は雨が降っていないけど，天気予報は後ほど雨が降り始めるかもしれないって言っているよ。

　now（今）と later on（後ほど）を手がかりに天気の変化を聞き分ける。現在は be not raining（雨が降っていない），その後は may start（…し始めるかもしれない）で，start のあとに raining が省略されている。正解は②。

(3) ①

🔊 shook hands は shook の最後の /k/ の音と hands の /h/ がどちらも子音のため，続けて読むと /h/ の音が脱落して「シュッキャンズ」のように聞こえることもある。

スクリプト	和訳
I introduced John to Lisa for the first time and they shook hands.	私はジョンをリサに初めて紹介し，彼らは握手しました。

　話し手 (I = speaker) が John を Lisa に紹介している。放送後半の they は John と Lisa を指すから，2 人が握手している図を選ぶ。speaker が紹介している様子で，John と Lisa が握手をしている①が正解。shake hands で「握手をする」で shake の過去形が shook。

(4) ④

スクリプト	和訳
The train status information has been updated. The 6:15 express has been delayed by ten minutes.	電車の運行状況が更新されました。6 時 15 分の急行は 10 分遅れています。

　6 時 15 分の列車が 10 分遅れているのだから，6 時 25 分に到着することになる。答えは④。by ten minutes の by は増減や遅れなどを表す動詞と共に使われて，「〜だけ；〜の差で」という意味を表す。

注
◇ status information「運用状況；運行状況」
◇ update「〜の最新情報を提供する」
◇ express「急行列車」

Training

答え

(1) The password is capital F, then i, l and e in small letters, forty dot seventeen. ↘

(2) It's not raining now but the weather forecast says it may start later on. ↘

(3) I introduced John to Lisa for the first time and they shook hands. ↘

(4) The train status information has been updated. The 6:15 express has been delayed by ten minutes. ↘

6

Let's Speak!

答え

1 (1) then i, l and e in small letters　　(2) it may start later on
(3) they shook hands　　(4) ① status information has been updated
② delayed by ten minutes

📖 **Words & Expressions**　道案内 ─────────

☐ corner	名曲がり角；角
☐ intersection	名交差点
☐ T-junction	名T字路, 丁字路
☐ traffic light	名信号
☐ crossing	名横断歩道
☐ go straight	まっすぐ進む
☐ go past ～	～を通り過ぎる
☐ go along ～	～に沿って進む
☐ turn right at ～	～を右折する
☐ take the <u>first</u> left	最初の角を左折する

Training

答え

(1) You still have two days. ↘

(2) I'm practicing for Saturday's game tomorrow and the day after. ↘

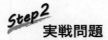

実戦問題

答え

1 (1) ④　(2) ①　(3) ②　(4) ②

解説

1 (1) ④

🔊 got sick の /t/ と /s/ は子音が続くため，/t/ の音は脱落しがちである。

スクリプト	和訳
M: Are you still going to that concert on Saturday?	男性：君はまだ，土曜日に例のコンサートへ行くつもりでいる？
W: Didn't you hear? <u>The singer got sick</u>.	女性：聞いてないの？　歌手が病気になっちゃったのよ。
M: Really? Well, are you free on that day, then? Would you like to come to the movies with us?	男性：本当？ それなら，その日は空いている？ 僕らと映画に行かないかい？
W: I <u>don't feel like seeing a movie</u>, but I'll <u>meet you for dinner</u> after.	女性：映画を見る気分じゃないけど，あとで一緒に夕飯を食べましょう。
M: Sounds good. See you later at the restaurant.	男性：いいね。レストランで会おう。

設問訳　女性は土曜日に何をするつもりか。

① コンサートとレストランに行く。　② 映画とレストランに行く。
③ 映画だけに行く。　④ レストランだけに行く。

女性は「コンサートは歌手が病気（のため中止）」，「映画は見る気分ではない」，「夕飯は一緒に食べよう」と発言しているから，土曜日の予定はレストランだけである。答えは④。

注

◇ feel like *doing*「…したい気がする」
◇ meet ～ for dinner〔lunch〕「～と一緒に夕食〔ランチ〕をとる」

(2) ①

スクリプト	和訳
M: What shall we do first when we get to the Holiday Park?	男性：ホリデーパークに着いたら，まず何をしようか。
W: I want to try the pool, but I think I'll be tired after the journey.	女性：プールを試してみたいけど，旅のあとで疲れていると思うわ。
M: Well, how about taking a rest at the café? We can enjoy the beautiful scenery from there.	男性：じゃあカフェで休憩するのはどう？　そこから美しい景色を楽しめるよ。
W: Really? We can see the beautiful forest, can't we? Okay, let's go to the café and then go swimming.	女性：本当？　美しい森を見ることができるのよね。いいわ，カフェへ行って，それから泳ぎに行きましょう。

設問訳　ホリデーパークでの初日に彼らは何をするか。

① 休憩したあとで泳ぎに行く。
② プールへ行き，それから夕食前に休憩する。
③ 夕食まで休憩し，それからカフェへ行く。
④ 森の中を歩き，あとで休憩する。

　何をするかを相談している場面。いろいろ提案しているが，最終的な結論としては go to the café and then go swimming「カフェへ行ってそのあと泳ぎに行く」。男性は taking a rest at the café と言っているので，正解は①。「カフェ」と café の発音の違いに注意しよう。café は元はフランス語。

(3) ②

スクリプト	和訳
W: I'm just studying math tonight as we have a test in the morning. Are you doing the same?	女性：午前中にテストがあるから，今夜は数学だけを勉強しているのよ。あなたもそう？
M: I think I've already prepared well for it. History is harder for me.	男性：僕はもうその準備がちゃんとできていると思う。歴史の方が僕には難しいよ。
W: We have the history test next week. This week is math and science.	女性：歴史のテストは来週よ。今週は数学と理科でしょ。

M: Those are my strongest subjects. I'm just going to <u>prepare for next week</u>, then go to bed early.	男性：それらは僕は大得意な科目だ。僕は来週の準備だけして，早く寝るよ。

設問訳　男性は今晩何を勉強しますか。

① 歴史と理科
② 歴史のみ
③ 理科のみ
④ 歴史と数学

　男性は最後に just going to prepare for next week「来週の準備だけをする」と述べており，その前の女性の発言から来週は歴史のテストがあることがわかる。数学と理科については Those are my strongest subjects.「それらは僕の大得意科目だ。」として，これらのテスト勉強をするとは言っていない。答えは②。対話中の the same や代名詞（it, those）がどの教科を指しているのかをきちんとつかむことが大切。

(4) ②

◀€ on the <u>list</u> for the <u>lunch</u> set では名詞の list と lunch が強くはっきりと，前置詞や冠詞は弱く速く発音される。下線部を強調してリズムに乗って読むと英語らしい発音になる。

スクリプト	和訳
W: A <u>tuna sandwich and a coffee</u>, please.	女性：ツナサンドとコーヒーをお願いします。
M: For just 50 cents more, you can add a dessert.	男性：あと 50 セントだけ足せばデザートをつけられますよ。
W: Okay. I'll have the <u>carrot cake</u>, please.	女性：そう。キャロットケーキをお願いします。
M: I'm afraid it's not on the list for the lunch set.	男性：すみませんが，それはランチセットのリストにはありません。
W: Okay. Then, I'll <u>pay extra</u>.	女性：そう，じゃあ追加料金を払います。

設問訳　女性の最終的な注文は何か。

① コーヒーとキャロットケーキ
② コーヒーとサンドイッチとキャロットケーキ
③ コーヒーとサンドイッチ
④ コーヒーのみ

　女性は最初にツナサンドとコーヒーを注文し，デザートを勧められてキャロットケーキを頼んでいる。キャロットケーキはランチセットのリストにないことを告げられても，追加料金を払うと言っているので，そのまま注文していることになる。よって答えは②。

注
◇ extra「图追加〔割り増し〕料金, 形余分の；追加の」

Training

答え

(1) Didn't you hear? ↗ The singer got sick. ↘

(2) Okay, let's go to the café and then go swimming. ↘

(3) I'm just going to prepare for next week. ↘

(4) I'm afraid it's not on the list for the lunch set. ↘

Step 3
Let's Speak!

答え

■ (1) ① The singer got sick　② meet you for dinner
(2) ① taking a rest at the café　② then go swimming
(3) ① We have the history test　② I'm just going to prepare
(4) ① for the lunch set　② I'll pay extra

📖 Words & Expressions　混同しやすい語

☐ desert [dézərt]	图砂漠
☐ desert [dızə́ːrt]	動〜を見捨てる；〜を去る
☐ dessert [dızə́ːrt]	图デザート　※ desert 動と同音
☐ adapt [ədǽpt]	動〜に適合させる；順応する
☐ adopt [ədɑ́ːpt, ədɔ́pt]	動〜を採用する；〜を養子にする
☐ beside	前〜のそばに
☐ besides	前〜のほかに；〜に加えて, 副その上
☐ every day	毎日
☐ everyday	形毎日の；日常の　ex. everyday clothes（普段着）
☐ personal [pə́ːrsənl]	形個人の；個人的な
☐ personnel [pə̀ːrsənél]	图職員；社員；人事（課）
☐ advise [ədváız]	動（〜に）助言する
☐ advice [ədváıs]	图助言；忠告

Training

答え

(1) The goal is in the way. Try somewhere near the center. ↘

(2) You're right, let's move them back from the field a little. ↘

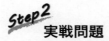

実戦問題

答え

1 (1) ② (2) ① (3) ④ (4) ③

解説

1 (1) ②

🔊 Won't you はつながって「ウォゥンチュー」のように発音される。

スクリプト	和訳
M: I'm thinking of driving to your house on Friday.	男性：金曜日に君の家まで車で行こうと思っているんだけど。
W: Won't you be tired after work? Why not come on Saturday or Sunday?	女性：仕事のあとで疲れていない？　土曜か日曜に来るのはどう？
M: You're right, but traffic on Saturday is terrible, and Sunday is too late. I'd rather take a day off on Friday and drive.	男性：君の言うとおりだけど，土曜は渋滞がひどいし，日曜では遅すぎるし。むしろ，金曜日に休みを取って車で行きたいよ。
W: That sounds good.	女性：いいわね。

設問訳　　いつ男性は車で出かけるか。

　金曜日を提案した男性に対し，女性は土曜か日曜を提案したが，結局金曜日に仕事を休んで行くことになったので，答えは②。

注
◇ Why not ...? (= Why don't you ...?)「…したらどうですか」※提案や軽い命令
◇ take a day off「1 日休みを取る」

12

(2) ①

🔊 would like（want の丁寧表現）の would は弱く短く発音される。主語が代名詞の場合は I'd，You'd のように短縮されることが多い。handle（取っ手）と「ハンドル」の発音の違いに注意しよう。

スクリプト	和訳
W: Which handbag do you think Mom would like?	女性：お母さんはどのハンドバッグを欲しがると思う？
M: It's Mother's Day, so let's get something nice. Those ones with a ribbon look nice.	男性：母の日だから，いいものを選ぼう。リボンが付いているのが素敵に見えるよ。
W: Yeah, but the ones with the long handles are over our budget.	女性：そうね。でも長い取っ手が付いているのは予算オーバーよ。
M: Those two with a pocket are out of fashion. Why don't we get this and give her some flowers, too?	男性：ポケット付きの2つは流行遅れだ。これを買って，花もあげるのはどうかな。

設問訳 彼らはどのカバンを買うだろうか。

　最後の発言の this がどのカバンを指すかが問題である。「取っ手が長いのは予算オーバー」，「ポケット付きは時代遅れ」という発言から，取っ手が短く，ポケットが付いていないカバンを選べばよい。①が正解。

注
◇ budget「予算」

(3) ④

🔊 bottles, out of の t は「バロウズ」「アウロヴ」のようにラ行音に聞こえる。（基礎編 Lesson 14）

スクリプト	和訳
M: Right! We've got bread, jam, milk, one of each. That's everything! How much will that cost?	男性：よし。パン，ジャム，牛乳を1つずつ買ったね。これで全部だ。いくらになる？
W: Let's see. Oh, we need two bottles of milk.	女性：どれどれ。あ，牛乳は2瓶必要よ。
M: I almost forgot. And use this coupon. You can get ten percent off.	男性：忘れるところだった。それとこの割引券も使おう。10 パーセントオフになるよ。
W: Great. Oh, no. It's expired.	女性：いいね。あらまあ，期限切れよ。

Lesson 4

> 対話から購入する品物と個数を聞き取り，イラストからそれぞれの価格を見て計算する。さらに 10 パーセントオフになる割引券を使ったかどうかもポイントとなる。購入した品物はパン，ジャム，牛乳 2 瓶で，割引券は最後に expired（期限切れで）であることがわかったから割引はない。$4 + $6 + ($3 × 2)=$16 で④が正解。

(4) ③

スクリプト	和訳
W: We've both got classes in the languages building this afternoon. Why don't we meet outside there before class?	女性：今日の午後は私たち 2 人とも言語棟で授業があるね。授業の前に言語棟の外で待ち合わせない？
M: Sounds good, but why don't we have lunch before?	男性：いいね。でもその前にランチを食べようよ。
W: Okay. You're in the sports arena in the morning, right? Meet me at the central fountain.	女性：いいよ。あなたは午前中は競技場にいるのよね。中央噴水のところで会いましょう。
M: It gets pretty busy there after class. <u>If you come to the arena</u>, I'll walk with you to the cafeteria in the main hall. We can get something and eat in the student center.	男性：授業のあとはそこはかなり混むよ。君が競技場へ来てくれたら，メインホールのカフェテリアまで君と歩いて行こう。何か買って学生センターで食べることができるよ。

設問訳　彼らはどこで会う予定か。

> 女性が言語棟の外，次に中央噴水を提案したが，最終的には男性が If you come to the arena（競技場に君が来てくれたら）と提案している。the arena は the sports arena を指すから③が正解。

注
◇ pretty「副 かなり：相当」
◇ busy「（場所が）にぎやかな：ごった返した」

音声

Training

答え

(1) Won't you be tired after work? ↗
(2) Which handbag do you think Mom would like? ↘
(3) Oh, we need two bottles of milk. ↘
(4) If you come to the arena, I'll walk with you to the cafeteria in the main hall. ↘

Lesson 4

Step 3
Let's Speak!

答え

■ (1) ① Won't you be tired ② I'd rather take a day off
　(2) ① do you think Mom would like ② with the long handles
　(3) ① two bottles of milk ② get ten percent off
　(4) ① It gets pretty busy ② If you come to the arena

📖 **Words & Expressions**　数え方・単位 ―――――――

□ a bottle of	1 瓶の	ex. a bottle of water（1 瓶の水）
□ a bowl of	1 椀の	ex. a bowl of rice（茶碗 1 杯のご飯）
□ a block of	1 塊の	ex. a block of ice（氷 1 塊）
□ a bunch of	1 房の	ex. a bunch of grapes（ブドウ 1 房）
□ a loaf of	1 斤の	ex. a loaf of bread（パン 1 斤）
□ a slice of	1 切れの	ex. two slices of bread（パン 2 枚）
□ a piece of	1 切れの	ex. three pieces of cake（ケーキ 3 切れ）
□ a pair of	1 組の	ex. a pair of chopsticks（箸 1 膳）
		two pairs of scissors（はさみ 2 丁）

15

Training

答え

(1) Mountain biking seems to be the most popular activity today. Richard, Joanne,

Max and I would like to join this ride. ↘

(2) Nicholas wants to relax but the other two are doing kayaking. ↘

Step 2
実戦問題

答え

1 (1) No　(2) No　(3) No　(4) Yes

2 (1) ②　(2) ③　(3) ①　(4) ③

解説

1 (1) No　(2) No　(3) No　(4) Yes

◀ What do you mean?「どういう意味ですか？」は「ワッドゥユミン」のように続けて聞こえる。よく使われる言い回しは1語1語明瞭に発音されることは少なく，ひとまとまりでも聞き取れるようにしたい。

〔指示文〕本問の4つの文を見なさい。これから，家事に関する男性と女性の会話が放送されます。各文が正しいか正しくないかを答えなさい。

スクリプト	和訳
W: What are you doing today, Jack? If you aren't busy, why don't you help me in the garden?	女性：ジャック，今日は何をするの？　忙しくなければ，庭仕事を手伝ってくれない？
M: Oh, I remember you telling me that you liked gardening. Sure, I'd love to help. But, I'm new to this. What do we have to do?	男性：ああ，君がガーデニングが好きだって話していたのを覚えているよ。もちろん手伝いたいけど，庭仕事には不慣れなんだ。何をすればいいの？
W: I think we have two main jobs. First of all, we need to tidy up around the	女性：大事な仕事が2つあると思う。まず，植物や花の周りを片付ける必要があるの。

16

plants and flowers. <u>We've had quite a bit of rain, so there's no need to water anything.</u> But there are a lot of weeds.

M: <u>What do you mean?</u>

W: If you look at the garden, you'll see all the flowers that I have grown. But because of the rain, you'll see some plants that shouldn't be there. They are the weeds, and we need to pull them out.

M: That sounds fine, but I'm worried that I won't know which ones are the flowers, and which ones are the weeds.

W: You'll be fine. I'll show you what to do. After we've finished that, we'll move on to the vegetable garden.

M: Oh, so you are growing things to eat, too? What are you growing now?

W: I have a lot of different vegetables and some fruit. You'll see strawberry plants and even an apple tree.

M: I love strawberries!

W: Everyone loves strawberries, but <u>they are not ready yet.</u> We need to check some of the vegetables. I'd like you to see if the carrots are ready, and if they are, I'd like you to take them out.

M: How will I know?

W: They will be orange, not green or yellow. We also need to check the broccoli to see if there are any flowers.

M: Are flowers good?

かなり雨が降ったから，水やりの必要はないわ。でも雑草がたくさんあるわね。

男性：どういうこと？

女性：庭を見ると，私が育てたすべての花が見えるでしょう。でも雨のせいでそこにあるべきではない植物も見えるの。それが雑草で，雑草は抜く必要があるの。

男性：わかったけど，僕はどれが花でどれが雑草かわからないんじゃないかと心配だよ。

女性：大丈夫よ。私どうすればいいか見せるから。それが終わったら，野菜畑に移りましょう。

男性：おお，じゃあ君は食べられるものも育てているの？ 今は何を育てている？

女性：いろいろな野菜をたくさんと，いくつかの果物よ。イチゴもあるし，リンゴの木だってあるわよ。

男性：僕はイチゴが大好きなんだ。

女性：みんなイチゴが大好きよ。でもまだ時期ではないわ。野菜をいくつかチェックしなくちゃ。あなたには人参がもう収穫できるか見てほしいの。大丈夫だったら抜いてちょうだい。

男性：どうしたらわかる？

女性：緑や黄色じゃなくて，オレンジ色になるよ。ブロッコリーも花が出ていないかチェックしなくちゃ。

男性：花があるといいの？

Lesson 5

W: Not for us. It's best to pick <u>broccoli before you see the flowers.</u> Actually, let's check that first. M: Fantastic. Lead the way.	女性：私たちにとっては良くないわ。花が出る前に収穫するのがいいの。それを最初にチェックしましょう。 男性：すてきだ。案内してよ。

(1)

問　ジャックはときどき庭仕事を手伝う。

男性は 1 つ目の発言の最後に I'm new to this.「僕はこれには不慣れなんだ。」と言っている。this は gardening を指しており，庭仕事には慣れていないということになる。「ときどき庭仕事を手伝う。」は「いいえ」。

(2)

問　彼らはまず庭に水やりをする必要がある。

女性の 2 つ目の発言に We've had quite a bit of rain, so there's no need to water anything.「かなり雨が降ったから，何にも水をやる必要はない。」とある。a bit of は「少しの；わずかの」という意味だが，quite a bit of は「かなりの」という意味になる。水やりをする必要はないから，答えは「いいえ」。

(3)

問　彼らは今日，果物を収穫するだろう。

果物については，女性の 5 つ目の発言にイチゴとリンゴが出てくるが，女性は 6 つ目の発言で，they are not ready yet「それら（イチゴ）はまだ準備ができていない」と言っており，まだ収穫の時期ではないことがわかる。リンゴについても，収穫の話は出ていないから，正解は「いいえ」である。

(4)

問　ブロッコリーは花が出る前に収穫するべきだ。

女性の最後の発言 It's best to pick broccoli before you see the flowers.「花が出る前にブロッコリーを摘むのが一番いい。」と一致する。「はい」が正解。

注
◇ tidy up「整頓する；片付ける」
◇ weed「雑草」
◇ lead the way「案内する」

2 (1)② (2)③ (3)① (4)③

◖◖ used to は続けて [júːsttə] と発音する。「（以前は）よく…したものだ」という過去の習慣を表す。be used to [bi júːst tə]「〜に慣れている」と混同しないように。used to のあとは動詞の原形，be used to のあとは名詞または動名詞が続く。

〔指示文〕これから，作家でありドキュメンタリー制作者であるエレン・ライトへのインタビューが放送されます。各質問に適切な解答を選びなさい。

スクリプト

M: Please welcome author and documentary maker Ellen Wright.

W: Thank you, Peter. It's great to be here.

M: Now, we'll cover your latest TV series in a moment. But let me just ask, what was it that really began your interest in nature?

W: Well, I guess I've always been fascinated by wildlife, ever since I was a little girl. My grandparents lived on a farm and I used to spend every summer holiday there, playing in the fields and local river. It was my grandfather who taught me the names of all the plants and animals.

M: And you actually live on the same farm now, is that right?

W: When I'm not traveling around the world, yeah. It's been passed down in my family for four generations now.

M: We all know you, of course, from the Wild World Show on kids TV, back in the 1990s. How did that all come about?

W: I was working as an advisor to the show in the beginning. I was teaching at a university and they needed someone to give advice on the different animals each week. Then the producer said to me one day that one of the hosts had become sick. He asked me to appear on the

和訳

男性：作家でありドキュメンタリー制作者であるエレン・ライトさんをお迎えしましょう。

女性：ありがとう、ピーター。ここに来られてうれしいです。

男性：さて、あなたの最新のテレビシリーズについてはあとですぐに話しますが、まず質問させてください。あなたが自然に興味をもつようになったきっかけは何ですか。

女性：ええ、私はほんの小さな頃から野生生物にいつも魅了されていたように思います。祖父母が農場に住んでいて、夏休みはいつもそこで、野原や川で遊んで過ごしたものです。すべての植物や動物の名前を私に教えてくれたのは祖父でした。

男性：そして、あなたは今、その同じ農場に実際に住んでいるのですよね。

女性：ええ、世界中を旅している時以外は。農場はこれまで家族4世代に渡って代々引き継がれてきました。

男性：もちろん我々はあなたのことを1990年代にさかのぼってキッズテレビのワイルド・ワールド・ショーから知っています。どうしてそうなったのですか。

女性：初めはアドバイザーとしてその番組で働いていました。私は大学で教えていて、番組では毎週さまざまな動物についてアドバイスをする人物を必要としていました。ある日、プロデューサーが私に、司会者の1人が病気になったと言いました。彼は私に2、3回分、番組に出るよう頼み、それで気に入ってもらえたよう

show for a couple of episodes, and I guess they liked me.

M: I'd say they liked you very much, as you went on to host the Wild World Show until 2010. Now, tell us a little about the new show.

W: It's called Our Planet. It tells the tale of how we are slowly destroying nature. We are trying to show people how they can help the planet to become healthy again.

です。

男性：大いに気に入られたのでしょう。2010年までワイルド・ワールド・ショーの司会を続けたのですから。さて，新しい番組について少しお話しください。

女性：「私たちの惑星」という番組です。私たちがどのように自然をゆっくり破壊しているかということを扱います。いかにして地球がまた健全になるよう助けられるかを人々にお見せしたいのです。

(1)

問　エレンはどのように自然に興味をもつようになったか。

① 両親が科学者だった。

② 農場で休暇を過ごした。

③ 学校で動物について学ぶのが大好きだった。

男性の２つ目の発言の「あなたが自然に興味をもつようになったきっかけは何か」という質問に，エレンは My grandparents lived on a farm and I used to spend every summer holiday there「祖父母が農場に住んでいて，夏休みはいつもそこで過ごした」と答えている。②が正解。両親の職業や，学校での学習についてはふれられていない。

(2)

問　誰がエレンに最初に自然に関するすべてを教えたか。

① 大学

② テレビ番組

③ 祖父

エレンの２つ目の発言の最後に It was my grandfather who taught me the names of all the plants and animals.「すべての植物や動物の名前を私に教えてくれたのは祖父だった。」とある。正解は③。

(3)

問　彼女は最初どのようにしてテレビの司会者になったか。

① 別の司会者が病気になった。

② 自然に関する本を書いた。

③ 大学でテレビ番組を始めた。

> エレンの4つ目の発言の後半に着目。one of the hosts had become sick「司会者の1人が病気になった」, He asked me to appear on the show「彼（＝番組のプロデューサー）が私に番組に出るよう頼んだ」とある。正解は①。4つ目の発言の前半に大学で教えていたとあるが、大学でテレビ番組を始めたわけではない。また、自然に関する本を書いたという発言はない。

(4)

問　彼女は今、何をしているか。

① 農場で働いている。

② ワイルド・ワールド・ショーで新しい回を作っている。

③ テレビで、人々に地球を守ることを教えている。

> 男性の最後の発言 tell us a little about the new show「新しい番組について少し話してください」から、エレンは現在新しい番組を作っていることがわかる。その内容はエレンの最後の発言 We are trying to show people how they can help the planet to become healthy again「いかにして地球がまた健康になるよう助けられるかを人々にお見せしたい」から、③が該当する。

注

◇ what was it that really began your interest in nature?（男性の2つ目の発言）
　強調構文〈It is ～ that ...〉の変形で、疑問詞 what が強調された形。

◇ fascinate「～の心を引きつける；魅了する」

◇ pass down「（伝統、知識など）を次の世代に渡す」

◇ come about「（事が）起こる；生じる」

◇ destroy「～を破壊する」

Training

答え

(1) What do you mean? ↘

(2) It's best to pick broccoli before you see the flowers. ↘

(3) My grandparents lived on a farm and I used to spend every summer holiday there, playing in the fields and local river. ↘

(4) It was my grandfather who taught me the names of all the plants and animals. ↘

Lesson 5

Step 3 Let's Speak!

答え

1 (1) ① I'm new to this　② What do you mean
　(2) ① Not for us　② before you see the flowers
　(3) ① used to spend every summer holiday　② It was my grandfather
　(4) ① had become sick　② help the planet to become healthy

📖 Words & Expressions　報道

☐ documentary	图ドキュメンタリー；記録作品
☐ non-fiction	图ノンフィクション（伝記, 史実, 紀行など実話に基づく作品） ⇔ fiction「フィクション」
☐ biography	图伝記
☐ reportage	图ルポルタージュ；報道（記事）
☐ journalism	图ジャーナリズム；報道；報道界
☐ news program	图ニュース番組
☐ comedy show	图お笑い番組

Lesson 6
比較・整理1（ビジュアル）

問題冊子 p.36 ／
音声はこちらから➡

Training

答え

(1) I usually walk to school, but I left my house a little late, so I decided to go by bicycle. ↘

(2) Luckily my father was leaving for work by car, so he dropped me off at school just in time. ↘

Step2 実戦問題

答え
1 ③→④→①→②
2 a② b④ c② d④
3 a② b② c① d 810

解説
1 ③→④→①→②

🔊 hide-and-seek の and はかなり弱く発音され，「ハイダンスィーク」のように聞こえる。

スクリプト	和訳
On Saturday, my little brother Ben and his friend Mike asked me to play a game of hide-and-seek. As I was the oldest, I decided to count first. After counting to fifty, I heard a sound in the living room. I quickly opened the living room curtains and found Mike standing there. Mike and I started to seek Ben, but we couldn't find him anywhere. The two of us looked all over and after an hour my parents	土曜日，弟のベンと弟の友だちのマイクが僕にかくれんぼをしようと言ってきました。僕が一番年上だったので，最初に数を数えることにしました。50まで数えたあとでリビングから音が聞こえました。すぐにリビングのカーテンを開け，マイクがそこに立っているのを見つけました。マイクと僕はベンを探し始めましたが，どこにも見つけることができませんでした。僕たち2人はあちこち探し，1時間後には両親も加わりました。僕たちは心配になってきました。僕は自分のベッドに座

| joined us. We started to get worried. I sat on my bed and thought about where he could be. Suddenly something moved and I found him asleep under the blanket. | り，彼がいそうな場所を考えました。突然，何かが動き，弟が毛布の下で眠っているのを発見しました。 |

エピソードが時系列で語られるので，順を追ってイラストに番号を振っていくとよい。かくれんぼで最初に話者が数を数える（③）→カーテンの後ろを見る（④）→（マイクを見つける）→マイクと共に弟を探す（①）→毛布の下で寝てしまった弟を見つける（②）という流れである。

注
◇ hide-and-seek「かくれんぼ」 *cf.* hide「隠れる」, seek「探す」

2 a② b④ c② d④

🔊 get on は t と o がつながって「ゲロン」のように聞こえることがある。ここでは on と off を対比させるため，on もはっきりと発音される。

スクリプト

Welcome to the Royal River Cruise, the best way to visit the city. We have seats on the lower deck starting from $25 for a one-way journey from City Bridge to Docklands Park, or $35 round-trip. We recommend the open top deck for a better sightseeing experience, at just $10 more than the lower deck. In addition, we offer a day pass for $50 that allows you to sit anywhere on the boat and to get on and off at any of our six stops between the bridge and the park, between 9 a.m. and 6 p.m.

和訳

街を訪れる最上の手段，ロイヤルリバークルーズへようこそ。シティブリッジからドックランズ公園まで，片道 25 ドルもしくは往復 35 ドルからの下甲板の席がございます。より素晴らしい景色を体験するには屋根のない上甲板をおすすめします。下甲板よりほんの 10 ドル高いだけです。さらに午前 9 時から午後 6 時まで，橋から公園の間の 6 つの乗り場のどこでも乗り降り自由で，船のどの場所にも座ることができる 50 ドルの 1 日券もご提供しています。

選択肢訳

① 20 ドル ② 35 ドル ③ 45 ドル ④ 50 ドル

下甲板の片道料金，往復料金，上甲板の料金，1 日券の料金の順に説明される。下甲板の席は $25 for a one-way journey（片道 25 ドル），$35 round-trip（往復 35 ドル）だから a は②。上甲板の席は下甲板の席より 10 ドル高いので，片道 35 ドル（25 ＋ 10），往復 45 ドル（35 ＋ 10）になる。したがって，c は②。1 日券は 50 ドルで，これは船のどの場所でも座ることができるから，下甲板も上甲板も同じである。b，d は④が正解。

3 a② b② c① d 810

スクリプト	和訳
Thank you for asking about the summer language courses at City College. We are proud to have held English courses here for over twenty years and we have taught classes to students from over seventy countries around the world. This year we are offering two language courses: the standard course and the premium course.	シティカレッジの夏の語学研修についてお問い合わせいただきありがとうございます。我々は 20 年以上ここで英語コースを開講してきたことを誇りに思います。世界中の 70 を超える国々の学生に教えてきました。今年は 2 つの語学コース，標準コースとプレミアムコースをご用意しています。
Both courses run for the first three weeks of August. The premium course has six hours of classes per day, split into three-hour blocks in the morning and afternoon. Students on the standard course attend the morning sessions only. As afternoon sessions include presentation classes, students will be expected to prepare for a minimum of two hours each evening, including around one hour for the daily writing task. Standard course students are only expected to cover the writing homework.	どちらのコースも 8 月の初めの 3 週間に行われます。プレミアムコースは 1 日に 6 時間の授業があり，午前と午後で 3 時間ずつに分かれています。標準コースの学生は午前中の授業のみに参加します。午後の授業にはプレゼンテーションの授業もあるので，学生は少なくとも毎晩 2 時間は準備にあてることが求められます。2 時間の中には毎日の作文のための約 1 時間が含まれています。標準コースの学生は作文の宿題をやることだけが求められます。
We believe both courses offer great value for students. Not only are the classes held in our modern facilities, but we only employ highly qualified staff with experience teaching students from around the world. The fees for the standard course come to $900 dollars and the premium course is $1,500. In addition, we can offer a 10% discount on both courses if you register before June 1st.	どちらのコースも学生にとって非常に価値のあるものをご提供できると確信しています。現代的な設備の中で授業が行われるだけでなく，世界中の学生を指導する経験を積んだ優秀なスタッフだけを採用しています。標準コースの料金は 900 ドルで，プレミアムコースは 1500 ドルです。加えて，どちらのコースも 6 月 1 日より前にご登録いただければ，10％の割引が可能です。

Lesson 6

① 2　② 3　③ 4　④ 6

	期間	授業時間 （1日当たり）	自習時間 （1日当たり）	料金 （早期申込）
標準コース	3週間	[b]　時間	1時間	[d]　ドル
プレミアムコース	[a]　週間	6時間	[c]　時間 以上	1,350 ドル

　　第2段落に注目する。どちらのコースも for the first three weeks of August（8月の最初の3週間）に行われるとあるので，a は②。授業時間はプレミアムコースは1日に6時間授業で，午前3時間と午後3時間に分かれている。スタンダードコースは午前中だけだから1日の授業時間は3時間ということになる。b は②。自習時間は，プレミアムコースはプレゼンテーションの準備と作文課題の1時間を合わせて少なくとも2時間の自習が必要である。c には①が入る。標準コースの料金は900ドルとあるが，早期申込みの場合は10%割引きが適用されるので，810ドル。

注
◇ split「〜を分ける」
◇ a minimum of 〜「最低でも〜；少なくとも〜」

Training

答え

(1) On Saturday, my little brother Ben and his friend Mike asked me to play a game of hide-and-seek. ↘

(2) In addition, we offer a day pass for $50 that allows you to sit anywhere on the boat and to get on and off at any of our six stops between the bridge and the park, between 9 a.m. and 6 p.m. ↘

(3) Both courses run for the first three weeks of August. ↘

(4) Standard course students are only expected to cover the writing homework. ↘

Let's Speak!

答え

■ (1)① play a game of hide-and-seek ② Mike and I started to seek
　　③ found him asleep under the blanket
(2)① starting from $25 for a one-way journey ② just $10 more
　　③ get on and off
(3)① Both courses run ② morning sessions only
　　③ including around one hour

📖 Words & Expressions　旅行

☐ one-way 　　　形片道の　*ex.* one-way ticket「片道切符」
☐ round-trip 　　形・名往復（の）
☐ sightseeing 　名観光
☐ business trip 名出張
☐ reservation 　名（ホテル，乗り物などの）予約
☐ exchange 　　動・名両替（する）
☐ timetable 　　名時刻表
☐ souvenir 　　　名土産

Lesson 6

Lesson 7
比較・整理2（複数話者）

問題冊子 p.41 ／
音声はこちらから➡

Training

答え

(1) Connect to friends anywhere on Earth with Talk Pal. ↘

(2) This app can support groups of six on one screen with incredibly clear sound and images. ↘

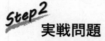

実戦問題

答え
1 ① **2** ④ **3** ②

解説
1 ①

🔊 barbecue と「バーベキュー」，pizza と「ピザ」のアクセント位置，日本語との発音の違いに注意。

スクリプト	和訳
①: Stanley's Natural Food Deli offers a two-course dinner with a drink at $20 per head. <u>Three courses are available for an extra charge of $8,</u> which includes a salad starter. This is a natural food restaurant with <u>no animal products</u> used in any dish.	①: スタンリーズ・ナチュラルフードデリは，1 名あたり 20 ドルの飲み物付きの 2 皿のディナーコースをご用意しています。もう 8 ドル加えれば，3 品料理になり，前菜のサラダを含みます。本店は，どの料理にも動物性の食品を使わない自然食品の店です。
②: Simon's Barbecue offers a vegetarian and a non-vegetarian course, each including drinks. Either course costs $30 and includes our special	②: サイモンズ・バーベキューはベジタリアンコースとベジタリアンではないコースがあり，すべて飲み物付きです。どちらも 30 ドルで，前菜に特別なカボチャ料理がついています。メ

28

Lesson 7

pumpkin starter. You can choose steak or vegetarian curry for the main course. Desserts can be added for an extra $4.50 per person.

③: At Maria's Italian we take pride in our traditional $28 Mediterranean course. Starting with a choice of salad, we have the best range of pizza and pasta with a wonderful homemade ice cream dessert. Drinks can be added for an extra $7 per head. Please feel free to order the vegetarian course, of course!

④: The Fish Shack brings you the finest fresh fish in the area. Our $35 three-course fish dinner is out of this world and comes with drinks. If you don't need a starter, we can offer the same quality for $28.

イン料理としてステーキかベジタリアン・カレーをお選びいただけます。お1人あたりもう4ドル50セントでデザートを追加できます。

③：マリアズ・イタリアンでは28ドルの地中海伝統料理が自慢です。選べるサラダで始まり，さまざまなピザやパスタ，自家製の素晴らしいアイスクリームデザートもございます。お1人7ドルで飲み物も追加できます。もちろんベジタリアン用のコースも遠慮なくご注文ください。

④：フィッシュ・シャックはこの地域の素晴らしい新鮮な魚料理をご提供します。3品で35ドルの魚料理のディナーは天下一品で，飲み物付きです。前菜がいらない場合は，同じ品質で28ドルのコースもあります。

選択肢訳

① スタンリーズ・ナチュラルフードデリ　② サイモンズ・バーベキュー
③ マリアズ・イタリアン　④ フィッシュ・シャック

	A. 値段	B. ベジタリアン対応	C. シーフードアレルギー
① スタンリーズ・ナチュラルフードデリ	× 2品+飲み物 20 ドル ○ 3品+飲み物 28 ドル	○	○
② サイモンズ・バーベキュー	× { 2品+飲み物 30 ドル +デザート 4.5 ドル	○	不明
③ マリアズ・イタリアン	× { 3品 28 ドル +飲み物 7 ドル	○	不明
④ フィッシュ・シャック	× 3品+飲み物 35 ドル × 2品+飲み物 28 ドル	不明	不明

「料理3品と飲み物で1人あたり30ドル未満」という条件を満たしているのは①のスタンリーズ・ナチュラルフードデリ。③マリアズ・イタリアンで28ドルなのは飲み物が含まれない。③マリアズ・イタリアンはシーフードアレルギーについてはふれていない。スタンリーズ・ナチュラルフードデリは動物性の食品は使っていないので，ベジタリアン，シーフードアレルギーの両方に対応できる。よってすべての条件を満たしている。①が正解。

◇ course「コース料理の一品」*ex.* a two-course dinner「2品のディナー」
◇ take pride in ～「～に誇りをもつ」
◇ feel free to *do*「遠慮なく…する」

2 ④

◀ suite「スイートルーム（一続きになった複数の部屋）」は発音注意。sweet「甘い」と同音。

<table>
<tr><td>

スクリプト

</td><td>

和訳

</td></tr>
<tr><td>

①：The Woodland Apartments offer comfortable living spaces in a large accommodation block. Rooms are $250 and up to four guests can stay in each room. These rooms have nice kitchens and guests can prepare meals in the small kitchen. The rooms do not have private bathrooms, but you can use the large common bath with a nice view.

②：The Woodland Executive suite suits those who wish to have a relaxing time. Situated in the forest, these suites each contain a private bathroom and accommodate two to three guests. Rooms start from $350 per night, including breakfast.

③：Our Garden Chalets offer spacious rooms located off a public lounge. Rooms are $190 per night for two persons with toilet and sink, without meals. Bathrooms are shared between four rooms.

④：The Garden Lakeside Apartments have a peaceful view over the lake or gardens where you can enjoy the free breakfast. Each apartment has

</td><td>

①：ウッドランド・アパートは大きな宿泊施設地区の中にある快適な居住空間をご提供します。部屋は250ドルで，各部屋4名様まで滞在できます。すてきなキッチンもあり，お客様がその小さなキッチンでお食事の用意をすることも可能です。各部屋に浴室はございませんが，素晴らしい景色の共同大浴場をご使用いただけます。

②：ウッドランド・エグゼクティブのスイートルームはゆったりとした時間をお望みの皆様にぴったりです。これらのスイートルームは森の中にあり，それぞれ専用の浴室がついていて，2〜3名が宿泊できます。1泊350ドルからで，朝食が含まれています。

③：ガーデン・シャレーは共用ラウンジから離れた広々としたお部屋を提供します。2名様1泊190ドルで，トイレと洗面台がついています。お食事はついておりません。浴室は4部屋で共用します。

④：ガーデン・レイクサイド・アパートは湖または庭園の穏やかな景色があり，無料の朝食をお楽しみいただけます。専用の浴室もご利用いただけます。3つのダブルベッドと2つのシン

</td></tr>
</table>

its own private bathroom. Able to accommodate up to eight guests in three double and two single beds, second floor apartments with a lake view are available at $650, with first floor garden view apartments $100 less.

グルベッドがあり 8 名様まで宿泊できます。湖が見える 2 階のお部屋は 650 ドル，庭園が見える 1 階はそれより 100 ドルお安くなっています。

選択肢訳

① ウッドランド・アパート　　② ウッドランド・エグゼクティブ
③ ガーデン・シャレー　　④ ガーデン・レイクサイド・アパート

	A. 予算合計	B. 専有できる風呂	C. 朝食
① ウッドランド・アパート	○ 500 ドル (250 ドル× 2)	×	不明
② ウッドランド・エグゼクティブ	× 700 ドル (350 ドル× 2)	○	○
③ ガーデン・シャレー	○ 570 ドル (190 ドル× 3)	× （4 部屋で共有）	×
④ ガーデン・レイクサイド・アパート	× 650 ドル（2 階）○ 550 ドル（1 階）	○	○

「予算 600 ドル未満」の条件に当てはまるかどうかを調べるためには，参加人数と部屋の収容人数から必要な部屋数を割り出し，部屋ごとの値段と掛け合わせて合計金額を計算する必要がある。計算結果は表のとおりで，予算の条件に合うのは①のウッドランド・アパートと④のガーデン・レイクサイド・アパートの 1 階である。両者のうち，他の 2 つの条件を満たしているのはガーデン・レイクサイド・アパートだから，正解は④。

注
◇ apartment「（保養地などの短期間滞在用）貸室」
◇ accommodation「宿泊施設」　　accommodate「（建物が人を）収容する」
◇ spacious「広々とした；ゆったりとした」
◇ with first floor garden view apartments (available at) $100 less と補って考える

3 ②

スクリプト

①: The basketball club plays in one of the strongest leagues in the country. We receive support from some companies, so students do not need to pay for uniforms or equipment. We practice

和訳

①：バスケ部は国内で最も強いリーグの 1 つでプレーしています。複数の会社から支援を受けているので，学生はユニフォームや用具の費用を負担する必要はありません。月曜から金曜に練習があり，試合は通常土曜日の夜に行われま

from Monday to Friday, and games are usually in the evenings on Saturdays. First and second year students play an active part in supporting the team and the best players often enter the games in their second year.

②: Join our new soccer club. We hold competitions most weekends, so if you are available either Saturday or Sunday, this is the club for you. We believe in active training, so all new members participate in matches from early on. The university covers our court costs; students just need to cover transport to away games.

③: Learn a traditional Japanese sport with the university karate club. We have a long tradition and have won the national championship several times. Once you purchase your karate suit and protective gear, usually two or three hundred dollars, there are no further costs. We practice from Monday to Friday. Students who train hard often enter the championships from the first year.

④: Softball is one of the most popular mixed male/female activities on campus. Join a friendly club and play in mixed matches. We have a great atmosphere and often hold Sunday matches which any members from first years to fourth years can join. All costs and equipment are provided by the club.

す。1，2年生はチームのサポートに積極的な役割を果たし，優れた選手は2年生で試合に出ることが多いです。

②：我々の新しいサッカー部へどうぞ。大会はほとんど週末に行われるので，土曜か日曜のどちらかに参加できるなら，我が部は君のための部活だと言えます。我々は積極的なトレーニングを信じているので，新人は全員早いうちから試合に参加してもらいます。大学がコート代を出してくれるので，学生はアウェイの試合に出かける交通費だけ負担すればいいです。

③：大学の空手部で伝統的な日本のスポーツを学びましょう。僕らには長い伝統があり，全国大会で何度も優勝しています。空手着と防具は通常は200～300ドルですが，いったん購入すれば，あとはお金はかかりません。月曜日から金曜日に練習します。一生懸命鍛えている選手は，1年生から試合に出ることが多いです。

④：ソフトボール部は学内で最も人気のある男女混合の活動の1つです。友好的な部活に入って，男女混合で試合をしましょう。とてもいい雰囲気で，1年生から4年生までどの部員も参加できる試合を日曜日によく行います。部費や用具はすべて部から提供されます。

選択肢訳

① バスケ部　　　　② サッカー部
③ 空手部　　　　　④ ソフトボール部

	A. 日曜休み	B. 道具と部費	C. 試合や大会への参加
① バスケ部	○（練習は月〜金，試合は土）	○	×早くて2年から
② サッカー部	○（土日のどちらか）	○（交通費のみ）	○
③ 空手部	○（練習は月〜金）	×（初期費用200〜300ドル）	○
④ ソフトボール部	×（試合あり）	○	○

　1つ目の条件「日曜日に部活がない」に当てはまるのは①のバスケ部と③の空手部。②のサッカー部の either Saturday or Sunday は土日のどちらかに参加すればよいということなので，これも条件に当てはまる。2つ目の費用に関しては空手部のみが初期費用がかかり，条件を満たさない。1年生からの試合参加については，バスケ部が「優れた選手は2年生で試合に出られる」とあり条件を満たさないが，あとの部活は新人，1年生も試合に出られると言っている。条件を3つとも満たしているのは②のサッカー部。

注
◇ purchase「〜を購入する；買う」
◇ protective gear「防具；防護服」

Training

答え

(1) Simon's Barbecue offers a vegetarian and a non-vegetarian course, each including drinks. ↘

(2) Starting with a choice of salad, we have the best range of pizza and pasta with a wonderful homemade ice cream dessert. ↘

(3) The Woodland Executive suite suits those who wish to have a relaxing time. ↘

(4) We hold competitions most weekends, so if you are available either Saturday or Sunday, this is the club for you. ↘

$Step^3$
Let's Speak!

1 (1) ① Barbecue offers a vegetarian and ② an extra $4.50 per person

(2) ① the best range of pizza ② order the vegetarian course

(3) ① suite suits those who wish ② from $350 per night, including breakfast

(4) ① you are available either Saturday or Sunday ② all new members participate in matches

---

📖 **Words & Expressions** お金 ────────

☐ cost	動（費用）がかかる 名費用；値段
☐ budget	名予算
☐ fee	名料金，会費；謝礼，報酬；授業料
☐ charge	名料金，手数料 動（金額）を請求する；〜を充電する
☐ price	名（品物などの）価格；値段
☐ fare	名運賃；料金
☐ coin	名硬貨
☐ bill（米），note（英）	名紙幣
☐ electronic money	名電子マネー

Lesson 8
書き取り 1 （メモ空所補充）

問題冊子 p.47 ／
音声はこちらから➡

Training

答え

(1) We'd like tickets for the early evening show, please. ↘

(2) Please be aware that there is a booking fee of one dollar per ticket. ↘

Step 2
実戦問題

答え

1 (1) 15th August　(2) Friday　(3) two　(4) a single and a double room
　(5) $164　(6) 10 a.m.

2 (1) new information　(2) five years ago　(3) fifth 〔top〕 floor
　(4) a 〔one〕 million　(5) student center

3 (1) keep their helmets on 〔wear helmets〕　(2) 40 meters　(3) raise our
　hand　(4) 10 seconds　(5) small, medium, large, extra large

解説

1 (1) 15th August　(2) Friday　(3) two　(4) a single and a double room
　(5) $164　(6) 10 a.m.

◀: 重要な情報は強くはっきりと発音される。ホテルの予約では宿泊数，人数，料金
　などが特に強調される。

スクリプト	和訳
M：Good evening, Royal Hotel. How may I help you?	男性：こんばんは。ロイヤルホテルです。どのようなご用件ですか。
W：Good evening. I'd like to make a reservation for the 15th August.	女性：こんばんは。8 月 15 日の予約をとりたいのですが。
M：Certainly! Let me see.... Is it just one room?	男性：かしこまりました。少々お待ちを。1 部屋だけでしょうか。
W：No, we'd like to book two single rooms, if possible.	女性：いいえ，できればシングルルームを 2 部屋予約したいです。

M：Sure. How many nights are you staying? I'm afraid we have a minimum of two nights stay.	男性：わかりました。何泊のご予定ですか。すみませんが当ホテルでは少なくとも2泊からとなっております。
W：That's perfect for us. We're arriving Friday and leaving Sunday.	女性：ちょうどよかった。金曜に着いて日曜に出発します。
M：Great. For those dates, we only have one single room left. Would you be okay with a single and a double? The single is $30 per night and the double $40.	男性：素晴らしい。その日程はシングルルームが1部屋しか残っていません。シングル1部屋とダブル1部屋でもよろしいですか。シングルは1泊30ドル，ダブルは40ドルです。
W：Yes, that will be fine. Is breakfast included in those charges?	女性：ええ，それでかまいません。その料金に朝食は含まれていますか。
M：These prices are for room only but include free tea and coffee. We can add breakfast for $6 per head for each day.	男性：この価格はお部屋代のみですが，無料のお茶とコーヒーが含まれます。朝食はお1人様1日につき6ドルでお付けすることができます。
W：That sounds good. We'll take the single and double rooms with breakfast included.	女性：よかった。シングルルームとダブルルームを朝食付きでお願いします。
M：Very well. Check in is from 3 p.m. and check out at 10 a.m. You can also book a late check out and extend your stay until 12 for $10 per room.	男性：承知しました。チェックインは3時から，チェックアウトは10時です。チェックアウトを12時まで延長する予約も1部屋につき10ドルでできます。
W：Not for us, thank you. We need to catch the train at 10:30 on the Sunday.	女性：ありがとう。でも延長はしなくていいです。日曜日は10時半の電車に乗らなければならないので。
M：Understood. Could I just take a few personal details?	男性：わかりました。では，お客様の情報について2，3伺ってもよろしいですか。

設問訳　女性がホテルの予約をする音声が流れます。

聞いて，抜けている情報(1)～(6)を記入しなさい。

(1) 滞在を始める日：〔　　　　〕

(2) 到着する曜日：〔　　　　〕

(3) 宿泊日数：〔　　　　〕

(4) 予約する部屋のタイプ：〔　　　　〕

(5) 合計金額：〔　　　　〕

(6) 彼女たちは_____前にチェックアウトするだろう。

会話はメモの順番に進む。女性は最初の発言で8月15日の予約を頼んでいる。女性の3番目の発言では金曜日に到着し日曜日に出発することがわかる。金曜日から日曜日だから2泊の滞在である。女性はシングルルーム2部屋を希望していたが，ホテルから提案されたシングル1部屋，ダブル1部屋を予約することになった。料金はシングル30ドル×2泊，ダブル40ドル×2泊，朝食6ドル×2人×2日分で合計164ドルである。ホテルのチェックアウト時刻は10時で，女性は延長を断っているので，10時までにはチェックアウトする予定である。the 15th August は，音声上はイギリス英語式に the 15th of August と読んでいる。

注
◇ head「（数を数えるときの）1人」 per head「1人当たり」

2 (1) new information　(2) five years ago　(3) fifth〔top〕floor
　(4) a〔one〕million　(5) student center

■ house は名詞［háus］と動詞［háuz］で発音が異なるので注意。名詞の複数形と，動詞に3単現の s が付いた houses は同じ発音［háuzɪz］。

スクリプト	和訳
Welcome to your first day orientation at Reed College.	リード大学の初日オリエンテーションへようこそ。
I hope you will enjoy the three years you will spend with us. We'll begin with a guided tour of the campus.	我々と共に過ごす3年間を君たちが楽しんでくれるよう望んでいます。キャンパスのガイド・ツアーから始めましょう。
As we go through the security gates on the left, you can see the college office. You will need to visit here to find out new information and apply to join clubs and courses.	左手にある防犯ゲートを通り抜けると大学事務室が見えます。新しい情報を見つけたり，部活や課程に参加する申請をしたりするにはここを訪れる必要があります。
To the right are the three science buildings. These are pretty new; they were built just five years ago, and we are lucky to have such modern facilities.	右手に科学棟が3棟あります。これらはかなり新しく5年前に建てられたばかりです。このような近代設備があるとは，我々は幸運ですね。
Moving on, you can see the student center. It is set in the very middle of the campus and has five floors, as well as a concert hall in the basement. There is a restaurant on the first floor and a coffee shop at the top, which has a great view over the whole college.	先へ進むと学生センターが見えます。ここはキャンパスのちょうど中央にあり5階建てです。地下にはコンサートホールもあります。1階にはレストラン，最上階にはコーヒー店があり，そこからの眺望は素晴らしく，大学全体を見渡すことができます。
Behind the student center we have	学生センターの後ろには中央図書館がありま

the main library. The library, at three hundred years old, is the oldest building here. However, as we'll see, although the outside looks old, the interior is very modern and <u>houses</u> over a million books.	す。図書館は築 300 年で，ここでもっとも古い建物です。ご覧のように外観は古びていますが，室内は非常に近代的で 100 万冊を超える蔵書があります。
Please feel free to look through the library and meet me back <u>in the student center in thirty minutes.</u>	遠慮なく図書館の中を見学してください。30 分後に，学生センターに戻ってまたお会いしましょう。

設問訳　リード大学に関する情報の音声が流れます。
聞いて，抜けている情報(1)～(5)を記入しなさい。

(1) _____ を見つけるために大学事務室を訪れる。
(2) 科学棟がに建てられた時期：〔　　　　〕
(3) コーヒー店の所在：〔学生センターの〔　　〕にある〕
(4) 図書館の蔵書数：〔　　　を超える〕
(5) 彼らは 30 分後に_____で会う。

本問と次問は，対話文ではなくアナウンスを聞いて，必要な情報を書き取る問題である。今まで同様，メモの順に情報が与えられるので，聞きながらメモを完成させよう。初めに大学事務室が紹介される。ここは<u>新しい情報</u>を見つけ，部活や課程を申請するために訪れる。次に科学棟が紹介され，建てられたのは five years ago（5 年前）と言っていた。学生センターは 5 階建てでコーヒー店はその最上階にあるから，コーヒー店の場所は<u>5 階</u>ということになる。five ではなく fifth とすることに注意する。中央図書館の蔵書数は <u>100 万冊</u>を超える。図書館を自由に見学したあと，30 分後に会う場所は<u>学生センター</u>である。

注
◇ basement「地階」
◇ house「～を所蔵する；収容する」

3 (1) keep their helmets on 〔wear helmets〕　(2) 40 meters　(3) raise our hand　(4) 10 seconds　(5) small, medium, large, extra large

スクリプト	和訳
Thank you all for coming to Brigham Forest Woodland Activities today. Looking at your entry forms, it seems all of you are visiting for the first time.	本日はブリガムの森ウッドランドアクティビティーズにお越しいただきありがとうございます。参加用紙を拝見したところ，すべてのお客様が初めていらしたようです。
In a moment, we'll talk about our safety features and we'll fit you for helmets and safety belts. Please make sure to <u>keep your helmet on at all times</u> while you are here.	すぐに安全機能についてご説明し，ヘルメットと安全ベルトのサイズをお客様に合わせます。ここにいらっしゃる間は常にヘルメットを着用することを確実に心掛けてください。

After you see the safety video, we'll take you out to the first activity, which is the treetop walk. You'll climb 40 meters to the start point, from where we will cross rope bridges to the finish point, which is 50 meters high. The journey usually takes between thirty and forty minutes, but you may go at your own pace.

If you feel sick at any time, please raise your hand and a guide will come to assist you.

After the treetop walk, we will move on to the rope slide. Hold the rope with two hands until you reach the bottom and stop moving. Try to move out of the way within 10 seconds so that the next person can come down smoothly. Again, if you have any problems, our guides will help you.

Okay, we are ready with the helmets now. Please choose small, medium, large or extra large from the box over here.

安全ビデオをご覧になったあと，最初の活動である樹上散歩に皆様をお連れします。出発点まで 40 メートル登り，そこから 50 メートルの高さにある終着点まで吊り橋を渡ります。行程にかかる時間は通常 30 分から 40 分ほどですが，ご自分のペースで進んでくださってけっこうです。

もし気分が悪くなったらいつでも手を挙げてください。ガイドが助けに伺います。

樹上散歩のあとは，ジップラインに移ります。下に着いて止まるまで，両手で縄をつかんでいてください。次の人がスムーズに降りてこられるよう，10 秒以内にその場から移動するようにしてください。繰り返しになりますが，もし何か問題がある場合は，ガイドがお客様を助けます。

では，ヘルメットの準備ができました。こちらへ来て箱から小・中・大・特大のサイズを選んでください。

Lesson 8

設問訳　ある活動に関する情報の音声が流れます。
聞いて，抜けている情報(1)～(5)を記入しなさい。
(1) 訪問者は常に_____しなければならない。
(2) 樹上散歩のスタート地点の高さ：〔　　〕
(3) 気分が悪くなったらすべきこと：〔　　〕
(4) ジップラインのあと，〔　　〕以内に移動すべきである
(5) ヘルメットのサイズの種類：〔　　〕

　野外活動の事前説明である。(1)にある at all times（常に）という言葉は第 2 段落の最後に出てくる。keep your helmet on（ヘルメットを着用したままにする）と言っている。treetop walk の説明では出発点まで 40 メートル登ると言っている。樹上散歩の説明の次の段落で，気分が悪くなった時は raise your hand（手を挙げる）ように言っている。rope slide の説明は最後から 2 段落目にある。within 10 seconds（10 秒以内）に移動するよう指示している。ヘルメットのサイズは最後の段落で説明される。小・中・大・特大の 4 サイズである。

Training

(1) We can add breakfast for six dollars per head for each day. ↘

(2) Not for us, thank you. ↘ We need to catch the train at 10:30 on the Sunday.

(3) Please feel free to look through the library and meet me back in the student center in thirty minutes. ↘

(4) If you feel sick at any time, please raise your hand and a guide will come to assist you. ↘

Step3 Let's Speak!

1 (1) ① We're arriving Friday and leaving Sunday　② $30 per night and the double $40
(2) ① are the three science buildings
② in the very middle of the campus and has five floors　③ and a coffee shop at the top
(3) ① move out of the way within 10 seconds　② or extra large from the box over here

Words & Expressions　迷いやすい自動詞・他動詞

□ raise [réɪz] 他 ～を上げる		raise － raised － raised
□ rise 自 上がる；立ち上がる		rise － rose － risen
□ lay 他 ～を置く；横たえる		lay － laid － laid
□ lie 自 ～に横たわる；～に位置する		lie － lay － lain
□ lie 名 うそ 自 うそをつく		lie － lied － lied

Lesson 9
書き取り2（短文空所補充）

問題冊子 p.52 ／
音声はこちらから➡

Training

答え

(1) Starting from Tuesday, for five days only we are offering a huge range of electronic devices at great discounts. ↘

(2) Find amazing prices on our PC floor, where you can buy a desktop computer with a printer for only $400. ↘

Step2
実戦問題

答え
■ (1) Friday　(2) warm and sunny　(3) Monday, Tuesday　(4) 25 (degrees)
　　(5) near the coast　(6) very cloudy
② (1) different music　(2) 1 p.m.　(3) May　(4) helper dogs
　　(5) the cake shop　(6) a performance by the film club
③ (1) Japanese　(2) have a discussion (about Japanese and Taiwanese culture)　(3) it is raining　(4) have [eat] lunch　(5) science　(6) Monday

---

解説
■ (1) Friday　(2) warm and sunny　(3) Monday, Tuesday　(4) 25 (degrees)
　　(5) near the coast　(6) very cloudy

スクリプト	和訳
It's 7:55 on this warm Sunday evening, so now let's take a look at the weather over the whole country from Monday to Friday. Starting in the southwest, it's going to be a warm and sunny week. The warm weather will continue throughout the south of the country, but the southeast will also experience some rain over the first two	暖かい日曜の夜7時55分です。月曜から金曜の全国の天気を見ていきましょう。南西部から始めます。暖かく晴れる週となるでしょう。暖かい天気が南部全体で続きますが，南東部は週の初めの2日間はいくらか雨も降るでしょう。

days of the week.

Moving into the central regions, we can see some high pressure bringing the warmest weather, with a high of 30 degrees midweek, although this will drop to 25 by Friday.

Going through to the north, rain is forecast for the northwest, especially near the coast. The northeast may escape the rain but there will be heavy clouds. It is likely to be a little cold as not much sunshine will get through.

中央部に移ります。かなり暖かい天気をもたらす高気圧があり，週の中ほどには最高気温が30度になりますが，金曜までには25度まで下がるでしょう。

北部へかけては，北西部，特に海岸付近が雨の予報です。北東部は雨は降りませんがどんよりとくもるでしょう。日の光があまり射さないため，少し寒くなりそうです。

設問訳　日曜日に天気予報が流れます。
各質問の空所に抜けている情報を入れなさい。

○天気予報
(1) この予報は〔　　　〕まで及んでいる。
(2) 南西部：〔　　　〕になりそうだ。
(3) 南東部：〔　　　〕雨が降る。
(4) 中央部：気温は金曜日までに〔　　　〕まで下がりそうだ。
(5) 北西部：〔　　　〕で特に雨が降りそうだ。
(6) 北東部：空は〔　　　〕。

地方ごとの天気予報が順に語られる。天気予報が放送されているのは日曜の夜で，月曜から金曜の予報である。初めに南西部が warm and sunny と予報される。南東部は the first two days of the week が雨，つまり翌 Monday と Tuesday が雨である。中央部は気温が高いが，金曜日には25度まで下がると言っている。北西部で特に雨が降るのは，especially（特に）に続く near the coast。北東部は there will be heavy clouds と言っているからくもりである。

注
◇ high pressure「高気圧」
◇ high「最高記録（ここでは最高気温）」

2 (1) different music　(2) 1p.m.　(3) May　(4) helper dogs
　(5) the cake shop　(6) a performance by the film club

🔊 energy と「エネルギー」，theme と「テーマ」は発音が大きく違うので注意。

スクリプト	和訳
Welcome to Sakura High School Festival! As we have students visiting	サクラ高校の学校祭へようこそ。今年はさまざまな国から訪れた生徒がいるので，英語で放

from different countries, we are holding our announcements in English this year.

We have many amazing events, so please try to see as much as you can.

In the main hall we have events in the morning and afternoon. From 9 a.m. you can hear the school orchestra. They will be playing two thirty-minute concerts. Each concert features different music, so why not listen to both?

The dance club will perform on the same stage from 1 p.m. They have been practicing very hard, so help to give them some energy by clapping for them.

On the main sports field, the school soccer team are playing games against both Midori High School and Nishi High School. As you know, Sakura High soccer club won the city competition in May, so why not cheer them today as well?

In front of the school, by the entrance, the first-year students are collecting money for helper dogs. They will be doing face painting for younger visitors, and also playing some music.

Each classroom will hold a themed presentation. As every room is different, we ask you to visit each one. There is so much to enjoy, including a haunted house, a game center and a cake shop. In the cake shop, you can enjoy hot tea, coffee, or orange juice.

Finally, if you go to the school gymnasium, you can see a performance by the film club. They have put up a

送を行っています。

多くの素晴らしいイベントがありますので，できるだけたくさん見学してみてください。

メインホールでは午前も午後もイベントがあります。午前9時からは学校オーケストラを聞くことができます。オーケストラは30分のコンサートを2回行います。どちらも違う音楽を呼び物としますから両方聞いてはいかがでしょう。

同じステージで午後1時からダンス部が演技をします。部員たちはとても厳しい練習をしてきたので，拍手をして彼らに力を与えるお手伝いをしてください。

中央運動場では，サッカー部がミドリ高校とニシ高校との試合をします。ご存知のとおり，サクラ高校サッカー部は5月に市の大会で優勝しました。今日も応援よろしくお願いします。

校舎の前の入り口そばでは，1年生が介助犬のための募金活動をしています。年少の来場者にフェイス・ペインティングをしたり，音楽を演奏したりもします。

各クラスではテーマに沿った展示をします。クラスごとに違うので，それぞれに行ってみてください。お化け屋敷，ゲームセンター，ケーキ屋など楽しめるものがたくさんあります。ケーキ屋では熱いお茶やコーヒー，オレンジジュースが楽しめます。

最後に，体育館に行くと映画部による上映があります。映画部では大きなスクリーンを掲げ，部員が作成した映画をお見せしています。バラ

Lesson 9

| giant screen and they are showing the films made by their members. There is a large variety and two of the members won prizes this year in a national competition. | エティに富んでいて，部員のうち2人は全国大会で今年の賞を取りました。 |
| To learn more about the festival, please pick up an information leaflet by the main gate. | 学校祭についてもっと知りたい方は，正門にあるパンフレットをお取りください。 |

設問訳　高校の学校祭についてのアナウンスが流れます。

各質問の空所に抜けている情報を入れなさい。

サクラ高校学校祭

○メインホール

(1) 学校オーケストラのそれぞれのコンサートでは〔　　　〕を呼び物としている。

(2) ダンスイベントは〔　　　〕から催される。

○中央運動場

・サッカーチームが試合をする。

(3) サッカー部は〔　　　〕に市の大会で優勝した。

○入り口そば

(4) 1年生は〔　　　〕のために募金を集めている。

○テーマに沿った展示

(5) 飲み物は〔　　　〕で手に入れられる。

○体育館

(6) 〔　　　〕を見ることができる。

学校祭の案内で，構内のどこで何が行われるかが説明される。オーケストラのコンサートは2回行われ，それぞれ different music を呼び物にすると言っていた。ダンスイベントはオーケストラと同じステージで行われると言っており，時間は午後1時からである。サッカー部の紹介は第5段落にある。大会で優勝したのは5月。1年生が募金を集めているのは helper dogs のためである。飲み物は第7段落の各クラスの出し物の中のケーキ屋で hot tea, coffee, or orange juice が出されると言っている。体育館で見られるのは第8段落の1文目で説明されている，映画部による上映である。

注

◇ themed「特定のテーマを持つ」 *cf.* theme「テーマ；主題」

3 (1) Japanese　(2) have a discussion (about Japanese and Taiwanese culture)　(3) it is raining　(4) have〔eat〕lunch　(5) science　(6) Monday

| スクリプト | 和訳 |
| Good morning to all the students who are visiting our school from Taiwan. We are very happy that you are | 台湾から我が校へお越しの学生の皆さん，おはようございます。皆さんがこの学校で過ごされることをとてもうれしく思います。本日のス |

spending time at our school. I will talk about today's schedule, so please listen carefully.

Before our first class, the principal of our school will give a speech. <u>He doesn't speak English, so we will translate his speech from Japanese to English</u>.

After the speech you will go with your group for a tour of our school. We will show you the sports ground and the classrooms.

At 9:30 you will join our English class. <u>We will have a discussion about Japanese and Taiwanese culture</u>, and after this we will listen to your school song and school presentation. We are looking forward to it very much. The English class lasts until 11:30, so we will have plenty of time to learn about each other.

After the English class, our sports teacher will take us to the gymnasium. We will have a choice of playing either basketball or badminton. We were going to play soccer, but <u>it's raining today</u>. I'm sure we can enjoy indoor sports together.

<u>We will have lunch at 12:30</u> in the cafeteria. The sports teacher will take us there.

After we have lunch you will join our regular classes for the two afternoon lessons. We have a math class and a science class. <u>Group A will do math first, then science. Group B will do the other way around.</u>

After school there will be a welcome

ケジュールをお話ししますのでよく聞いてください。

　1 時間目の前に，我が校の校長先生がお話されます。校長先生は英語を話さないので，私たちが日本語から英語に通訳します。

　お話のあと，皆さんはグループで学校ツアーに出かけます。運動場や教室をお見せします。

　9 時 30 分に英語の授業に参加します。日本と台湾の文化について話し合い，そのあと皆さんの校歌と学校発表を聞きます。私たちはとても楽しみにしています。英語の授業は 11 時 30 分までですから，お互いのことを学ぶ時間はたっぷりあります。

　英語の授業のあとは，体育の先生が体育館に連れて行ってくれます。バスケットボールとバドミントンのどちらをやるかを選びます。サッカーをする予定でしたが，今日は雨が降っています。室内スポーツを一緒に楽しむことができるでしょう。

　12 時 30 分にカフェテリアでランチを食べます。体育の先生がカフェテリアまで連れて行ってくれます。

　昼食後は午後の 2 時間，通常授業に参加します。数学と理科の授業があります。グループ A の皆さんは数学を先にやって次に理科です。グループ B の皆さんはその逆の順です。

　放課後は会議室で歓迎会があります。軽食と

Lesson 9

reception in the meeting room. We will have some snacks and drinks and you will meet your host families. Please enjoy the two days over the weekend with your family and we will see you back at school on Monday.

Now, over to our school principal.

飲み物をご用意します。皆さんはホストファミリーに会います。週末の2日間をホストファミリーと楽しんでください。そして，月曜にまた学校でお会いしましょう。

では，校長先生お願いします。

設問訳 外国から来た生徒たちへの案内が流れます。

各質問の空所に抜けている情報を入れなさい。

学校紹介

○授業の前

(1) 校長先生は〔　　　〕でスピーチをする。

・スピーチのあと，学校ツアーに出かける

○9時30分

・英語の授業に参加

(2) 生徒たちはまず〔　　　〕。

○体育館で

(3)〔　　　〕なので，室内スポーツをする。

○12時30分

(4) 生徒たちは〔　　　〕。

○午後

・グループ A はまず数学の授業を受ける。

(5) グループ B はまず〔　　　〕の授業を受ける。

○放課後と翌週

・歓迎会が開かれる。

(6) 生徒たちは〔　　　〕に再会する。

　第2段落で，校長先生は英語を話さず，話者が日本語から英語に通訳すると言っているので，校長先生が話すのは日本語。英語の授業ではまず日本と台湾の文化について討論すると言っていた。体育館の話題は第5段落で，雨が降っているので室内スポーツを楽しもうと言っていた。12時30分はカフェテリアでランチを食べる時間である。午後の授業ではグループ A は数学，理科の順，グループ B は the other way around（その逆）だから理科が先である。最後に週末の2日間のあとまた月曜日に会いましょうと言っている。

注
◇ the other way around「あべこべに；その逆で」
◇ reception「宴会；（会社，病院などの）受付」
◇ over to 〜「次は〜の番で」

Training

答え

(1) Starting in the southwest, it's going to be a warm and sunny week. ↘

(2) They have been practicing very hard, so help to give them some energy by clapping for them. ↘

(3) Each classroom will hold a themed presentation. ↘

(4) Group A will do math first, then science. Group B will do the other way around. ↘

Step³ Let's Speak!

答え

1 (1) ① over the whole country from Monday to Friday ② over the first two days of the week
(2) ① hold a themed presentation ② the cake shop, you can enjoy
(3) ① Group A will do math first ② enjoy the two days over the weekend ③ see you back at school on Monday

Lesson 9

📖 Words & Expressions　音楽

☐ orchestra	图オーケストラ, 管弦楽団
☐ brass band	图ブラスバンド, 吹奏楽団
☐ concert	图コンサート
☐ conductor	图指揮者
☐ soloist	图ソロ奏者, 独唱者
☐ classical music	图クラシック音楽
☐ instrument	图楽器

Lesson 10
比較・整理3（講義）

問題冊子 p.58 ／
音声はこちらから➡

Training

答え

(1) Many organizations use number of citations as a tool to rank universities. ↘

(2) While there are some ranking organizations that focus on student welfare and
experiences, many of the larger organizations pay less attention to these
matters. ↘

Step 2
実戦問題

答え

1 Part A (1)③　(2) a)②　b)①　c)④　d)③　Part B ③
2 Part A (1)⑤　(2) a)①　b)②　c)④　d)③　e)④　f)③　g)③　h)④
　　　(3)③　Part B ②

解説

1 Part A (1)③　(2) a)②　b)①　c)④　d)③

🔊 roughly の gh の発音は [f]。同様に [f] と発音するのは enough, laugh, tough
などがある。一方，high, eight, weigh などの gh は発音しない。

スクリプト	和訳
Although airplanes account for roughly 2.5% of global CO_2 emissions, it has been hard for customers in the past to imagine the actual pollution of a flight. All things considered, a flight in economy class produces around as much pollution per mile as driving a car. However, if one were to drive the 3,000 miles from New York to Los Angeles in	飛行機は地球上の二酸化炭素排出量の約2.5％を占めますが，従来の乗客がフライトによる実際の汚染を想像することは難しいことでした。あらゆる点を考慮すると，エコノミークラスの1回のフライトは，1マイルあたり1台の車で移動するのと同じくらいの汚染を生じます。けれども，仮に車でニューヨークからロサンゼルスまで3,000マイルを移動するとしたら，平均時速50マイルだと1行程に約60

a car, at an average speed of 50mph, the journey would take around 60 hours to complete. The driver would certainly notice how much fuel they had used. But making the same journey by plane takes only five hours, which makes it difficult for the passenger to feel how much fuel the journey uses. As it is difficult to reduce the amount of fuel, airlines and consumers are starting to look at carbon offsetting.

Carbon offsetting basically means trying to take back the CO_2 produced by the flight. The most common way to do this is to plant trees. The new trees are able to take CO_2 out of the atmosphere, and people can calculate how much they should pay to offset the carbon they use by calculating the cost of planting trees. This can be done indirectly using websites which provide the calculations, and also, increasingly, is done as a service directly by the airlines, which offer you the chance to pay the extra to plant trees when you buy your ticket.

However, alternatives do exist, especially for the consumer who may not trust that the money they pay goes directly into a forest. Many websites offer to invest money into a fund which looks at renewable energy and other green technology.

Currently the consumer is free to choose whether or not they offset their carbon. The future may see more regulation and airlines forced to find a way to make up for the CO_2 they produce.

時間かかります。運転手はどのくらいの燃料を使ったか確実にわかるでしょう。しかし，同じ行程を飛行機で移動するとわずか5時間で，乗客がその行程でどのくらいの燃料を使うのか感じることは困難です。燃料の量を減らすことは難しいので，航空会社や消費者はカーボンオフセットに注目し始めています。

カーボンオフセットは，基本的にフライトによって生じた二酸化炭素を取り消そうとする試みを意味します。その最も一般的な方法は木を植えることです。新しい木は大気中の二酸化炭素を取り除くことができ，人々は木を植えるコストを計算することで，自分たちが使う炭素を相殺するのにいくら払うべきかを計算することができます。これは計算してくれるウェブサイトを使って間接的に行うことができます。また，次第に直接航空会社によるサービスとしてできるようにもなっています。航空会社はチケット購入時に木を植えるための特別費を支払う機会を提供しています。

けれども，特に自分が払ったお金が森に直接使われているかを信用していない乗客に対して，別の方法もあります。多くのウェブサイトが再生可能エネルギーやその他の環境保全技術に注目しているファンドにお金を投資することを提案しています。

現在のところは，乗客は炭素を相殺するかどうかを選ぶのは自由です。将来はもっと規制が厳しくなり，航空会社は生み出した二酸化炭素の埋め合わせをする方法を見つけなければならないかもしれません。

Lesson 10

選択肢訳

(1) ① 6　　　② 10　　　③ 12　　　④ 20

(2) ① 間接的　　② 直接的

　　③ 再生可能エネルギー　　　④ 植樹

○ワークシート

車で 3000 マイル移動するのは，飛行機で移動するより＿＿倍の時間がかかる。

フライトによって生じた二酸化炭素を取り消す	① 間接的／② 直接的		③ 再生可能エネルギー／④ 植樹
一般的な方法	a)	航空会社に支払う	c)
別の方法	b)	ファンドに投資する	d)

(1)　第1段落3文目に，ニューヨークからロサンゼルスまで3,000マイル移動するのに，車では60時間かかるとある。5文目には，同じ距離を移動するのに飛行機では5時間とある。60 ÷ 5 = 12 だから，車の移動は飛行機の移動より<u>12</u>倍の時間がかかることになる。

(2)　第2段第2文に一般的な方法として木を植えることが挙げられている。また最終文に，直接航空会社に特別費を支払うことができる，とある。3段落目では，支払ったお金が直接森へ行くかどうかを信用できない人にはファンドという方法があると紹介し，カーボンオフセットの代わりに，再生可能エネルギーなどの環境保全に役立てるため，間接的にお金を使うこともできるとしている。

注

◇ emission「排出（量）；放出」　*cf.* emit「～を放つ；出す」
◇ all things considered「すべてを考慮すると；結局」
◇ if S were to ...「仮に…するとしたら」
◇ renewable「再生可能な」
◇ regulation「規則；規制」
◇ make up for ～「～を補う；～の埋め合わせをする」

① Part B ③

スクリプト	和訳
Look at this graph, which shows typical carbon offsetting figures for flights from London to other destinations (figures as of 2018). This shows the difference in carbon offsetting depending on the class of flight used, based on the percentage of fuel used per seat.	グラフを見てください。ロンドンから別の目的地までのフライトに対する典型的なカーボンオフセットの値段です（数値は 2018 年現在のもの）。これは，席ごとに使用される燃料の割合を基にした，フライト内の席のクラスによるカーボンオフセットの違いを表しています。

選択肢訳

① 飛行機は，フライト距離が短いほど乗客1人当たりの二酸化炭素を多く産出する。

② ビジネスクラスでの旅行は，エコノミークラスやファーストクラスの旅行より二酸化炭素の使用量が少ない。

③ 値段の高いクラスほど乗客1人当たりの二酸化炭素を多く産出する。

④ エコノミークラスの席しかない飛行機は乗客1人当たりの二酸化炭素をより多く産出するだろう。

> グラフ：カーボンオフセットの値段（アメリカドル）
>　　　　ロンドン－ジュネーブ（短距離），ロンドン－ドバイ（中距離）
>　　　　エコノミークラス，ビジネスクラス，ファーストクラス

　グラフから，フライト距離の長短にかかわらずエコノミークラスよりビジネスクラス，ビジネスクラスよりファーストクラスの方が1席当たりのカーボンオフセットの費用がかかることがわかる。つまり値段の高い席の方が乗客1人当たりの二酸化炭素排出量が多いということになる。これに当てはまるのは③のみ。

注
◇ destination「目的地，行先」
◇ as of ～「～の時点で；～現在での」

2 Part A (1)⑤　(2) a)①　b)②　c)④　d)③　e)④　f)③　g)③　h)④　(3)③

スクリプト

　The Eurasian red squirrel (Sciurus vulgaris) is a species of tree squirrel native to Europe and northern Asia which has seen serious population crashes in Italy, Great Britain and Ireland. These crashes are mainly due to the introduction in the 19th century of the eastern grey squirrel (Sciurus carolinensis) from North America. The population of red squirrels in the UK has come down from 3.5 million to around 150,000. The remaining squirrels survive mostly in Scotland, with the population in England only around 10% of the total.

　The grey squirrel has a negative impact on red squirrel populations in a variety of ways. The larger grey squirrel has a greater ability than the red squirrel to live at higher levels of population density. Grey squirrels

和訳

　ユーラシア・アカリス（学名 Sciurus vulgaris）は，ヨーロッパや北アジア原産の樹上性リスで，イタリア，イギリス，アイルランドで深刻な集団的急減に直面しています。この急減は主に19世紀に北アメリカから移入してきたトウブハイイロリス（学名 Sciurus carolinensis）のためです。イギリスのアカリスの個体数は350万匹から約15万匹に減っています。残っているリスは主にスコットランドで生きのびており，イングランドにいる個体数は全体のわずか10%に過ぎません。

　ハイイロリスはさまざまな面でアカリスの個体数に悪影響を与えます。アカリスより大きいハイイロリスは，個体密度が高くてもアカリスよりも生存できる能力があります。ハイイロリスは1ヘクタール当たり約15匹の個体が住むことができます。これは主に食べ物の選択肢の

can live at a density of around 15 individuals per hectare, mainly due to their wider range of food choices. In comparison, red squirrels manage only two or three individuals in the same hectare.

Grey squirrels are also able to eat green acorns before they turn brown, as they can resist tannins, the defensive chemicals found in many unripe plants. Red squirrels must wait until the acorns have turned brown before they can be digested, meaning most will have already been taken by the grey squirrels.

However, perhaps the most damaging impact the grey squirrels have is as carriers of the squirrel pox virus. Being immune to the disease, grey squirrels carry the virus everywhere, infecting red squirrels, which do not have immunity. Whole populations of red squirrels can be destroyed by this disease.

Recent years have seen attempts to conserve the red squirrel in the UK and Ireland. One method employed is indirect action involving the reintroduction of the pine marten to areas of England and Wales. The pine marten hunts grey squirrels more effectively than red squirrels as they spend more time on the ground and are more easily caught, and it is this behavior that is thought to be one reason for the greater numbers of red squirrels in Scotland, where many pine martens live. Conservationists hope the spread of this animal will lead to

範囲が広いからです。対照的に，アカリスは同じ広さに 2，3 匹の個体しかいることができません。

ハイイロリスは茶色くなる前の緑色のどんぐりも食べることができます。ハイイロリスは多くの未熟な植物にある，防御的な化学物質であるタンニンに耐性があるからです。アカリスはドングリが茶色く熟すまで待たなければドングリを消化することができません。それは，ほとんどのどんぐりがハイイロリスにすでに取られてしまっているということを意味します。

けれども，おそらくハイイロリスによる最大の悪影響は，ハイイロリスがリス痘ウィルス（※リスの感染症）の保有者であることです。ハイイロリスはその病気に免疫があるので，ウィルスをあちこちに運び，免疫を持たないアカリスに感染させるのです。アカリス全体が，この病気によって滅ぼされる可能性があります。

近年は，イギリスやアイルランドでアカリスを保護する試みが見られています。利用されている 1 つの方法は，イングランドやウェールズへのマツテン（※イタチの一種）の再導入を伴う間接的な行動です。マツテンは，アカリスよりもハイイロリスを効果的に捕まえます。ハイイロリスのほうが地上にいる時間が長く，捕まえやすいからです。この行動が，多くのマツテンが生息するスコットランドではアカリスがより多くいることの 1 つの理由だと考えられています。自然保護活動家は，マツテンの広まりがイギリスの他の地域のアカリスの個体数の自然な回復につながることを期待しています。

a natural recovery in the red squirrel
population in other areas of the UK.

選択肢訳

(1) ① 150 万　　② 35 万　　③ 10 万
　　④ 3 万 5 千　⑤ 1 万 5 千　⑥ 1 万
(2) ① 在来種　　　② 外来種
　　③ 比較的耐性がある　　④ 比較的耐性がない
(3) ① アカリスの個体数はハイイロリスが到来するしばらく前に減少していた。
　　② アカリスはハイイロリスより体が小さいのでハイイロリスからえさを取ることができない。
　　③ ハイイロリスはリス痘ウィルスの影響を受けにくい。
　　④ マツテンはハイイロリスの行動のせいで数が減っている。

○ワークシート
イギリスのアカリスの個体数
急減前＝ 350 万匹　　　急減後＝ 15 万匹（主にスコットランド内）
（イングランド内の個体数＝ A ）

		アカリス	ハイイロリス
①在来種／②外来種		a)	b)
③比較的耐性がある／ ④比較的耐性がない	強いタンニン	c)	d)
	高い個体密度	e)	f)
	マツテンの存在	g)	h)

Lesson 10

(1)　第 1 段落の最後の方で，アカリスの個体数は 350 万匹から約 15 万匹に減ったこと，そのほとんどがスコットランドに生息し，イングランド内には 10％ほどしかいないことが説明されている。15 万匹のうちの 10％だからイングランド内には約 1 万 5 千匹ということになる。⑤が正解。

(2)　イギリスにもともといたのがアカリス，北アメリカから移入してきたのがハイイロリスである。a が在来種，b が外来種。タンニンについては第 3 段落でえさとなるどんぐりの説明の中に出てくる。ハイイロリスはタンニンが多い緑色のどんぐりも食べることができ，アカリスは熟してタンニンが減ったどんぐりしか食べることができない。c が④，d が③である。個体密度については第 2 段落にある。生息できるのは，ハイイロリスは 1 ヘクタール当たり 15 匹，アカリスは 1 ヘクタール当たり 2，3 匹だから，e が④，f が③となる。マツテンは最終段落に出てくる。ハイイロリスの天敵として導入されているので，g は③，h が④である。

(3)　第 4 段落 2 文目にハイイロリスはリス痘ウィルスの免疫を持っているとあるから，③が本文の内容と一致する。ハイイロリスが入ってきたことでアカリスが減少しているのだから，その前から減少していたという①は不適切。アカリスの体が小さいためにハイイロリスからえさを取ることができないという説明はないから②も不適切。マツテンはハイイロリスの天敵だから，ハイイロリスの行動のせいでマツテンが減少するということはない。④も不適切。

◇ density「密度」 *ex*. population density「人口密度」
◇ in comparison「対照的に」
◇ acorn「どんぐり」
◇ resist tannins「タンニンに耐性がある」
◇ defensive「防御の」
◇ immune「免疫がある」

2 Part B ②

スクリプト	和訳
Look at this graph which shows relative percentages of red squirrel, grey squirrel and pine marten sightings at three different locations in the UK, one in the center of the country, one in the east and one in a zone between the two. This graph is based on data collected by Sheehy and Lawson, 2014.	イギリスの異なる3つの地点，国の中央，国の東部，その2カ所の中間地でのアカリス，ハイイロリス，マツテンの目撃数の相対的割合を示すグラフを見てください。このグラフは2014年にシーヒィとローソンによって集められたデータを基にしています。

選択肢訳

① アカリスの個体数が多いとハイイロリスの個体数を低く保つ傾向にある。
② マツテンの個体数の多さは，ハイイロリスの個体数を抑えるのに役立つ。
③ ハイイロリスの数が少ないほどえさが減るということになり，その結果マツテンの数が減る。
④ 辺りにアカリスが少ない方がハイイロリスはより繁栄する。

> グラフ：目撃数の割合
>
> 東部／中間地／中央部
> アカリス／ハイイロリス／マツテン

ハイイロリスの増加により，アカリスの数は減少することが講義からわかるが，アカリスの数がハイイロリスの数に影響を与えるかどうかは述べられていないので①，④は不適切。マツテンの数の減少については述べられていないので③も不適切。講義の最終段落とグラフに合う②が正解。

注
◇ sighting「目撃」

Training

答え

(1) Although airplanes account for roughly 2.5% of global CO_2 emissions, it has been hard for customers in the past to imagine the actual pollution of a flight. ↘

(2) Many websites offer to invest money into a fund which looks at renewable energy and other green technology. ↘

(3) The remaining squirrels survive mostly in Scotland, with the population in England only around 10% of the total. ↘

(4) The grey squirrel has a negative impact on red squirrel populations in a variety of ways. ↘

Step3
Let's Speak!

答え

1 (1) ① if one were to drive the 3,000 miles ② would take around 60 hours to complete ③ takes only five hours
(2) ① This can be done indirectly using websites ② as a service directly by the airlines
(3) ① Being immune to the disease ② can be destroyed by
(4) ① hunts grey squirrels more effectively ② the greater numbers of

📖 Words & Expressions　環境問題

☐ environmental problem　名環境問題
☐ global warming　名地球温暖化
☐ carbon　名炭素
☐ carbon dioxide　名二酸化炭素
☐ emission　名放出(量)
☐ pollution　名汚染；公害　*ex.* air pollution「大気汚染」
☐ greenhouse effect　名温室効果
☐ fossil fuel　名化石燃料
☐ renewable energy　名再生可能エネルギー

Lesson 11
比較・整理4（対話）

問題冊子 p.70／
音声はこちらから➡

Training

答え

(1) Oh, I just mean that I thought, well I still think, that killing animals for meat is wrong. ↘

(2) It is certainly wrong to eat the meat of animals that have been raised inside factories, where they live inside a cage inside a building. ↘

実戦問題

答え

1 Part A (1) ③　(2) ②　Part B ③
2 Part A (1) ①　(2) ④　Part B (1) ③　(2) ②

解説

1 Part A (1) ③　(2) ②

🔊 don't you は t と y の音がつながって「ドンチュー」のように発音される。

スクリプト	和訳
Brian：Emi, don't you bring a tablet or laptop computer to school?	ブライアン：エミ，タブレットかノートパソコンを学校へ持って行かないの？
Emi ：No, I don't. I have my smartphone.	エミ：うん，持って行かない。スマートフォンは持って行くよ。
Brian：How about using a computer in class? Don't you use technology in your classes at school?	ブライアン：授業でコンピューターを使ってはどう？ 学校の授業でテクノロジーは利用しないの？
Emi ：Sometimes, but it depends on the class. But no, we don't bring our own devices to school. We have some classrooms with computers, so if the teacher	エミ：ときどきは使うけど，授業によるかな。でも自分のデジタル機器は学校へは持って行かないよ。いくつかコンピューターのある教室があって，先生が使いたいと思った

wants to use one, we go to these rooms. Do you take something to school, Brian?

Brian : Usually I use a tablet. In most classes we have to do some research on a tablet. Most homework is done through the Internet.

Emi : But don't some students look at the Internet instead of listening to the teacher? I can imagine some people doing that if we had tablets in all our classes.

Brian : It's true, some people do that. Some people even play games on their tablets in class. But I think that if the teacher is careful, it can help us to learn more in class if we have access to the Internet.

Emi : I'm not sure. I think there is a place for technology, but in some classes we should keep our devices away and think by ourselves. We have to keep our smartphones in our lockers and I also think that is a good thing. I prefer our system here.

Brian : Yes, it's probably best not to use smartphones in class.

時に私たちはその部屋へ行くの。ブライアン，あなたは何か学校へ持って行く？

ブライアン：普段はタブレットを使うよ。ほとんどの授業でタブレットで調べ物をする必要があるんだ。宿題はほとんどネットを使ってやるよ。

エミ　　：でも，先生の話を聞かないでインターネットを見ている生徒はいないの？　もし私たちがすべての授業でタブレットを持っていたら，何人かはそうすると思うな。

ブライアン：そのとおり，そういう人もいるよ。授業中にタブレットでゲームをやっている生徒さえいるよ。でも先生が気をつけていれば，ネットに接続すると授業でもっと多くのことを学ぶのを助けてくれるよ。

エミ　　：どうかな。テクノロジーの出番もあると思うけど，いくつかの授業ではデジタル機器は脇に置いて，自分自身で考えるべきよ。私たちは自分のスマホはロッカーにしまっておかなければならなくて，私もそれはいいことだと思う。このやり方が気に入っているよ。

ブライアン：うん，授業でスマホを使わないのがたぶん一番だね。

Lesson 11

設問訳 選択肢訳

(1) ブライアンの発言の要点は何か。

① スマホを使うことは，テクノロジーを何も使わないよりもよい。

② ゲームをやる人がいるので，タブレットは教室には適さない。

③ テクノロジーは教室で役に立つ。

④ 先生はもっとコンピューター室で授業をやるべきだ。

(2) エミの発言の要点は何か。

① スマホは学校では禁止されるべきだ。

② テクノロジーを使わない授業もあることが一番いい。

③ 生徒はノートパソコンかタブレットを学校へ持ってくることを始めるべきだ。

④ 生徒はネット上で宿題をやれば，もっと宿題ができるだろう。

(1) ブライアンは自分のタブレットを学校へ持って行って使用しており，授業でのコンピューター使用に賛成の立場である。ブライアンの最後から2番目の発言に it can help us to learn more in class if we have access to the Internet「ネットに接続すれば，授業でもっと多くのことを学ぶのを助けてくれるよ」とある。これは③の内容と一致する。ブライアンのスマホについての意見は最後の発言にあり，「授業でスマホを使わないのが一番」と言っているので①は不適切。ブライアンもゲームをやる生徒がいることは認めているが，先生が気をつけていればいいと述べているので②はブライアンの主張とは言えない。コンピューター室の話をしたのはエミだから④も不適切。

(2) エミはスマホを学校へ持って行っているが，授業では使わず，授業で常にコンピューターを使うことには否定的である。エミは最後の発言で in some classes we should keep our devices away and think by ourselves「いくつかの授業ではコンピューターは脇に置いて，自分自身で考えるべき」と言っており，②の意見と合致する。これが正解。スマホはエミ自身も学校へ持って行っているので①は不適切。③，④のような主張はしていない。

注

◇ device「装置；器具；デジタル機器」

　　　　※ここでは laptop computer, tablet, smartphone などの総称として使用されている

① Part B ③

スクリプト	和訳
Moderator：Today we will hear from some students and some teachers, including myself, about using technology in the classroom. Roy, what do you feel about using a tablet in class?	司会：本日は生徒たちと私を含めた先生方に，教室でテクノロジーを使うことについて意見を伺います。ロイ，教室でタブレットを使うことについてどう思いますか？
Roy：My school allows us to bring technology into the classroom, and most people use tablets or smartphones. They can be useful, but to be honest, they have a negative side.	ロイ：僕の学校では，教室にテクノロジーを持ち込んでもよくて，ほとんどの人がタブレットかスマホを使っています。便利なこともあるけれど，正直なところ，よくない面もあります。
Moderator：I've got to say, I agree with you. But in what way?	司会：私も君に賛成だと言わざるを得ません。でもどんな点で？
Roy：Well, there are some lessons where we need those devices. For	ロイ：はい。それらのデジタル機器が必要な授業もあります。例えば，異なる意見を調

example, looking up different opinions or using certain programs that go with the class. But in most classes, <u>they are not necessary</u>. The teachers should probably use technology more, though.

Moderator：Mary, you're a math teacher. Don't you think students will have difficulty in concentrating on math if they have technology?

Mary：You make a good point, Mike, but in the end, technology is already a huge part of our lives. I think <u>it's our job to help students use it responsibly</u>. We are lucky that we have class tablets in our school.

Moderator：How does that work, exactly?

Mary：Well, we can pass them out at the beginning of class, but only if we need to. Then we take them back in. I control what is on these tablets, so there are no games or music streaming apps. I find I use them about fifty percent of the time.

Moderator：How about you, Jane? What does your school do?

Jane：We bring our own devices, but <u>I really like the idea from Mary's school</u>. It's great to use a device when we need to, but sometimes they get broken. If we had school devices, we wouldn't need to worry about that.

べたり，授業に合ったプログラムを使ったりする場合です。でも，ほとんどの授業では，デジタル機器は必須ではありません。それでもおそらく先生はもっとテクノロジーを使うべきなのでしょう。

司会：メアリー，あなたは数学の先生ですね。生徒がテクノロジーを持っていると，数学に集中するのが難しいと思いませんか？

メアリー：マイク，よい点をついていますね。でも結局，テクノロジーはすでに私たちの生活の大きな部分を占めています。生徒がテクノロジーを責任を持って使う手助けをするのが，私たちの仕事だと思います。幸いにも私たちの学校には授業用のタブレットがあります。

司会：厳密には，どんな具合ですか。

メアリー：タブレットは授業の初めに配りますが，必要な場合だけです。その後返却させます。それらのタブレット上にあるものはコントロールしているので，ゲームや音楽配信のアプリは入っていません。タブレットを使う時間は約50％くらいだと思っています。

司会：ジェーンはどうですか。あなたの学校ではどうしていますか。

ジェーン：私たちは自分のデジタル機器を持って行きますが，メアリーの学校の考えがとてもいいと思います。必要な時にデジタル機器を使うのは素晴らしいことですが，機器はときどき故障します。学校のデジタル機器があれば，それを心配する必要がありません。

Lesson 11

選択肢訳

① 司会者（マイク）とロイ
② ロイとメアリー
③ メアリーとジェーン
④ ジェーンと司会者（マイク）

ロイは初めの発言で they have a negative side「それら（タブレットやスマホ）にはよくない面もある」，2番目の発言で they are not necessary「それらは必要なものではない」と言っているので，デバイス使用を支持していない。司会者もロイに対して I agree with you「あなたに賛成」と言っているので，教室でのデジタル機器の使用には否定的である。メアリーはテクノロジーはすでに生活で大きな部分を占めているので，生徒たちが責任を持って使えるよう先生が手助けをするべきだと言っており，教室での使用に肯定的である。ジェーンはメアリーの発言を受け，今は自分のデバイスを授業中に使っているが，学校のデバイスを使うことに賛成する意見を述べている。メアリーとジェーンが教室でのデジタル機器の使用を支持していると言える。

注

◇ to be honest (with you)「正直に言って」 *cf.* to be frank「率直に言って」
◇ have got to = have to
◇ responsibly「責任を持って」

2 Part A (1) ① (2) ④

スクリプト	和訳
Martha：Takashi, do you rent your apartment, or do you own it?	マーサ：タカシ，あなたはアパートを借りている？ それとも所有している？
Takashi：My apartment? Um, I rent it. How about you? Do you rent your apartment in the States, Martha?	タカシ：アパート？ 借りているよ。君は？ マーサ，アメリカのアパートは借りているの？
Martha：No, I bought a small apartment about three years ago. It was my dream to stop renting and have my own place.	マーサ：いいえ，3年くらい前に小さなアパートを買ったの。賃貸をやめて自分の家を持つのが夢だったのよ。
Takashi：Don't you worry that you will always have to live there?	タカシ：ずっとそこに住まなくてはならないって心配はないの？
Martha：No, it's just my first apartment. When I have more money, I'll sell it and buy a bigger one. It shouldn't be so difficult. The cost of renting	マーサ：ないよ。私の最初のアパートっていうだけ。もっとお金持ちになったら売って，もっと大きなアパートを買うわ。そんなに難しいことじゃないはずよ。賃貸料だって高いでしょう？

60

	is also high, isn't it?
Takashi :	Yes, renting is very expensive. But I prefer to be flexible. If I change my job, I can leave and rent a new place. I'm afraid that apartments in some areas are difficult to sell.
Martha :	But another thing about having your own apartment is that you can decorate it however you want. In a rented apartment this is difficult.
Takashi :	I guess I never thought about decorating. It's a pretty new apartment so I don't need to do that. If you rent somewhere, you can choose a place that you like, so maybe you don't need to decorate.
Martha :	I guess we are happy with our different choices.

タカシ：	うん。とても高いね。でも僕は融通が利くほうがいいな。もし仕事を変えたら，ここを離れて新しい場所を借りることができる。場所によってはアパートを売るのが難しいのも心配だし。
マーサ：	でももう1点，自分のアパートを持てば，自分のやりたいように飾ることもできるよ。賃貸アパートだとそれは難しいでしょ。
タカシ：	部屋を飾り付けることは僕は考えたことがない気がするよ。かなり新しいアパートだからそうする必要がないんだ。どこかを借りるなら好きなところを選べるから，飾る必要はないんじゃないかな。
マーサ：	私たち，自分たちそれぞれの選択に満足してるってことよね。

Lesson 11

設問訳 選択肢訳

(1) マーサはアパートについてどう考えているか。

① アパートを購入することによって，もっと自由に飾り付けできると考えている。

② アパートを購入するのは借りるよりもずっとお金がかかると考えている。

③ アパートを借りることは不安定だと心配している。

④ 自分のアパートにできるだけ長く住みたいと望んでいる。

(2) アパートを借りることについて，タカシはどう考えているか。

① アパートを買うよりもずっと安い。

② 新しいアパートを借りると生活がより快適になる。

③ 借りたアパートを自分が好きなように飾り付けることができる。

④ 住む場所をより容易に選ぶことができる。

(1) マーサの最後から2番目の発言に「自分のアパートを持てば、それを飾り付けること
　　ができる」とあり、①と一致する。3番目の発言の最後に「賃貸料も高い」と述べている
　　ことから、アパートの購入費が借りるよりずっと高いとは考えていないので、②は正し
　　くない。アパートの住み方と安定性については言及していないので③は不適切。3番目の
　　発言で、お金ができたら今のアパートを売ってもっと広いアパートを買うと言っている
　　ので、今のところに長く住みたいと望んではいない。④も不適切。

(2) タカシはアパートを借りており、3番目の発言で I prefer to be flexible.「僕は融通が
　　利くほうがいい。」、I can leave and rent a new place「今の場所を離れて新しい場所を借
　　りることができる」と言っている。これが賃貸アパートに住んでいる理由の1つだから、
　　④が正解。マーサの「賃貸料も高い」という意見に同意して「とても高い」と言ってい
　　るから①は不適切。②については最後の発言で新しいアパートだから飾り付ける必要は
　　ないと述べているが、快適になるとは言っていない。そもそもタカシは部屋を飾り付け
　　ることは考えたことがないと言っているので、③も不適切。

注
◇ flexible「融通の利く；柔軟な」

2 Part B (1) ③ (2) ②

スクリプト	和訳
Presenter (male)：On our show today, we are looking at the buy-verses-rent debate, especially for young people who have just started working.	司会（男）：今日の番組では、家を買うか借りるか、特に働き始めたばかりの若者にとってどちらがいいかの討論を見ていきます。
Presenter (female)：That's right, Paul. Remember, we are not thinking about parents in their thirties and forties, who want to buy a home for their families, but rather people in their early twenties who have just finished college.	司会（女）：そうね、ポール。心に留めておいてほしいのは、30代や40代の親たち、家族のために家を買いたい人たちではなく、大学を卒業したばかりの20代前半の若者について考えているということです。
Presenter (male)：So, we've invited two people in their twenties onto the show today, Mark and Nicole. Now, most young people at this age choose to rent and not to buy their own houses. <u>Young people should be out enjoying themselves, not worrying about buying a house.</u> Isn't that right, Nicole?	司会（男）：そこで、本日の番組には2人の20代の方をお招きしました。マークとニコルです。さて、この年代のほとんどの若者は自分の家を買うのではなく賃貸を選びます。若者は外で楽しむべきで、家を買おうと悩むべきではありません。そうではありませんか、ニコル。

Nicole：<u>Well, for me, that's kind of where I am now.</u> I'm just starting work, and I don't know if I'll stay here or move in the future. A couple of my friends have recently bought, but for me, you know, I just don't want to save up money now. I mean, I don't really earn that much, yet.

Mark：But that's exactly why you should do it!

Presenter (female)：Why do you say that, Mark?

Mark：You just don't know where you'll be in ten years, five years, or even two years. But if you start to buy somewhere now, you won't have so much to pay in the future. Your house is your fortune. You know, when you have kids or something, you don't want to suddenly have to think about buying a house, too.

Presenter (male)：But then, you're stuck in that house, aren't you? What if you want to move?

Mark：You've got two options: sell it or rent it out. If you buy your house in a good area, you'll always be able to do this.

Presenter (female)：I actually did just that when I was in my twenties. You can help yourself later in life if you buy early. Let's hear from some of our viewers.

ニコル：ええ，私には，ちょうど今，私がいる立場がそうです。働き始めたばかりで，将来はここにいるのか引っ越すのかわかりません。2, 3 人の友達は最近買いましたが，私は今はお金を貯めたくないだけです。つまり，まだそれほど稼いでいないということです。

マーク：でも，それこそ君がそうすべき理由なんじゃないですか！

司会（女）：どういうことですか，マーク。

マーク：10 年後，5 年後，2 年後だってどこにいるかなんてわかりません。でも，もし今どこかを買うことを始めたら，将来お金がそれほどかからないでしょう。家は財産ですからね。ほら，子どもができた時などに，突然家を買うことを考えなければならない事態にはなりたくないでしょう。

司会（男）：でもそうすると家に縛りつけられることになりませんか。引っ越したくなったらどうしますか。

マーク：2 つの選択肢があります。売るか貸すかです。よい場所に家を買ったら，いつでもそうすることができるでしょう。

司会（女）：私が 20 代の時，まさにそうしていました。早いうちに買えば，将来の自分自身を助けることができます。視聴者からの意見も伺いましょう。

Lesson 11

(1) ① 男性司会者（ポール）とマーク
　　② 女性司会者とニコル
　　③ 男性司会者（ポール）とニコル
　　④ ニコルとマーク

グラフ

(2) ① アメリカの住宅物価指数
　　② アメリカの人々の純資産
　　　　　住宅所有者の純資産は賃貸居住者の 31 ～ 46 倍相当
　　③ 住宅所有者と賃貸居住者（の割合）
　　④ 賃貸居住者が好む建物の種類
　　　　　■大きなマンション　■一戸建て　■小さなアパート

(1) 男性司会者は 2 番目の発言で，「若者は外で楽しむべきで，家を買おうと悩むべきではない」と言っている。それに対し，ニコルは自分はまさにその状態で，お金を貯めたいと思っていないし，それほど稼いでもいないと言っている。つまり男性司会者とニコルは家を買うことに反対している。一方，マークは早いうちに買えば，将来払うお金はそれほど多くなく，引っ越したい時は売るか貸せばよいと考えている。また女性司会者も自分はそうしたとマークに賛成している。この 2 人は若者が家を買うことに賛成だと言える。したがって，正解は③。

(2) マークは，家を買えばそれは財産になると考えている。グラフ②は，借家住まいの人と持ち家の人の財産を比較したもので，持ち家の人の方が財産がずっと多いことが読み取れる。これがマークの意見を示すグラフである。①の住宅物価指数，③の住宅所有者と賃貸居住者の割合，④の賃貸居住者が好む建物の種類は，どれも若いうちに家を購入することとは関連がない。

Training

答え

(1) Don't you use technology in your classes at school? ↗

(2) They can be useful, but to be honest, they have a negative side. ↘

(3) But I prefer to be flexible. ↘

(4) But if you start to buy somewhere now, you won'(t) have so much to pay in the future. ↘

Step 3

Let's Speak!

> **答え**
>
> **1** (1) ① it can help us to learn more   ② keep our devices away
>
> (2) ① I agree with you   ② they are not necessary
>
> (3) ① leave and rent a new place   ② can decorate it however you want
>
> (4) ① A couple of my friends have recently bought   ② that's exactly why

📖 Words & Expressions   コンピューター

☐ desktop computer	图デスクトップコンピューター（机上型）
☐ laptop computer	图（大きめの）ノートパソコン *cf.* lap「ひざ」
☐ notebook computer	图（小型の）ノートパソコン
☐ tablet computer	图タブレット型コンピューター
☐ smartphone	图スマートフォン
☐ VR	Virtual Reality：仮想現実
☐ AR	Augmented Reality：拡張現実
☐ wearable device	图ウェアラブル（体に装着できる）端末
☐ folder	图フォルダ（コンピューターでファイルを保存する場所）
☐ scroll	動スクロールする（コンピューターなどの画面を上下に動かす）
☐ sign up	動登録する；申し込む

Lesson 12
長めの聞き取り（対話）

問題冊子 p.80 ／
音声はこちらから➡

Training
答え

(1) Hi, I'd like to sign up to use the college sports center. I think I need to **register**
for the year. ↘

(2) Is that necessary? I **already took** the course last year. ↘

Step 2
実戦問題

答え
1 (1)③ (2)④ (3)①
2 (1)② (2)④ (3)③

解説
1 (1)③ (2)④ (3)①

🔊 timetable の語尾の [l] は舌の先を上あごに軽くつけて発音され，「～テイボウ」
のように聞こえる。email の場合も同じ。looks like のように語頭にくる [l] との
違いに注目しよう。

スクリプト	和訳
W：Hi, can I speak to someone on the IT help desk?	女性：こんにちは。IT のヘルプデスクのどなたかとお話しできますか。
M：Actually, IT and library services are combined so we can all assist you. Are you registering a new account?	男性：実は IT と図書館サービスは統合されているので, 私たちがお手伝いできますよ。新しいアカウントを登録しているのですか。
W：No. I actually registered online before the opening week, but I'm having a problem accessing some areas of my account.	女性：いいえ。開校週の前にネットで登録したのですが, 自分のアカウントのいくつかの部分へのアクセスがうまくいかないのです。

66

M : Just wait for a second.... Okay, do you have your student ID or library card on you?

W : Sure, here it is.

M : Okay..., just a moment.... Right, here you are! So, what are your problems?

W : I can get online and see my timetable and grades. But, I'm not getting messages from my study group and I can't seem to access printing services.

M : Okay, so you signed up, but it looks like you haven't set up your account. See, you should put some money into the account before using the printing service.

W : Oh, so I have to prepay before I can print.

M : You need a minimum of $5 in your account before you can access printing options. You can pay by credit card or use one of our prepaid cards, which you can get from the machine over there.

W : That one by the door? Okay, I'll do that in a second. Do you know why I'm not getting messages from my study group? I just thought they'd come through to my main email folder.

M : Um..., oh! Here it is. You need to go into your messages folder, here. Can you see any links from your study group?

W : Let me just scroll down. I'm sorry, I didn't think to look here. Oh, maybe this one?

男性：少々お待ちください。はい，学生証か図書館カードをお持ちですか。

女性：もちろんです。どうぞ。

男性：はい，少々お待ちを。よし，ありました。何にお困りですか。

女性：ネットに接続して自分の時間割と成績は見ることはできます。でも，学習グループからのメッセージを受け取ることができず，印刷サービスにも接続できないようです。

男性：わかりました。あなたは登録はしているのですが，アカウントの設定がまだのようです。ご覧ください。印刷サービスを利用する前にアカウントに入金しなければなりません。

女性：まあ，印刷する前にあらかじめ支払う必要があるのですね。

男性：印刷オプションにアクセスするにはアカウント内に少なくとも5ドル必要です。クレジットカード，またはいずれかのプリペイドカードで支払うことができます。プリペイドカードは向こうの機械で手に入ります。

女性：ドアのそばの機械ですね。わかりました，すぐにやってみます。学習グループからのメッセージが届かないのはなぜかわかりますか。私のメインのメールフォルダーに来ていると思うのですが。

男性：うーん，ああ！　ここです。ここのご自分のメッセージフォルダーに入る必要があります。ご自分の学習グループからのリンクが見えますか。

女性：下へスクロールしますね。ごめんなさい，ここを見るなんて思わなかったわ。ああ，これかしら。

Lesson 12

M：If you click it, you should get an <u>option to accept.</u>	男性：それをクリックすれば，受け取るオプションが得られます。
W：Okay, I checked it. Nothing is happening..., oh, wait.	女性：わかりました。チェックしました。何も起こりません…，あ，待って。
M：Your mail box will probably start to fill up.	男性：あなたの受信箱はおそらくいっぱいになり始めます。
W：Oh, wow. There's, like, a hundred messages here.	女性：あらあら。100通ものメッセージがここにあるみたい。
M：It looks like you are on your way, now. If there is anything else, I'm just over here.	男性：もうご自分で大丈夫そうですね。もし何か他にありましたら，私はすぐここにいますから。
W：Sure, thanks a lot!	女性：はい。本当にありがとう！

設問訳 選択肢訳

(1) 女性はなぜヘルプデスクへ来たのですか。

① 図書館のアカウント登録をしたい。

② ネットで自分のアカウントにアクセスできない。

③ 自分のアカウントのある部分にアクセスするのに手助けが必要である。

④ 最初の週にアカウントを設定する締切を過ぎてしまった。

(2) この施設では印刷サービスはどうすれば作動しますか。

① アカウントを開設したら，いくつかの印刷オプションを利用できる。

② IT サービスは，あなたが書類を手にしたあとで，印刷したものについて請求するだろう。

③ クレジットカードを持っていなければ印刷サービスは利用できない。

④ 印刷する前にお金を入れておく必要がある。

(3) 学習グループからのメールを受け取れなかった原因で最も可能性があるのは何ですか。

① 学習グループのメールが受け入れられる前に許可が必要である。

② 印刷のアカウントに 5 ドルを入れていない。

③ メールサーバーがいくつかのアドレスを受信箱からブロックしている。

④ すでに受信箱にメールがたくさんありすぎる。

(1) 女性は2番目の発言で，自分のアカウントのいくつかの部分にアクセスできないと言い，4番目の発言でネットに接続して一部のサービスは見られるが，メールの受信と印刷サービスに接続できないことを説明しているから，すでに登録はできている。①，④は不適切。一部は接続できているので②も正しくない。③が正解。

(2) 印刷サービスについては男性の4番目，5番目の発言で説明されている。印刷サービスを利用するにはあらかじめ5ドル以上の入金が必要だと言っている。④が一致する。事前の入金について述べていない①，②は不適切。入金方法はクレジットカードの他にプリペイドカードも使えると言っているから③も不適切。

(3) 男性の最後から3番目の発言のなかに,「それ(学習グループからのリンク)をクリックすればメールを受け取るオプションが得られる」とあり,女性がチェックすると受信箱にメールがたくさん届き始める。そのグループからのメールを受け取るという設定が必要だったことがわかる。正解は①。印刷のアカウントとメールの受信は関係がないので②は不適切。アドレスをブロックしているという説明はないので③も適さない。受信箱へメールがたくさん届いたのは,男性に言われた場所をクリックしたあとだから④も正しくない。

注
◇ combine「~を統合させる」
◇ charge O for ~「O に~の料金を請求する」

2 (1)② (2)④ (3)③

スクリプト	和訳
M : Good morning! Those look like heavy bags!	男性：おはようございます。カバンが重そうですね。
W : Oh...yes. They are a little heavy. Is this Derwent Hall?	女性：ええ,ちょっと重いです。ここはダーウェント寮ですか。
M : You're in the right place. Sit down here for a moment. <u>Are you here to register your stay?</u>	男性：そのとおりです。ちょっとここへお座りください。入寮するためにここへ来たのですか。
W : <u>Yes</u>, I'm transferring from Japan for this academic year. <u>I should have a room here for the year.</u>	女性：はい。本年度,日本から編入します。その1年間のための部屋がここにあるはずです。
M : Let's see..., Ms. Yamaguchi, is that right?	男性：ええと,ヤマグチさんですね。
W : Yes. I think I'm in room 205.	女性：ええ。私は 205 号室だと思います。
M : Here it is! Now, you are aware that rooms in our hall are shared accommodation, aren't you?	男性：ありました! さてと,この寮の部屋は相部屋なことはご存知ですね。
W : Yes, I'm quite excited to meet my roommate.	女性：ええ。ルームメイトに会うことにとてもわくわくしています。
M : Ah! Actually, you are kind of lucky! At the moment, the room is completely vacant. You'll have the place to yourself until the end of October, when we have a new student coming.	男性：おお,実はあなたはラッキーかもしれません。現在のところ,その部屋は完全な空き部屋です。10 月末まであなただけの空間です。10 月末に新しい学生がやってきます。
W : Oh, that's a surprise. Can you tell	女性：まあ,驚きました。設備について少し教

me about the facilities a little?

M : Oh, it's not too complicated. You're on the second floor and there are ten rooms to each floor. There are bathroom areas at each end of the floor, with shared showers and toilets. These are cleaned each week, but we do ask you to clean up after yourself as much as possible.

W : Right..., sure, that's no problem.

M : Other than that, <u>students here must come back to the Hall before 11</u>. If you need to stay out past this time, you need to get permission from Mrs. Wilson, the supervisor of the Hall. Oh, and you know this is an all-female dormitory, right?

W : That's no problem, I'm used to that. How about meals? Are they served here?

M : Trent Hall, next to us, has a large cafeteria area. We don't include meals in the price, but they are very reasonable. Breakfast starts at 6.

W : Thank you, I think that's everything. Where do I go?

M : Just over there, on the left. Sorry, we don't have an elevator, but you've only got one floor to go up. Oh, one more thing : laundry. There are three washers and two dryers in the room just behind me. They're open twenty-four seven, but <u>you'll need some coins, so make sure to get some change beforehand</u>. This desk closes at 9.

W : Thank you for the advice.

えていただけますか。

男性：それほど複雑ではありません。あなたは2階の部屋で，各階に10部屋ずつあります。各階の端にバスルームがあり，共用のシャワーとトイレがあります。これらは毎週掃除されますが，ご自分の使用後はできるだけきれいにしてくださるようお願いします。

女性：はい，もちろんです。問題ありません。

男性：それ以外では，学生は11時前に寮へ戻ってこなければなりません。もしそれ以降も外出している必要がある場合は，寮の監督者であるウィルソンさんの許可を得なければなりません。あ，それからここは女性専用の寮であることはご存知ですね。

女性：大丈夫です。それには慣れています。食事についてはどうですか。ここで出されますか。

男性：隣のトレント寮に大きなカフェテリアコーナーがあります。寮費に食事代は含まれていませんが，カフェテリアはとてもお手頃です。朝食は6時に始まります。

女性：ありがとう。これで大丈夫だと思います。どちらへ行けばいいですか。

男性：左側のすぐそこです。すみません，エレベーターはありませんが，あなたは1階分上がるだけです。ああ，もう1つ，洗濯について。洗濯機が3台と乾燥機が2台，ちょうど私の後ろの部屋にあります。24時間年中無休で使えますが，硬貨が必要ですからあらかじめ小銭を忘れずにご用意ください。この受付は9時に閉まります。

女性：アドバイスありがとうございます。

音声

設問訳 選択肢訳

(1) 女性は何をしようとしていますか。

① この寮の部屋を予約する。

② 1年間を過ごす部屋に入る手続きをする。

③ 10月まで自分の部屋をシングルに変更する。

④ カバンを部屋まで運んでくれる人を探す。

(2) 寮での生活について，受付の男性は何と言っていますか。

① 学生はバスルームを毎日掃除しなければならない。

② 女性は10月よりも前に別の学生と部屋をシェアするだろう。

③ 朝食はダーウェント寮の2階で供される。

④ 外出する学生は11時までに戻らなければならない。

(3) 受付の男性は洗濯室について何を伝えていましたか。

① その部屋は受付が開いている時だけ利用できる。

② 洗濯機や乾燥機は多くないので，学生は早く来なければならない。

③ あらかじめ硬貨を準備するのはよい考えかもしれない。

④ エレベーターがないので，洗濯物を運ぶのは大変だろう。

(1) 男性の2番目の発言に「あなたは入寮するために来たのですか。」とあり，女性はYesと答えている。その後の会話からすでに予約はしてあることがわかるから，正解は①ではなく②。10月末まで同室の学生が来ないという話をしていたが，シングルに変更したわけではないので③は正しくない。カバンについても最初に話題になっているが，運んでくれる人を探している様子はないので④も不適切。

(2) 男性の6番目の発言でお風呂とトイレは毎週掃除されると言っているので①は不正解。その前の男性の発言で，女性と同室の学生は10月末まで来ないと言っているから②も不適切。朝食は，男性の最後から2番目の発言にトレント寮のカフェテリアで出されるとあり，ダーウェントン寮ではないから③も不適切。④は男性の7番目の発言の1文目で「ここの学生は11時までに寮へ戻らなければならない」と言っているのに一致する。④が正解。

(3) 洗濯については男性の最後の発言で説明されている。you need some coins（硬貨が必要）と言っているから，③が正解。open twenty-four seven は店やヘルプデスクなどのサービスでよく使われる表現で，週7日，1日24時間，つまりずっと休みなく開いているという意味である。受付は午後9時に閉まるが洗濯室はいつでも利用できるので①は不適切。②，④のような言及はない。

注
◇ accommodation「宿泊施設」
◇ vacant「（部屋，家などが）空いている；使用されていない」
◇ facility「施設；設備」
◇ dormitory「寮，寄宿舎」

Training

答え

(1) I actually registered online before the opening week, but I'm having a **problem** **accessing** some areas of my account. ↘

(2) If you click it, you should get an **option to accept.** ↘

(3) Other than that, students here must come back to the Hall **before eleven.** ↘

(4) They're open twenty-four seven, but you **need some coins,** so make sure to get some change beforehand. ↘

Step 3
Let's Speak!

答え

1 (1) ① Are you registering a new account   ② I'm having a problem accessing some areas
   (2) ① you should put some money   ② before you can access printing options
   (3) ① Are you here to register your stay   ② have a room here for the year
   (4) ① clean up after yourself as much as possible   ② come back to the Hall before 11

📖 Words & Expressions 住居

- [ ] accommodation 名宿泊施設
- [ ] facility 名設備；施設
- [ ] toilet 名トイレ；洗面所
- [ ] laundry room 名洗濯室
- [ ] dormitory 名寄宿舎；寮《米》
- [ ] hall 名寄宿舎；寮《英》
- [ ] apartment 名アパート《米》
- [ ] flat 名アパート《英》

Lesson 13
長めの聞き取り（講義）

問題冊子 p.87／
音声はこちらから➡

Training

答え

(1) The first is what we call live-attenuated, or weakened vaccines. ↘

(2) The influenza vaccine is an example, and these vaccines ten(d) no(t) to give
life-long immunity due to the weaker immune response. ↘

Step2
実戦問題

答え
1 (1)② (2)② (3)①
2 (1)③ (2)① (3)④

解説
1 (1)② (2)② (3)①

🔊 flatter（flat「平らな」の比較級），sharper（sharp「急激な；鋭い」の比較級）な
ど，原形の単語は知っていても比較変化していると聞き取れないことがあるので
注意。

スクリプト	和訳
We'll pick up where we left off last week with the idea of our stereotypical river running through a landscape. Our river begins high up in the hills and carries sand and rocks, which scrape the land. As we said last time, this forms a v-shaped notch which eventually becomes a valley. The process is called erosion. Due to the process of erosion by the water, the valley becomes deeper, and when ice around the river melts, the rocks from the sides of the valley fall	風景の中を流れていく典型的な川がどんなものかについて，先週中断したところから始めましょう。川は山の高い部分から始まり，砂や岩を運び，それが陸地を削ります。前回言ったように，これが結果的に谷となるV字型の切れ込みを形作ります。この過程を浸食と言います。水による浸食の過程が原因で，谷はより深くなり，川の周辺の氷が溶ける時に，谷の側面の岩が川へ落ち，最後には海岸へと運ばれます。

into the river and eventually are carried to the coast.

This is where I'd like to turn our attention today, as the river flows wider and more slowly over flatter land on its journey to the coast. As you can imagine, the rocks don't move smoothly out into the sea. Many stay in the slower waters and form obstacles, which affect the rate and flow of water. As the water moves at different speeds due to these obstacles, it starts to wind from side to side. Faster moving water has basically more energy, and the force of this faster moving water is found on the outside of bends in the river, causing erosion and leading to the formation of a cliff. The water keeps cutting into the cliff, the sand of which eventually falls into the river. This creates a sharper bend in the river. On the other bank, the slow-moving water on the inside drops sand and mud, leading to the formation of a beach or slope. These two processes, fast water on the outside and slow-moving water inside cause the river to bend more and more over the flatter low-lying land.

You can see now what is going to happen. The more energy the outside of the bend has, the more the outside bends are scraped, which makes sharper and sharper bends. These bends are eventually cut from the river and turn into separate ox-bow lakes. These lakes eventually dry up, leaving circular marks across the land as the river constantly shifts and changes shape on its path to the sea.

これが，本日私が注目したいところです。川は海への旅の過程で，より平らな土地をより幅広くよりゆっくりと流れます。ご想像のとおり，岩はスムーズに海へと移動するわけではありません。ゆっくり動く水の中では多くが残り，障害物となります。それは水の速度や流れに影響します。これらの障害物のせいで水はさまざまな速度で移動するので，左右に曲がりくねり始めます。より速く移動する水は基本的にエネルギーが多く，この速く移動する水の力は川の湾曲の外側で見られ，浸食を引き起こし崖を作ることになります。水は崖を削り続け，その砂は最終的に川の中に落ちます。これによって川により急なカーブができます。反対側の岸では，内側でゆっくり動く水が砂や泥を落とし，砂浜や斜面を作ることになります。これらの2つの過程，外側の速い水と内側のゆっくり動く水が，より平らな低地では，川がますます曲がりくねる要因となります。

皆さんは今や何が起こるのかわかりますね。カーブの外側のエネルギーが大きくなればなるほど，外側のカーブはより多く削られ，それがますます急なカーブを作ります。これらのカーブは最後には川から切り離され，独立した三日月湖となります。これらの湖は最後には干上がり，川が海への道の途中で常に移動したり形を変えたりするのにつれて，陸地に円形の跡を残します。

設問訳 選択肢訳

(1) この講義の話題の中心は何ですか。

① 世界中にはさまざまな種類の川がある。

② 川がどのように地形に影響を与えるか。

③ 川は山の高い部分に谷を作り出す。

④ 川は海まで流れる間にさまざまな段階を通り抜ける。

(2) なぜ講師は水の速い動きと遅い動きを比較しているのですか。

① 川は水源では下流に比べて速く流れる。

② スピードが異なると周りの陸地に異なる影響を与える。

③ 彼は岩を越えて流れる水によって生み出されるエネルギーに興味がある。

④ 水の流れが遅くなると岩はもっとゆっくり動く。

(3) 講師はなぜ「皆さんは今や，何が起こるのかわかりますね。」と言ったか。

① 講師は学生が想像できる筋書きの説明をしてきた。

② 講師は学生に図を見るように頼んでいる。

③ この項目は学生が過去に学習したと講師が考えている。

④ 講師は学生によく注意をしてほしいと思っている。

(1) 川がどのように地形に影響を与えるかについての講義である。第1段落では浸食の仕組み，第2段落では平らな土地で川が蛇行する過程，第3段落ではその結果起こることが説明される。したがって，講義全体の話題の中心は②である。①は本講義ではふれられていない。③は講義の一部であり，全体を通しての中心的話題ではない。④については，講義の力点は，川が地形を変えていることに置かれているので，正解とは言えない。

(2) 水の速い動きと遅い動きの比較は第2段落にあり，水の速度が異なるカーブの外側と内側では川が陸地に与える影響が異なることを説明している。したがって，正解は②である。その他の①，③，④は水の速度を比較する理由ではない。

(3) 当該の発言は第3段落の冒頭である。発言中の now は「今や，今では」という意味で，「今までの説明を聞いた今なら何が起こるかわかるだろう」というニュアンスである。①が正解。「何が起こるか」について学生がすでに学習しているからではなく，今までの説明から判断して予測できるだろうという意味なので③は不適切。

Lesson 13

注

◇ scrape「～をこする；こすり落とす」

◇ notch「V字型の切れ込み」

◇ erosion「浸食」

◇ turn one's attention「注意を向ける」

◇ obstacle「障害（物）」

◇ cliff「崖」

◇ wind [waind]「曲がる；曲がりくねる」※発音注意

◇ ox-bow lake「三日月湖」　cf. ox「牡牛」, bow「弓（状のもの）」※牡牛の角の形の湖の意

2 (1)③ (2)① (3)④

In today's talk, I'd like to cover the eight plays by William Shakespeare known as the Henriad. Now, the term Henriad comes from a 1969 book by Alvin Kernan. Kernan linked the eight plays concerning the lives of English kings from Richard II in the 14th century, through to the overthrow of Richard III by the first Tudor king, Henry VII, in the late 15th century.

These works are more commonly split into two tetralogies, a tetralogy being a series of four plays. The first tetralogy to be written by Shakespeare was the second in terms of historical order, and contains the plays *Henry VI* parts 1, 2 and 3, and *Richard III*. It records the period of history known as the Wars of the Roses, which ended when the Tudor dynasty (in which Shakespeare was writing) began. It's important to note that Shakespeare himself did not write the plays as a tetralogy; each play was an independent work, and this is merely a term we use to group the plays today for our own convenience.

While the first Henriad contains one of Shakespeare's better-known works, namely *Richard III*, it is the second Henriad that critics regard as a true masterpiece. Kernan cites the "large scale heroic action" of the plays. However, the human aspect of the characters, many of which appear many times throughout the tetralogy, are perhaps what makes

和訳

今日の話では，ヘンリアドとして知られる，ウィリアム・シェイクスピアの8つの劇を扱いたいと思います。さて，ヘンリアドという専門用語はアルビン・カーナンによる1969年の書籍に由来します。カーナンは，14世紀のリチャード2世から15世紀後半に最初のテューダー朝の王であるヘンリー7世によってリチャード3世が倒されるまでの，英国王の人生に関する8つの劇を関連付けました。

これらの作品は，より一般的には2つの4部作に分けられます。4部作とは4つの劇からなるシリーズのことです。シェイクスピアによって書かれた最初の4部作は，歴史的な順番で見ると2番目のもので，ヘンリー6世第1部，第2部，第3部とリチャード3世の劇から成っています。これは，バラ戦争として知られる歴史上の期間を記録しています。バラ戦争はテューダー朝（シェイクスピアが書いていた時代）が始まった時に終わりました。シェイクスピア自身はその劇を4部作として書いたのではないということに注意することが重要です。それぞれの劇は独立した作品で，4部作というのは現在便宜上，劇をグループ分けするために使っている用語にすぎません。

1番目のヘンリアドは，シェイクスピアのよく知られた作品の1つ，すなわちリチャード3世を含んでいますが，批評家たちが本当の傑作だとみなしているのは2番目のヘンリアドです。カーナンは劇の「スケールの大きい英雄行動」を引き合いに出しています。けれども，登場人物の人間的側面が，その多くが4部作を通して何度も現れますが，おそらくそれがこの劇のシリーズを真に偉大な作品にしているものでしょう。

this series of plays a truly great work.

The central character in the second Henriad is most definitely Prince Harry, and it is his growth and later victory in war against France as king, um, in *Henry V*, that gives us this powerful, heroic character.

These plays also contain the character of Falstaff as a contrast to Harry. While Harry becomes heroic, Falstaff represents many things that are wrong with society, such as drinking, having parties and being dishonest. One of the main stories is that of Harry at first enjoying his time with Falstaff but then becoming a good king to lead the country.

Critics in the past have sought to place a political story behind the Henriad. Shakespeare, writing in the time of Tudor queen Elizabeth I, certainly provides a narrative of historical chaos, which ends in the rise of order and modernity as the Tudor dynasty begins. However, the two tetralogies, especially the second Henriad, are so much more than just a political history. These plays represent one of the true peaks of English literature from a playwright at the height of his powers.

2番目のヘンリアドの中心人物はハリー王子で間違いありません。我々にこの力強く英雄的な人物像を与えるのは，うーん，ヘンリー5世の劇におけるハリー王子の成長と王として戦ったフランス戦での勝利です。

これらの劇にはハリーとの対比としてフォルスタッフという登場人物も出てきます。ハリーが英雄的になる一方で，フォルスタッフは酒を飲んだり，宴会をしたり，不誠実であったりといった社会的によくないこととされる多くのことを象徴しています。中心となる話の1つでは，ハリーは最初はフォルスタッフと楽しく時を過ごすのですが，国を率いるよい王になります。

過去の批評家たちはヘンリアドの背後に政治的な物語を置こうとしてきました。シェイクスピアはテューダー朝期の女王エリザベス1世の時代の作家で，確かに歴史的な混沌の物語を提供しています。その混沌はテューダー朝が始まった時に秩序と近代性の台頭によって終わりを告げました。けれども，2つの4部作，特に2番目のヘンリアドは，単なる政治的な歴史をはるかに超えるものです。これらの劇は，全盛期の劇作家による英文学の真の頂点の1つを代表しています。

 Lesson 13

設問訳　選択肢訳

(1) この話は主に何についての話か。

① シェイクスピアによるいくつかの劇の違い。

② 4部作を通して登場人物を保つことの重要性。

③ シェイクスピアによる2つの4部作の紹介。

④ 英文学における歴史劇の重要性。

(2) アルビン・カーナンは2番目のヘンリアドをどのようにほめているか。

① 4 つの作品には，より壮大で英雄的な物語がある。

② シェイクスピアの最盛期である後期に書かれた。

③ テューダー的な見方でより正確に歴史を我々に見せてくれる。

④ バラ戦争の背景を我々に教えてくれる。

(3) 教授によれば，なぜヘンリアドの劇に政治性があると感じる批評家がいたのか。

① それらは重要な王朝について書かれた。

② それらは偉大な登場人物の人間的な側面を我々に見せてくれる。

③ それらはテューダー朝を批判することを避けている。

④ それらは過去の問題とシェイクスピアの時代の国内の平穏を対比している。

(1) この講義は全体としてシェイクスピアの劇 8 つを 2 つの 4 部作にグループ分けし，その背景にある歴史的な出来事と結びつけながら説明している。よって正解は③。①は漠然としすぎているので不適切。登場人物の維持についても重要性を述べてはいないので②も正しくない。英文学における歴史劇の位置づけについては述べていないので④も不適切。

(2) カーナンは第 3 段落で 2 番目のヘンリアドの方を「大規模な英雄行動」に言及して傑作としているとあり，「より壮大で英雄的な物語がある」とほめている①と一致する。その他の選択肢は，ヘンリアドをほめる観点ではない。

(3) 批評家については最終段落でふれている。シェイクスピアはテューダー朝期に作品を書いており，テューダー朝の始まりによって終わりを迎えることになった歴史的な混沌を物語にしている。批評家たちはここに political story behind the Henriad「ヘンリアドの背後にある政治的な物語」を感じたのである。④の内容と一致する。①〜③は批評家が感じた政治性とは関連がない。

注
◇ split O into 〜「O を〜に分ける」 split − split − split
◇ tetralogy「(本，オペラ，劇などの) 4 部作」 cf. tetra-「4 つの」 + -logy「言葉；〜論；〜学」
◇ in terms of 〜「〜によって；〜の観点から」
◇ dynasty「王朝；〜王朝時代」
◇ for one's own convenience「〜の都合で；〜の都合に合わせて」
◇ masterpiece「傑作；名作；(ある人の) 最高傑作」

Training

答え

(1) This is where I'd like to turn our attention today, as the river flows wider and more slowly over flatter land on its journey to the coast. ↘

(2) This creates a sharper bend in the river. ↘

(3) However, the human aspect of the characters, many of which appear many times throughout the tetralogy, are perhaps what makes this series of plays a truly great work. ↘

(4) Critics in the past have sought to place a political story behind the Henriad. ↘

Step 3
Let's Speak!

答え

■ (1) ① the valley becomes deeper ② I'd like to turn our attention
(2) ① a sharper bend in the river ② to bend more and more
(3) ① regard as a true masterpiece ② what makes this series of plays
(4) ① in the rise of order and modernity ② one of the true peaks of English literature

Lesson 13

Words & Expressions カタカナ語と発音が異なる語

☐ vaccine [vӕksíːn] 名ワクチン
☐ virus [váɪrəs] 名ウイルス
☐ chaos [kéɪɑːs] 名無秩序；混沌；カオス
☐ vitamin [váɪtəmɪn] 名ビタミン
☐ herb [ə́ːrb, hə́ːrb] 名ハーブ
☐ Asia [éɪʒə] 名アジア
☐ theme [θíːm] 名テーマ

Lesson 14
技能融合1（Listening → Speaking）（短文での応答）

問題冊子 p.94 ／
音声はこちらから➡

Training

答え

(1) Do you often go to the library in your town, ♪ and why? ↘

Step2 実戦問題

1 解答例

(1) I would like to travel to Australia. I have never been there, but I am interested in Australian animals. I want to see some of these animals, for example, koalas and kangaroos.

(2) I enjoyed the school festival. I worked hard with my classmates to think about our class theme. It was hard to decide on the theme, but finally we did it. Many people said, "Your class theme is great!"

(3) I like spring best. There are many flowers, such as cherry blossoms, and the weather becomes warm. We also start a new school year in spring, so it is exciting.

(4) I prefer to go to the mountains. Summer is hot, but it is cool in the mountains. It is easy to relax and we can enjoy nature.

解説

1 (1)

🔊 would you は d と y がつながって「ウヂュー」のように聞こえる。

スクリプト	和訳
Where would you like to travel in the future, and why?	将来どこを旅行したいですか。それはなぜですか。

解答例

I would like to travel to Australia. I have never been there, but I am interested in Australian animals. I want to see some of these animals, for example, koalas and kangaroos.

解答例の和訳

私はオーストラリアを旅行したいです。そこへ行ったことはありませんが，オーストラリアの動物に興味があります。例えばコアラやカンガルーなどの動物をいくつか見たいです。

> 問われているのは旅行したい場所と，その理由。まず場所を答える。質問文に合わせて I'd like to travel to に続けて行きたい地名を入れるといいだろう。理由としてはそこでやりたいこと，興味があること，見たいものなどを挙げよう。

(2)

🔊 event と「イベント」の違いに注意。特にアクセント位置に気をつけよう。

スクリプト	和訳
What event at your school did you enjoy the most?	学校で最も楽しかった行事は何ですか。

解答例

I enjoyed the school festival. I worked hard with my classmates to think about our class theme. It was hard to decide on the theme, but finally we did it. Many people said, "Your class theme is great!"

解答例の和訳

学校祭を楽しみました。クラスメートと共にクラスのテーマについて考えようとがんばりました。テーマを決めるのは大変でしたが，最後にはやり遂げました。たくさんの人が「あなたのクラスのテーマはすばらしい！」と言ってくれました。

> school trip（修学旅行），sports festival（体育大会），music festival（音楽会）などの学校行事を答える。そして，その行事で自分が何をしたか，具体的に何が楽しかったかなどを付け加えよう。

(3)

スクリプト	和訳
Which season of the year do you like best, and why?	1 年の中でどの季節が一番好きですか。またそれはなぜですか。

解答例

I like spring best. There are many flowers, such as cherry blossoms, and the weather becomes warm. We also start a new school year in spring, so it is exciting.

解答例の和訳

私は春が一番好きです。桜などのたくさんの花があり，天候も暖かくなります。春には学校の新年度も始まりわくわくします。

Lesson 14

spring（春），summer（夏），fall/autumn（秋），winter（冬）の中で最も好きな季節を答える。I like 〜 (the) best. で文を始めるといいだろう。このときの best は副詞の最上級なので the はつけなくてもよい。

(4)

スクリプト	和訳
Do you prefer to go to the beach or the mountains in the summer?	夏には海へ行くのが好きですか。それとも山へ行くのが好きですか。

解答例

I prefer to go to the mountains. Summer is hot, but it is cool in the mountains. It is easy to relax and we can enjoy nature.

解答例の和訳

私は山へ行く方が好きです。夏は暑いですが，山は涼しいです。リラックスしやすく，自然を楽しむことができます。

prefer to *do* は「（〜よりむしろ）…することを好む」という意味。山と海のどちらが好きかを答える。理由や，その場所でやりたいことなどを付け加えるとよい。

注

◇ prefer to *do* ... rather than (to) *do* 〜「〜することよりも，むしろ…する方を好む」*cf.* prefer O₁ to O₂「O₂ より O₁ が好きである」

Training

(1) Where would you like to travel in the future, and why? ↘

(2) What event at your school did you enjoy the most? ↘

(3) Which season of the year do you like best, and why? ↘

(4) Do you prefer to go to the beach ↗ or the mountains ↘ in the summer? ↘

Step3
Let's Speak!

答え

■　(1) Where would you like to travel　(2) did you enjoy the most
　　(3) of the year do you like best
　　(4) prefer to go to

Words & Expressions　学校行事

☐ field trip 　　　　　　　　图遠足；校外見学
☐ excursion 　　　　　　　　图遠足；（団体の）小旅行
☐ swimming meet 　　　　　图水泳大会　*cf.* meet「（運動・競技の）大会」
☐ entrance ceremony 　　　　图入学式
☐ graduation ceremony 　　　图卒業式
☐ parents' day 　　　　　　　图授業参観日
☐ school festival 　　　　　　图学校祭

Lesson 14

Lesson 15
技能融合 2 （Reading → Listening（対話）→ Speaking）

問題冊子 p.97 ／
音声はこちらから➡

Training

答え

(1) I think a better system would be to allow you to take books out, but limit the length of time you can take the books out. ↘

(2) Imagine if the majority of textbooks, or at least the books recommended by tutors, were available online. ↘

Step2
実戦問題

解答例

1　The man disagrees with the college's decision to make second language classes elective. He thinks that even learning a little of a foreign language can help students to understand more about the world. His second point is that the foreign language classes help students from many different majors come together and meet new people. In fact, this is how he met his friend here. He worries that most students will not choose a foreign language in the future.

2　The student is shocked that he will need to enter a lottery to get a room at the university next year. He wants to stay in hall, but he is not sure if he will be able to stay or not, so he will need to look for a shared house, just in case. He thinks that the university should build more accommodation for students. He also wants information on the number of rooms available, so that he can understand more about the chance of getting a university room next year.

解説

1

◀ 最後の方の男性の発言中，had the choice の [d]，not to do の [t] の音は，次の音のかまえをするために発音されずに，「ハッザチョイス」「ナットゥドゥー」のようになる。

84

英文訳

大学が翌年から1年生の必要条件を変更しようとしています。100秒間で，変更に関する掲示を読んでください。

来年から第二言語は選択科目に

　ここ数年の学生数の変化に伴い，大学は第二言語の授業に関して変更をすることになりました。第二言語の授業はこれからもすべての学生に提供されますが，学生はこれらの授業を受講するかどうかを決めることができます。

　現在はフランス語，スペイン語，ドイツ語のクラスがあり，すべての1年生は，これらのうちの1つが必修となっています。今や学生の半数以上が海外から入学しているので，とりわけ第一言語として英語を話さない学生に対しては，言語学習の量は減らされるべきであると思われます。

　3言語すべての選択クラスは学習を望むどの学生にも残されます。もっとも，もし多くの1年生が1つの第二言語を選択したら，少し大きいクラスになることを覚悟してください。この新しいシステムは来年度中は試行期間として行われ，大学側は第二言語のクラスの需要を調査します。

スクリプト

Now listen to two students discussing the notice.

M：You know, I think this could be a kind of wrong step for the college.

W：What, you mean the second language classes? How come? To be honest, it was hard studying French in that first year.

M：Yeah, it was hard, but there were a lot of positives, too. I think a lot of students come here without having a strong view of the world. <u>Even just learning a little of another language can give you more understanding of the world.</u>

W：Well, you know, it says that a lot of students now are from all over the world.

和訳

では，この掲示について2人の学生が話し合うのを聞きなさい。

男性：ねえ，これは大学にとって悪い一歩になるんじゃないかと思うよ。

女性：え，第二言語の授業のこと？ どうして？ 正直に言うと，1年生でフランス語を勉強するのは大変だったわ。

男性：ああ，大変だったけど，いい面もたくさんあったよ。多くの学生が強い世界観を持たずにここへ来ていると思う。別の言語を少し学ぶだけでも，世界への理解を広げることができるよ。

女性：あら，ほら，多くの学生が世界中から来ているって書いてあるわよ。

M : But they could still benefit from learning another language. And there's another important point about these classes that goes beyond what you learn. <u>As these classes are not related to your major, you can communicate with many students from various majors.</u>

W : I guess so. Like, we actually did meet in that French class, now that you say it.

M : For sure! As I study history and you major in biology, we probably wouldn't have met outside of this class, you know? And that kind of meeting is more important for students that are coming from other countries. <u>It must be a great way to meet people and make friends.</u>

W : Well, the classes are still elective. Most students may still choose to take a second language.

M : You think? Would you? I mean, seriously, if you really had the choice not to do it.

W : Yeah, I guess not.

Give yourself 30 seconds to prepare your response to the following question. Then speak for 60 seconds.

The man gives his opinion on the college's notice. State his opinion and the reasons he gives for holding that opinion.

男性：でもそれでも別の言語を学ぶことから恩恵を得られるよ。それにこれらのクラスでは学ぶこと以上の大切な点が別にあるよ。これらのクラスは自分の専攻に関係ないから、いろいろな専攻の学生とコミュニケーションをとることができるよ。

女性：そうね。まあ実際言われてみれば、私たちもフランス語のクラスで会ったしね。

男性：確かに！ 僕は歴史を勉強していて、君は生物専攻だから、このクラス以外では会わなかったかもしれないね。この手の出会いは別の国出身の学生にはもっと大切だよ。人に出会って友達になるいい方法に違いないよ。

女性：まあ、クラスはまだ選択式でしょ。ほとんどの学生が第二言語の授業を選択するんじゃないかな。

男性：そう思う？ 君はそうする？ つまり、まじめな話、そうしなくてもいいという選択肢があったとしても？

女性：うーん、選択しないかも。

次の質問に答えるための準備時間が30秒間あります。次に答えを60秒間で話してください。

男性は大学の掲示について自分の意見を言っています。彼の意見とそのような意見を持った理由を説明しなさい。

解答例

The man disagrees with the college's decision to make second language classes elective. He thinks that even learning a little of a foreign language can help students to understand more about the world. His second point is that the foreign language classes help students from many different majors come together and meet new people. In fact, this is how he met his friend here. He worries that most students will not choose a foreign language in the future.

解答例の和訳

男性は第二言語を選択制にするという大学の決定に反対しています。彼は，少しでも外国語を学ぶことは学生が世界についてより理解する助けとなると考えています。2つ目の点は，外国語の授業は異なる専攻の学生が集まり，新しい人々と出会う助けになるということです。実際，このようにして彼はここにいる友人と会いました。彼はほとんどの学生が将来は外国語を選択しないのではないかと心配しています。

大学の掲示は，現在は必修科目である第二言語を来年は選択科目にするという内容である。男性の意見が求められているので，まず掲示の内容に賛成か反対かについて述べ，そのあとで理由を付け加えるとよい。男性は反対の立場である。その理由として，外国語を学習することで世界について考えるようになることと，外国語のクラスでは専攻の違う学生とも知り合いになれることを挙げている。

注

◇ requirement「必要条件」
◇ trial period「試用期間」
◇ major「専攻」，「専攻する」

2

英文訳

次年度，学生が部屋の申請をする規則にいくつか変更があります。学生通信の記事を読みなさい。記事を読む時間は100秒間です。

2年生から，大学学生宿舎は抽選に

先週，大学宿舎委員会が通知を出しました。2年生以上の学生は，大学寮内の部屋の確約を得るには，次年度から抽選をする必要があるかもしれません。多くの2年生は大学の部屋を出て，友人とのシェアハウスへ引っ越すことを好みますが，学内に住み続けることを好む学生も常に大勢います。

「新入生の数が標準より多いため，残りの部屋がわずかしかありません。」と，宿舎委員の1人がコメントしました。

特別な支援が必要な学生は別に考慮されますが，2年次も学生宿舎に入ることを希望するほとんどの学生は7月3日までに抽選に登録する必要があります。日程はまだ決定されていませんが，受け入れの可否に関する決定は8月末ごろに郵送される予定です。

Lesson 15

Now listen to two students discussing this article.

W : Hey, didn't you want to stay on for your second year in university halls?

M : I did! I was as surprised as anyone when I read that article. I called the accommodation office, but they basically said the same thing. If I want to remain living in university halls, I have to enter this lottery.

W : Did they say how many people will enter the lottery?

M : They said they don't know, but I guess they are hoping most people will decide to leave the halls so that they don't have too much competition for places. I just wish I'd known about it earlier.

W : So, what are you going to do?

M : Well, I'll apply for a place, but I suppose I'll need to look around for a shared house, not too far from the campus. I know they need to guarantee first-years' places, but if they are planning on taking more new first-years, you know, they should at least have built more accommodation first.

W : Maybe it's just a one-time event. Like, maybe the number of new students will go back down again next year.

M : Who knows? At least, if they let us know just how many places were available, we'd know what kind of

では，この記事について 2 人の学生が話し合うのを聞きなさい。

女性：ねえ，あなたは 2 年生も大学寮にいたいんじゃなかった？

男性：いたかったよ。この記事を読んだとき，僕は誰よりも驚いたよ。宿舎事務所に電話をしたけど，基本的に同じことを言っていたよ。もし大学寮に住み続けたかったら，この抽選に申し込まないといけないな。

女性：事務所の人は，何人が抽選に申し込むと言っていた？

男性：わからないと言っていたけど，彼らは部屋を求める倍率があまり高くならないように，多くの人が寮を出ると決めることを望んでいると思うよ。もっと早くわかっていたらよかった。

女性：それであなたはどうするの？

男性：うん，応募するつもりだけど，学校からあまり遠くないシェアハウスを探す必要が出てくると思う。1 年生用の部屋を確保する必要があるのはわかるけど，より多くの新入生を入れるつもりなら，少なくともまずもっと宿舎を建てるべきだったよ。

女性：まあたぶん一時的なことなのよ。また来年は新入生の数が減るとかね。

男性：誰にもわからないさ。少なくとも入れる部屋がどのくらいあるのかを僕らに知らせてくれたら，そのうちの 1 つを手に入

chance we have of getting one of the rooms. It could be a hundred, it could be only ten. A little more information would have helped. And sooner!

Give yourself 30 seconds to prepare your response to the following question. Then speak for 60 seconds.

The man has some opinions regarding the new accommodation policy. State his opinions and the reasons he has for holding them.

れられる機会がどのくらいあるかわかるのに。100 部屋かもしれないし 10 部屋だけかもしれない。もうちょっと情報があれば助かったのに。そしてもっと早いうちに！

次の質問に答えるための準備時間が 30 秒間あります。次に答えを 60 秒間で話してください。

男性は新しい宿舎制度に関していくつか意見があります。彼の意見とそのような意見を持った理由を説明しなさい。

解答例

The student is shocked that he will need to enter a lottery to get a room at the university next year. He wants to stay in hall, but he is not sure if he will be able to stay or not, so he will need to look for a shared house, just in case. He thinks that the university should build more accommodation for students. He also wants information on the number of rooms available, so that he can understand more about the chance of getting a university room next year.

解答例の和訳

その学生は次年度，大学で部屋を得るには抽選に参加する必要があることにショックを受けています。彼は残りたいと思っていますが，残ることができるかどうかわからないので，念のためシェアハウスを探さなければならないでしょう。彼は大学がもっと学生のための宿舎を建てるべきだと考えています。入れる部屋の数についての情報も欲しがっています。そうすれば次年度，大学の部屋に住む機会があるかどうかもっとわかるからです。

大学の掲示から，次年度は 2 年生以上の学生の宿舎は抽選になることがわかる。それに対する男子学生の意見とその理由が求められている。初めに彼は「驚いた」と言っており，次年度も宿舎に住むことを望んでいることが発言からわかる。彼の意見としては，「大学はもっと宿舎を建てるべきだ」と「どのくらい部屋数があるかを早く知らせてほしい」という 2 つを挙げている。

注

◇ lottery「抽選，くじ引き；宝くじ」
◇ accommodation「宿泊施設」

Training

答え

(1) Yeah, it was hard, but there were a lot of positives, too. ↘

(2) As these classes are not related to your major, you can communicate with many students from various majors. ↘

(3) I just wish I'd known about it earlier. ↘

(4) A little more information would have helped. ↘

Step3 Let's Speak!

答え

■ (1) ① there were a lot of positives
　　② can give you more understanding of
　(2) ① these classes are not related to
　　② we actually did meet
　(3) ① to look around for a shared house
　　② have built more accommodation
　(4) ① how many places were available　② A little more information

Words & Expressions　大学生活

□ university	名総合大学
□ college	名単科大学
□ junior college	名短期大学
□ campus	名構内，キャンパス
□ major	名専攻　動専攻する
□ graduate school	名大学院《米》　cf. postgraduate school《英》
□ thesis	名（卒論や修論などの）論文
□ professor	名教授
□ department	名学部，学科

Training

答え

(1) Hydrogen produced in this manner canno(t) be said to be environmentally friendly. ↘

(2) This basically means using electricity to split water into hydrogen and oxygen, with no harmful by-products. ↘

Step2 実戦問題

解答例

1 Peer-to-peer lending is a system in which people can lend money through websites as a way of investing and making money. The benefit to the lender is that they can make more money than with a traditional bank account. However, there is the possibility of losing their investment if the borrowers do not repay the loans. The peer-to-peer websites also charge a fee and lenders need to think carefully about these things before they invest money.

2 There are two different kinds of trees: angiosperms and gymnosperms. Gymnosperms have been on the earth much longer than angiosperms. However, there are many more species of angiosperms now. There are a number of ways we can distinguish these trees. Angiosperms produce seeds inside fruit, which are carried by animals that eat the fruit, but gymnosperms have seeds that are exposed, and use the wind to transport their seeds. Gymnosperms are evergreen [evergreens] and angiosperms lose their leaves in the autumn. Humans use many angiosperms for food. Wood from angiosperm trees is hardwood and is used for high quality products, but the softwood of gymnosperms is used for buildings and cheaper furniture.

1

🔊 本文第3文の check the background <u>of the</u> borrowers, reduce some <u>of the</u> risk の 2箇所の of the は弱く発音され，聞き取りづらい。また，background と of, some と of はつながって発音されることにも注意する。

英文訳

個人間融資に関する文章を読みなさい。文章を読んだあと，講義を聞き，続く質問に答えなさい。では，読み始めなさい。（制限時間：45秒）

個人間融資が主要な投資源になるにつれ，ここ数年オンライン上での貸し借りの仕組みがますます整ってきています。これらの個人間融資サービスは多くの専門のウェブサイトで提供されています。投資家と借り手は，双方に利益があるようにサイトを通して組み合わされます。投資家，つまり貸し手はたいてい，お金を貸すことで従来の預金口座に入れておくよりもお金をもっと増やしたいと望む人々です。借り手は従来の銀行ローンよりも払う金利を少なくしたい会社や個人でしょう。個人間取引のサイトはこれらの集団を取りまとめ，概念としてはビジネスとしてうまく成り立っていると思われます。

スクリプト

Now listen to an economics lecture on the advantages and disadvantages of peer-to-peer lending.

If we look at the lender, there are several positive points to this system. Firstly, <u>there is the chance of earning more than by saving money in a bank</u>. The interest rates are agreed in advance, so the income should be steady. Peer-to-peer companies generally check the background of the borrowers, and lenders are able to control who they lend their money to in order to reduce some of the risk. Many peer-to-peer sites offer additional protection such as insurance, and can put pressure on borrowers who do not pay money back.

There are, as you might have guessed,

和訳

では，個人間融資の利点と欠点に関する経済学の講義を聞きなさい。

貸し手に注目すると，このシステムにはいくつかのよい面があります。
まず，銀行に預金するよりも多く稼げる機会があります。金利はあらかじめ合意のもと決められるので，収入は確実なはずです。個人間取引の会社は，一般的に借り手の背景事情を確認し，貸し手はリスクをある程度減らすために，自分のお金を誰に貸すかをコントロールすることができます。多くの個人間取引サイトは保険など追加の保護対策を提供しており，お金を返さない借り手には圧力をかけることができます。

あなた方が推測するように，ある程度の欠点

certain disadvantages. <u>The main one is, of course, the risk of lending money to people you don't know.</u> Most governments do not offer protection for peer-to-peer lending in the way that they do for a regular savings account. <u>This means that there is the possibility of losing some, or even all, of your investment</u> if the borrowers do not repay the loan. Peer-to-peer websites work to minimize this risk, but the risk is certainly higher than investing with a bank. Additionally, <u>the websites do charge fees for these services</u>——this is, after all, how they make their money—— although a smart investor would take these fees into account when planning to lend money in this way. Lenders also need to be prepared to calculate by themselves taxes on any profits.

Despite the risks, growth in this industry has been steady, mainly due to poor rates of interest paid by banks.

Give yourself 30 seconds to prepare your response to the following question. Then speak for 60 seconds.

Explain what peer-to-peer lending is and how the professor outlines the advantages and disadvantages to the lender.

もあります。主な欠点は、当然のことながら知らない人々にお金を貸すリスクです。

ほとんどの政府は、通常の預金口座に設けているような保護政策を個人間融資には設けていません。つまり、借り手がローンの返済をしなければ、あなたは投資したお金の一部または全部を失う可能性があるということです。個人間取引サイトはこのリスクを最小限にするよう努めていますが、リスクは銀行へ投資するよりも確実に高くなります。加えて、取引サイトはこれらのサービスの手数料を、これが結局のところ取引サイトの収入源なのですが、取っています。賢明な投資家はこの方法でお金を貸す計画を立てる時に、これらの手数料を考慮に入れていますが。貸し手は利益にかかる税金も自分たちで計算する準備をする必要があります。

リスクにもかかわらず、この産業の成長は堅実で、これは主に銀行の金利の低さによるものです。

30秒間で以下の質問への答えを準備してください。その後60秒間であなたの答えを話してください。

個人間融資とは何か、また貸し手にとっての利点と欠点について教授がどう概説しているかを説明しなさい。

Lesson 16

解答例

Peer-to-peer lending is a system in which people can lend money through websites as a way of investing and making money. The benefit to the lender is that they can make more money than with a traditional bank account. However, there is the possibility of losing their investment if the borrowes do not repay the loans.

The peer-to-peer websites also charge a fee and lenders need to think carefully about these things before they invest money.

解答例の和訳

　個人間融資は，投資や金儲けの方法として，ウェブサイトを通じて人々がお金を貸すことができるシステムです。貸し手にとっての利点は従来の銀行口座よりも多くのお金を稼ぐことができることです。けれども借りた人がお金を返さなければ，投資したお金を失うという可能性もあります。個人間取引のサイトも手数料を取るので貸し手はお金を投資する前に，これらのことも慎重に考える必要があります。

　個人間融資の概要と，貸し手から見た利点と欠点を説明することが求められている。個人間融資の概要は読解資料から読み取れる。ウェブサイトを通じて個人間で直接貸し借りをする仕組みで，投資家（貸し手），借り手の特徴が説明されている。講義は貸し手から見た利点（positive points）で始まっている。銀行に預けるよりも高い金利で利益を得られるのが利点である。欠点（certain disadvantages）は後半で説明されている。欠点の main one として挙げられているのは知らない人にお金を貸すリスクで，具体的には，投資したお金が回収できない可能性があることである。また additionally に続けて手数料がかかることも欠点として挙げられている。

注

◇ investment「投資」　　cf. invest「～を投資する」，investor「投資家」
◇ savings account「預金口座」
◇ interest「利子，利息；金利」　ex. interest rate「金利」
◇ steady「着実な」
◇ minimize「～を最小にする」　⇔ maximize「～を最大にする」
◇ take ～ into account「～を考慮する；～を考慮に入れる」

2

英文訳

木の歴史に関する文章を読みなさい。文章を読んだあと，講義を聞き，続く質問に答えなさい。では，読み始めなさい。（制限時間：45 秒）

比較的最近，人類の活動によって破壊されるまでは，私たちの惑星は森の惑星で，ほぼ全世界に広がる木に覆われていました。そして何億年もの間，これらの木々はすべて裸子植物（gymnosperms の語義は naked seed『裸の種』）でした。その後，2 億年ほど前に花や実をつける被子植物が発達し始めました。今日では多くの木を含む何十万種類もの被子植物があります。一方，世界中でわずか千種類ほどの裸子植物しか残っていないと考えられています。

スクリプト

Now listen to a biology lecture on the differences between angiosperms and gymnosperms.

We've talked about the fact that the angiosperm group split off from gymnosperms around 200 million years ago. But, what are the main ways we can distinguish these two kinds of tree we see today? Well, most of you know that gymnosperms produce seeds that are not contained in a fruit, but are often found exposed in cones. In contrast, angiosperms usually produce seeds inside fruit. Thus, angiosperms mainly rely on animals when they reproduce or transport seeds, whereas gymnosperms tend to rely on the wind.

Another major difference is that most gymnosperms are evergreens, producing leaves in the shape of needles or scales, which remain on the tree throughout the year. Angiosperms follow a seasonal lifecycle, losing their often broad, flat leaves in the autumn and re-growing them again in the spring.

Finally we can divide these groups in terms of how we humans use them. Angiosperms are of far more importance to humans in terms of a food source. We eat the fruit and sometimes leaves and roots of angiosperm trees as a major part of our diet. Gymnosperms do not generally provide food for humans, although we use them to make products such as

和訳

では，被子植物と裸子植物の違いに関する生物学の講義を聞きなさい。

これまでに被子植物群は2億年ほど前に裸子植物から分かれたという事実について話してきました。しかし，現在私たちが見かけるこれら2種類の木々を見分ける主な方法は何でしょうか。さて，ほとんどの皆さんは，裸子植物は種が果実の中に含まれず，しばしば松かさの中など木の外側で見られる種を作るということを知っていますね。対照的に，被子植物は通常果実の中に種を作ります。ですから被子植物は再生産したり種を移動させたりする時に主に動物に頼りますが，裸子植物は風に頼る傾向にあります。

もう1つの大きな違いはほとんどの裸子植物が常緑で，針状やうろこ状の葉をつけ，その葉が年間を通して木に残っているということです。被子植物は季節ごとのライフサイクルに従い，秋には多くが広く平らな葉を落とし，春には再び葉を茂らせます。

最後に，我々人間がどう利用するかによって，これらのグループを分けることができます。被子植物は食料源という観点から人類にとってはるかに重要です。我々は食料の主要な部分として被子植物の果実や，時には葉や根も食べることがあります。裸子植物は，石鹸や香水といった製品を作るのに使いますが，一般的には人間の食料にはなりません。どちらの木も我々に木材を提供します。被子植物は固い木材を提供しますが，それらはゆっくり成長し，一般的に，

Lesson 16

95

soaps and perfumes. Both trees provide us with wood. Angiosperms produce hardwood, which grows slowly and is generally denser and used for higher quality products. For most buildings and for cheaper furniture, the softwood timber of gymnosperms is used because it grows faster.

より密度が高く高品質の製品に使われます。ほとんどの建物や安価な家具には，裸子植物の柔らかい木材が使われます。裸子植物の木は成長が速いためです。

Give yourself 30 seconds to prepare your response to the following question. Then speak for 60 seconds.

30 秒間で以下の質問への答えを準備しなさい。その後 60 秒間であなたの答えを話しなさい。

Give a brief history of the two types of tree and outline some ways the professor suggests for distinguishing angiosperms from gymnosperms.

2 種類の木の簡単な歴史と，教授が示している被子植物を裸子植物と区別するいくつかの方法の概要を説明しなさい。

解答例

There are two different kinds of trees: angiosperms and gymnosperms. Gymnosperms have been on the earth much longer than angiosperms. However, there are many more species of angiosperms now. There are a number of ways we can distinguish these trees. Angiosperms produce seeds inside fruit, which are carried by animals that eat the fruit, but gymnosperms have seeds that are exposed, and use the wind to transport their seeds. Gymnosperms are evergreen 〔evergreens〕 and angiosperms lose their leaves in the autumn. Humans use many angiosperms for food. Wood from angiosperm trees is hardwood and is used for high quality products, but the softwood of gymnosperms is used for buildings and cheaper furniture.

解答例の和訳

木には 2 つの異なる種類，被子植物と裸子植物があります。裸子植物の方が被子植物よりははるか昔から地球上にありました。けれども現在は被子植物の種類の方がずっとたくさんあります。これらの木々を区別する方法はいくつかあります。被子植物には果実の中に種ができ，種は，果実を食べる動物によって運ばれますが，裸子植物の種はむき出しで，種を運ぶには風を使います。裸子植物は常緑で，被子植物は秋に葉を落とします。人類は多くの被子植物を食料として利用します。被子植物の木材は固く，高品質の製品に利用されますが，裸子植物の柔らかい木材は建物や安価な家具に使われます。

被子植物と裸子植物という2種類の木の歴史と区別の仕方を説明することが求められている。歴史については読解資料で説明されている。裸子植物の方が古くからあり，被子植物があとから派生したこと，種類は現在では被子植物の方が多いことを述べるとよい。区別の方法は講義でいくつか述べられている。種が果実に包まれているかどうか，種を運ぶ方法，葉の形状，常緑か落葉するか，食料として使われるかどうか，木材としての利用方法の違いなどが挙げられている。

　本レッスンで取り上げたような，ある程度専門的な英文では，そのトピックに関する背景知識を持っていると理解がしやすい。日ごろから様々な分野に興味をもち教養を深めておくことも大切である。

注
◇ gymnosperm「裸子（らし）植物」
◇ angiosperm「被子（ひし）植物」
◇ split off from ～「～から離れる；分裂する」
◇ distinguish「区別する；識別する」
◇ cone「(裸子植物の) 球果，松かさ；円錐（形)」
◇ scale「うろこ；うろこ状のもの」
◇ dense「密集した；高密度の」

Training

(1) Firstly, there is the chance of earning more than by saving money in a bank. ↘

(2) The main one is, of course, the risk of lending money to people you don't know. ↘

(3) In contrast, angiosperms usually produce seeds inside fruit. ↘

(4) Angiosperms are of far more importance to humans in terms of a food source. ↘

Step 3 Let's Speak!

答え

1 (1) ① the income should be steady　② check the background of the borrowers
(2) ① there is the possibility of losing　② work to minimize this risk
　　③ take these fees into account
(3) ① remain on the tree　② losing their often broad, flat leaves
(4) ① used for higher quality products　② because it grows faster

1

答え
(1) ③ (2) ②

解説
(1) ③

スクリプト	和訳
M: Let's have a look in a furniture shop next. We have some visitors coming next week and I need to get two new chairs so we can all eat together.	男性：次は家具屋さんを見よう。来週お客さんが来るから，全員そろって食事ができるように新しい椅子を2脚買わないと。
W: Sure! Smith's Furniture Shop is on Bridge Street, but if it's only for a few days, why don't we just get some used furniture?	女性：そうね。スミス家具店がブリッジストリートにあるわね。でも数日だけのためなら，中古の家具を買うのはどうかしら？
M: That's a good idea, but I looked in Green's Used Furniture last week. They didn't have anything nice. I thought about trying the Jones' Department Store, too. But I think they will be too expensive.	男性：いい考えだね。でもグリーン中古家具は先週見た。いいものは何もなかったよ。ジョーンズデパートに行ってみるのもいいかと思ったんだ。でも，あそこは高すぎると思うんだ。
W: Usually they are. But there is a sale on at Jones' this week and some furniture is half price. <u>Why don't we check that out first?</u>	女性：普段はそうね。でもジョーンズデパートは今週セール中で半額の家具もあるのよ。まずそこを検討してみましょう。
Question: Which shop will they visit first?	

設問訳　彼らはまずどの店を訪ねるか。

99

女性の最後の発言 Why don't we check that out first? の that は直前の発言にある Jones'
(Department Store) を指している。正解は③。その前に男性はジョーンズデパートは高すぎ
ると言っているが，女性は今週はセール中で半額の家具もあることから，まずそこへ行く
ことを提案している。

(2) ②

スクリプト	和訳
M: Do you want cake with your coffee?	男性：コーヒーといっしょにケーキも欲しい？
W: You know, I'm going to say no. It looks too sweet.	女性：いいえと答えるってわかっているでしょ。甘すぎるように見えるわ。
M: Well, how about a sandwich, or something else light? You must be hungry after working all morning.	男性：じゃあサンドイッチとか何か軽いものはどう？ 午前中ずっと働いてお腹がすいているだろう？
W: Well, okay. I'll take <u>a piece of fruit with the coffee</u>.	女性：ええ，そうね。コーヒーとフルーツをひと切れもらうわ。
Question: Which of these pictures shows the woman's order?	

設問訳　これらのイラストのうち，女性の注文はどれか。

最後の発言から，女性はコーヒーと a piece of fruit を頼むことがわかる。イラストの中で
果物はバナナだから②が正解。

2

解答
(1) three　　(2) Kyoto　　(3) stadium　　(4) mountain　　(5) hot spring
hotel　　(6) shopping area　　(7) (limousine) bus

解説

スクリプト	和訳
First of all, welcome to Tokyo and the second part of your visit to Japan. I hope you enjoyed your journey <u>from Kyoto</u> aboard the bullet train. Our tour now continues <u>for three days</u> in Japan's exciting capital city. We'll begin the	まずは，東京，そして皆様の日本訪問の第二部へようこそ。京都からの新幹線の旅はお楽しみいただけたでしょうか。私たちのツアーは日本の刺激的な首都で，これから3日間続きます。はとバスと呼ばれる有名な黄色いツアーバスの1つで旅行を始めます。丸1日の東京巡りにお

trip on one of the famous yellow tour buses, called a *Hato Bus*. This will take you on a full one-day tour of the city, where we will stop at seven different spots, including lunch <u>near the sumo stadium</u>.

Tomorrow we will be spending the day at <u>a mountain resort</u>, about two hours from central Tokyo. You should have a chance to take some photos of Japan's greatest symbol, Mount Fuji. After that, we hope you can <u>relax in a hot spring hotel</u>. Spend the night here before heading back to Tokyo in the morning and take advantage of the opportunity to <u>walk around the shopping area</u> and take a river cruise.

After the third night we will take you in the comfort of <u>a limousine bus</u> to the airport and the end of what we hope will have been a wonderful tour of Japan.

連れし，相撲競技場（国技館）の近くでのランチも含めて7カ所のさまざまなスポットを訪れます。

明日は東京の中心地から2時間ほどの山のリゾート地で過ごします。日本の最も素晴らしい象徴である富士山の写真を撮る機会があるでしょう。そのあとは温泉ホテルでおくつろぎいただけると思います。一晩ここで過ごし，明朝東京へと向かいます。それからショッピングエリアを散策し，川のクルーズ船に乗ります。

3日目の夜ののち，空港まで快適なリムジンバスで皆様をお送りします。最後まで日本を巡る素晴らしいツアーとなりますように。

設問訳 ツアーについての女性のアナウンスを聞き，(1)〜(7)の空所を完成させなさい。

旅行の第2部：東京

・活動：日本の刺激的な首都で（ (1) ）日間過ごす

1日目

・（ (2) ）から新幹線で到着する

・相撲（ (3) ）の近くでランチを楽しむ

2日目

・（ (4) ）のリゾートで過ごし，（ (5) ）でくつろぐ

3日目

・（ (6) ）を散策し，川のクルーズ船に乗る

・（ (7) ）で空港へ行く

スクリプトの下線部を参照のこと。聞き取るべき語句は，案内の中で伝えるべきポイント部分なので，強くはっきりと発音されている。

◇ aboard「(乗り物) に乗って」

3

解説
Part A (1)④ (2)②

🔈 live close to 〜 の close は形容詞で発音は [klóus]。動詞の close [klóuz] との発音の違いに注意しよう。

スクリプト	和訳
Sarah: Kenta, how old were you when you got your first smartphone?	サラ：ケンタ，初めて自分のスマートフォンを持ったのは何歳の時？
Kenta: I got one when I entered junior high school, so I was twelve. But I had been asking my mother for one for a long time. How about you, Sarah?	ケンタ：中学校へ入った時だよ。だから 12 歳だ。でもずっと欲しいって母に頼んでいたんだ。サラはどう？
Sarah: I got one just last year, when I was fifteen.	サラ：私は去年，15 歳の時に買ったばかりよ。
Kenta: Don't you think that's a little late?	ケンタ：それって少し遅めだと思わない？
Sarah: Not really. Only a few of my friends had them, and I didn't really need one. We couldn't bring them to school, anyway. At home I had a tablet.	サラ：そうでもないよ。友だちで持っている子も少なかったし，それほど必要じゃなかったから。どうせ学校へは持って行ってはいけなかったし。家ではタブレットがあったの。
Kenta: But what if you needed to call your parents; if the train got stuck or if there was an emergency?	ケンタ：でもご両親に電話する必要があったら？ 電車が止まったり，何か緊急の時とか。
Sarah: Well, most people lived close to school. We didn't catch a train so we could always go home straightaway. Smartphones are	サラ：そうね，ほとんどの人は学校のそばに住んでいて，電車に乗らないからいつでもすぐに家に帰ることができたの。スマホは買う時だけでなく，月々の電話代も高いで

102

expensive, not only to buy but also the monthly payment for calls.

Kenta: My mom always complains about the cost, too. But I think it would be hard to contact friends and live well without a phone. I couldn't live without mine now.

しょ。

ケンタ：母もいつも料金について文句を言っているよ。でもスマホなしでは友だちと連絡をとったり快適に生活したりするのは難しいと思うな。もうスマホなしでは生活できないよ。

設問訳 選択肢訳

(1) サラの発言の要点は何か。

① タブレットは電話よりも便利だ。

② 電話に関する学校の規則は厳しすぎた。

③ 電話を持っていない時は不満だった。

④ 最近まで，日常生活にスマートフォンは必要だと思わなかった。

(2) ケンタの発言の要点は何か。

① 人々は若すぎるうちに電話を手に入れていると考えている。

② 若者はさまざまな理由で電話が必要だと感じている。

③ 電話は若者が買うには高すぎる。

④ 若者は電話で遊ぶ時間が多すぎる。

(1) サラは3番目の発言で，スマートフォンはそれほど必要ではなかったと言っている。その理由として，学校には持っていけなかったこと，家ではタブレットを使っていたこと，通学時に緊急の電話をする必要性がなかったことなどを挙げている。④が正解。サラの3番目の発言に，タブレットを家で使っていたとあるが，電話との便利さの比較はしていないので①は不正解。学校の規則についての不満は述べていない。また電話がない時も不便を感じていなかった様子なので②，③も不正解。

(2) ケンタは3番目の発言で，電話がないと困る場合を2つ挙げている。また最後の発言では友だちと連絡をとることや，快適な生活をするのに不可欠だと述べ，スマホなしでは生活できないとまで言っている。②が正解。電話を手に入れる年齢が早すぎるどうかは話題にしていないので①は不正解。料金の高さについては話しているが，それは母の不満でありケンタ自身は料金に対する意見は述べていない。またスマホで遊ぶ時間についても話題になっていないから③，④も不正解。

Part B (1) ③ (2) ③

🔊 サンドラは教授の発言に強く反対しているため，disagree, time, place, neither, that time などが強く長めに発音される。リズムと強弱に気をつけて聞いてみよう。

スクリプト	和訳
Moderator: We're discussing technology in schools today. I have with me	司会：本日は学校でのテクノロジーについて討論しています。シティ大学のカーマイケル

Professor Carmichael from City University, along with two school principals, John and Sandra. Now Professor Carmichael, you feel young people should have access to more technology, but when should this start?

Professor Carmichael: Well, as young as possible really. Look, the next generation of adults will be living in a world of artificial intelligence and advanced technology. There is evidence that children in kindergarten can benefit from using tablets or computers, as long as the software is at the right level for them.

Sandra: I'm sorry, but I completely disagree. There is a time and place for technology, and neither kindergarten nor elementary school are that time. Children are surrounded by many electronic devices when they are at home. At our school, we feel that children learn more by using a pencil and making calculations on paper, not on a screen.

Professor Carmichael: Please don't get me wrong. I also believe there is a time and place for writing with a pencil or learning numbers with a pen and paper. I just think that you can achieve both.

John: Our school began introducing tablets to children from six years old, and I have to say, it has been

---

教授，学校の校長先生であるジョンとサンドラのお2人にお越しいただいています。さて，カーマイケル教授，あなたは若い人たちはもっとテクノロジーを利用するべきだとお考えですが，これはいつ始めるべきでしょうか。

教授：そうですね，実際早いほどいいでしょう。ご覧ください。次世代の大人は人工知能や先進技術の世界で生きることになります。幼稚園の子どもたちが，自分たちのレベルに合ったソフトを使用していれば，タブレットやコンピューターを使用することで恩恵を受けるという証拠があります。

サンドラ：すみませんが，私はまったく反対です。テクノロジーには適した時と場所があり，幼稚園も小学校もその時ではありません。子どもたちは家にいる時は多くの電子機器に囲まれています。私たちの学校では，画面上ではなく，鉛筆を使ったり紙の上で計算したりすることによって，より多くのことを学んでいると感じています。

教授：誤解しないでください。私も鉛筆で書いたりペンと紙で計算したりするべき時と場所があることは信じています。ただ，2つは両立すると考えています。

ジョン：私たちの学校では，6歳からタブレットを導入し始めています。それは素晴らしい第一歩だと言わざるをえません。子供た

音声

a great step. Children can move through many tasks using the software, access a variety of music and movies and interact with people around the world.

Moderator: But, don't you think, as Sandra said, students get too much technology already at home. I have two young boys and I don't think I would like to see them using computers until they are teenagers, really.

John: As long as the teacher is careful and chooses the correct software, and also monitors the class carefully, I think technology is a tool we should use.

ちはソフトウェアを使って多くの課題を進め、さまざまな音楽や動画にアクセスし、世界中の人々と交流することができます。

司会：でも、サンドラが言ったように、生徒たちはすでに家で多量のテクノロジーにさらされていると思いませんか。私には2人の小さい息子がいますが、彼らがティーンエイジャーになるまでコンピューターを使うところを本当に見たくありません。

ジョン：教員が気を配り、適切なソフトウェアを選び、クラスを注意深く見守っている限り、テクノロジーは私たちが使うべき道具だと私は思います。

選択肢訳

(1)

① 司会者と教授
② 教授とジョン
③ 司会者とサンドラ
④ ジョンとサンドラ

(2)

グラフ

① 2歳までに子どもが使用するテクノロジー
   子どもの割合
   機器（左から）ノートパソコン，スマートフォン，デジタルカメラ，携帯型テレビゲーム
② スマートフォンでのSNSなどにかける時間
③ 教室での無線テクノロジー
   私たちには本当にそれは必要でしょうか？
   教師の4人に3人は…アプリは教育に有益だと言っています
   生徒の86%はタブレットはより効果的に学習するのに役立つと言っています
④ 教室内テクノロジーの問題点
   1. 変化のペース
   2. 費用
   3. 社会動学
   4. 注意散漫
   5. 目的

Lesson 17

(1) 教授は最初の発言で，テクノロジーの利用を始める時期を問われて，as young as possible（できるだけ早く）と答えているから，低年齢のテクノロジー利用に関して肯定的である。それに対しサンドラはまったく反対だと意見を述べており，幼稚園や小学校はテクノロジーを使う時と場所ではないと主張しているから，低年齢でのテクノロジーには否定的。ジョンは自分の学校では6歳からタブレットを導入していることを紹介し，配慮の上で使わせるべきだと主張しているから肯定的。司会者は2番目の発言で自分の子どもの例を挙げ，teenagers になるまでコンピューターを使わせたくないと言っているから否定的な立場である。以上より低年齢でのコンピューターを利用した教育に否定的なのは，司会者とサンドラである。したがって正解は③。

(2) 教授は低年齢のうちから教育にテクノロジーを利用するべきだという立場である。グラフ①は2歳までのデバイスごとの利用割合，②はスマートフォンでの SNS などの利用時間のグラフだから，教授の主張とは関係がない。④は教室でのテクノロジー利用の問題点を挙げている図なので，これも教授の主張とは異なっている。③は教室でテクノロジーを利用することに肯定的な教員や生徒が多いことを示す図だからこれが正解。

注
◇ artificial intelligence「人工知能」
◇ evidence「証拠；根拠」
◇ calculation「計算」
◇ get O wrong「O を誤解する；取り違える」
◇ monitor「～を監視する；チェックする」

4

解答例

(1) This sounds like a good idea, if it is just one or two hours. However, the school should link the volunteer work to other academic activities. Also, students shouldn't be forced to do volunteer work. There should be another activity for students who don't want to volunteer〔do volunteer work〕.

(2) No, I don't agree with this. It's true that more Japanese people need better English skills, but we shouldn't force people to learn. This idea would also cost too much money.

(3) I think it is important for Japan to have more foreign workers because we don't have enough young people to take all the jobs. However, people who come to Japan should receive good training on how to understand Japanese language and culture.

(4) I think this is very important. We can vote from eighteen now, but many people do not. If young people do not vote, their voices will not be heard.

解説

(1)

スクリプト	和訳
Do you think schools should introduce time for students to do volunteer work during the week?	学校は生徒がボランティア活動をする時間を平日の授業時間に取り入れるべきだと思いますか。

解答例

This sounds like a good idea, if it is just one or two hours. However, the school should link the volunteer work to other academic activities. Also, students shouldn't be forced to do volunteer work. There should be another activity for students who don't want to volunteer〔do volunteer work〕.

解答例の和訳

ほんの1，2時間ならいい考えだと思います。けれども，学校はボランティア活動を他の学術的活動と関連付けるべきです。さらに生徒はボランティア活動を強制されるべきではありません。ボランティアをしたくない生徒には別の活動を用意するべきです。

賛成か反対かの立場を明らかにし，その理由を述べる。平日の授業時間に行うことによる利点や問題点に対する考えなども付け加えるとよい。解答例1文目の if ～は条件付きで賛成の場合などに便利な表現。

(2)

スクリプト	和訳
Is it a good idea for Japan to have English as an official language, as well as Japanese?	日本が，日本語の他に英語を公用語とすることはよい考えですか。

解答例

No, I don't agree with this. It's true that more Japanese people need better English skills, but we shouldn't force people to learn. This idea would also cost too much money.

解答例の和訳

いいえ，私はこれには賛成ではありません。より多くの日本人がより優れた英語の技能を必要としていることは確かですが，学ぶことを強いるべきではありません。それに，この考えは費用がかかりすぎるでしょう。

official language「公用語」は公の場での使用が定められている言語。英語が公用語になると，公的な情報を発信する場合には英語も使わなければいけないことになる。賛成か反対かをまず述べ，その根拠を述べる。英語が公用語になった場合に起こりうることについてメリットやデメリットを挙げてもよい。

Lesson 17

107

注

◇ official language「公用語」　*cf.* common language「共通語」, second language「第二言語」

(3)

スクリプト	和訳
Should Japan allow more foreign people to work here?	日本はより多くの外国人が日本で働くことを認めるべきでしょうか。

解答例

I think it is important for Japan to have more foreign workers because we don't have enough young people to take all the jobs. However, people who come to Japan should receive good training on how to understand Japanese language and culture.

解答例の和訳

すべての仕事をまかなうだけの若者がいないので，日本は外国人労働者を増やすことが大切だと思います。けれども日本へ来る人々は日本語や日本文化を理解する方法についての訓練を十分に受けるべきです。

日本の現状（労働力が不足している職種がある等）を踏まえて賛成・反対を述べよう。解答例の enough 〜 to ...は「…するのに十分な〜」を表す。反対の場合は，現状の問題を他にどのような方法で解決するべきかにもふれておきたい。

(4)

スクリプト	和訳
Is it important for young people under 20 to vote in elections?	20 歳未満の若者が選挙で投票することは大切ですか。

解答例

I think this is very important. We can vote from eighteen now, but many people do not. If young people do not vote, their voices will not be heard.

解答例の和訳

これはとても大切だと思います。私たちは今では 18 歳から投票できますが，多くの人は投票しません。若者が投票しなければ，若者の声は聞いてもらえません。

若者に関わる制度の変更などは，問題として取り上げられることが少なくない。日ごろから自分の意見を英語で言えるよう考えておこう。なお，「20 歳以上」は 20 and over と言う。単に over 20 と言うと，20 歳を含まずそれ以上の年齢を指す。

5

解答例

The woman is unhappy about the new student center because she preferred the old system. The university seems to have four departments and each one had a small student center. She thought that the small centers were all different and unique. She also thought it was good to have a variety of student centers. She doesn't think the new CSC will have the same character and she wants some of the old student centers to stay open.

解説

英文訳

大学が学生向けのサービス棟について変更しようとしています。100秒間で，変更に関する注意書きを読んでください。

10月1日　新学生センター オープン

多くの皆さんがご存知のように，大学は昨年，新しい中央学生センター（CSC）に取り組み始めました。長年の間，我々は大学に「ハブ（拠点）」が欠けていると感じてきました。新しいセンターは最新テクノロジーを売りにしており，学生の皆さんの活発なキャンパスライフのまさに中心になることを強く望んでいます。

CSCは10月1日にオープン予定で，現在学科棟に配置されている4つの小センターに取って代わることになります。これらのうちの2つ，言語学科と経済学科の小センターはすでに閉鎖されています。科学学科と図書館の小センターは夏休みのあともCSCのグランドオープンまでそのまま利用できます。それ以降は4つの小センターは学生センターとしての役割を終え，主に会議室と展示センターとして使われます。

皆さんがCSCを楽しんでくださいますように。そして我々はシティ大学発展の新しいステージを楽しみにしています。

学生サービス部長　Gグラント

スクリプト	和訳
Now listen to two students discussing the notice:	では，この注意書きについて2人の学生が話し合うのを聞きなさい。
M : It's a pity the small centers are closing, but the new CSC sounds exciting.	男性：小センターの閉鎖は残念だけど，新しいCSCはおもしろそうだね。

W : I'm not so sure. Most universities have big student centers, but I always thought our department centers were great. They were a unique part of college life.

M : But, they really weren't that modern. And two of them were really small.

W : It's true, but each of them was different. That was a key point of studying at this university: <u>different centers that can be used by different departments.</u> It was great to have variety.

M : Well the CSC has four floors and three cafés. I'm sure each one is different.

W : Do you think so? I hear that the menu of each café is quite different from original ones. There won't be the same character. <u>The unique character of our university will be lost!</u> I think they should keep the old ones open.

M : You know, sometimes they were empty. They weren't that popular because they were kind of old. If we kept them open, I don't think many people would go.

W : Well then, <u>at least they could keep one or two open</u>. They could use them for parties or large study groups. I hope that we will be able to reserve them sometimes.

M : If they use them as meeting rooms, as it says here, maybe that is possible.

W : Don't get me wrong, I don't

女性：私にはよくわからないわ。ほとんどの大学が大きな学生センターを持っているけれど，私は学科のセンターが素晴らしいといつも思っていたから。大学生活の独特の部分だったわ。

男性：でも小センターはあまり現代的じゃないよ。それに2つのセンターは本当に小さかったし。

女性：そのとおりだけど，それぞれが違ったでしょう。それがこの大学で勉強する重要な点だったのよ。それぞれの学科で異なるセンターが利用できることが。多様性があるのがよかったのに。

男性：CSCは4階建てで3つのカフェがあるよ。それぞれが違っていると思うよ。

女性：そう思う？ それぞれのカフェのメニューはかなり元のメニューとは違うって聞いたけど。以前と同じ特徴はないでしょう。私たちの大学の独自性は失われるわ。古いセンターも開けておくべきだと思うな。

男性：ほら，ときどきあそこはがらがらだったよ。古い感じだからそんなに人気がなかったよ。開けておいても大勢は行かないと思うよ。

女性：じゃあそれなら，少なくとも1つか2つは開けておけないかな。パーティーや大きな学習会に使えるわ。ときどきそこを予約できるといいな。

男性：もしそこを会議室として使うなら，ここに書いてあるとおり，それは可能じゃないかな。

女性：誤解しないで。私は新しい中央棟に反対

disagree with the new central building. I just wish we could keep our smaller centers, too.

しているわけじゃないの。私たちの小センターも残しておいてほしいだけ。

Give yourself 30 seconds to prepare your response to the following question. Then speak for 60 seconds.

次の質問に答えるための準備時間が30秒間あります。次に答えを60秒間で話してください。

The woman is unhappy about the new student center. Explain her opinion and the reasons she has for holding this opinion.

女性は新しい学生センターに不満を持っています。彼女の意見とそのような意見を持った理由を説明しなさい。

解答例

The woman is unhappy about the new student center because she preferred the old system. The university seems to have four departments and each one had a small student center. She thought that the small centers were all different and unique. She also thought it was good to have a variety of student centers. She doesn't think the new CSC will have the same character and she wants some of the old student centers to stay open.

解答例の和訳

女性は古いシステムの方が好きだったので新しい学生センターに不満を持っています。この大学には4つの学科があるようで，それぞれに小さな学生センターがありました。彼女は小センターはどれもそれぞれ異なり独自性があると思っていました。多様な学生センターがあることはいいとも考えていました。新しいCSCに同じ特徴はないと考え，古い学生センターのいくつかはそのまま開いていてほしいと望んでいます。

大学の掲示は，新しい学生センターがオープンする予定で，それまであった学科ごとの4つの小さな学生センターの機能をそこに移すというもの。女性は2番目，3番目の発言で，小センターのよい点として，それぞれの学科で異なりバラエティがあること，それが自分たちの大学の独自性であることを挙げている。最後に古いセンターの利用法を提案し，小センターの一部は残してほしいと希望を述べている。

注
◇ cease「やめる；中止する」
◇ function as ～「(～の) 機能を果たす」
◇ pity「残念なこと」

Lesson 17

Lesson 18
まとめの問題2

問題冊子 p.116／
音声はこちらから➡

1

答え
(1)② (2)② (3)③ (4)①

解説

スクリプト	和訳
W: Welcome back, Tomoki. How did you enjoy your year in Australia?	女性：おかえりなさい，トモキ。オーストラリアでの1年はどうだった？
M: Oh, hi, Emma. It was great! Thank you for <u>sending me emails</u>, it helped me when I got a little homesick. I hope you got my postcards.	男性：やあ，エマ。素晴らしかったよ！ メールを送ってくれてありがとう。少しホームシックだった時に助けになったよ。僕の絵はがきが届いているといいんだけど。
W: Yes, I loved the pictures of the beach.	女性：ええ，海岸の写真が気に入ったわ。
M: I was staying near the beach, so I could go there every day. I loved swimming in the sea and even <u>tried surfing</u>, but I wasn't so good at it.	男性：僕は海岸の近くに滞在したんだ。だから毎日海岸へ行くことができたよ。海で泳ぐのが大好きで，サーフィンもやってみたけどそれはあまり得意じゃなかった。
W: And how about your studies? Was it difficult to study in a different country?	女性：勉強の方はどう？ 違う国で勉強するのは難しかった？
M: It helped that the year-abroad program was arranged between the two universities. When I went there, an Australian student came to my university in Japan. So, there was a lot of support. <u>My tutor met me twice a week</u> and they also arranged accommodation for me.	男性：年間留学プログラムが2つの大学間で準備されていたのが役立ったよ。僕が向こうに行った時，オーストラリアの学生が日本の僕の大学に来たんだ。だからたくさんのサポートがあったよ。僕の指導員は週2回僕と会ってくれて，大学では宿泊施設も手配してくれたよ。
W: Was it in a university dormitory?	女性：それは大学の寮？
M: No, it was <u>in a shared house with four other people</u>. I made two	男性：いや，別の4人といっしょのシェアハウスだったよ。デンマークとタイ出身の親

great friends from Denmark and Thailand. It was a very international university. W: Well it all sounds fantastic.	友ができたよ。とても国際的な大学だったんだ。 女性：まあ，何もかも素敵そう。

設問訳 選択肢訳

(1) エマはトモキに（　　　）を送った。

① はがき
② メール
③ 絵

(2) トモキは自由時間に（　　　）。

① 水泳を習った
② サーフィンに挑戦した
③ 海岸の写真を撮った

(3) オーストラリアにいる間，トモキは（　　　）。

① 外国の学生のサポートをした
② あるオーストラリア人が日本に行くのを手伝った
③ 指導員と毎週話をした

(4) トモキは（　　　）滞在した。

① 5人用の家に
② 国際的な寮に
③ 別の2人と国際的な家に

(1) トモキは1番目の発言で「メールを送ってくれてありがとう」と言っているから，送ったものはメール（②）。
(2) 自由時間にしたことは，トモキの2番目の発言から surfing。②が正解。「海で泳ぐのが大好き」と言っているが，水泳を習ったとは言っていない。エマの2番目の発言にある「海岸の写真」はその前のトモキの発言から「絵はがき」のものであるとわかるので，トモキが写真を撮ったわけではない。
(3) トモキの3番目の発言の最後で「指導員と週に2回会った」とあるから，毎週会っていたことになる。③が正解。学生のサポートや，オーストラリアの学生が日本へ来たのは大学間で準備されたサービスによるもので，トモキがしたことではない。
(4) トモキの最後の発言で「別の4人といっしょのシェアハウス」に滞在したと言っている。本人も合わせてそのシェアハウスには5人が住んだことになるから①が正解。大学の寮についてはエマが質問した時に否定している。デンマーク人とタイ人の2人が話題に出てくるが，この2人は親友になった人物。同室の4人のうちの2人と考えられる。

Lesson 18

2

解説

◀╏ her のように h で始まる人称代名詞は，h の音が脱落することがある。put her は「プター」のように聞こえる。

スクリプト

Last week we moved house. We began packing about two weeks before the move. On the day of the move, some men came to put our things into the truck. They took the larger furniture first, then the boxes. When the last box was in the truck, the house felt very empty. My father was driving us to the new house when I found that I had forgotten Becky. Becky is a bear that I have had since I was three years old. She is very precious to me. I asked my father to turn around and go back. He wasn't very happy, but we went back to the house and I searched all over. It was no good. I couldn't find her anywhere. Maybe she was lost. When we arrived at the new house, all the furniture and boxes were in the house. I looked through some of my boxes, but I still could not find Becky. Then I heard my mother calling me. She was in the kitchen and opening a box of cakes and cookies. There at the top of the box was Becky. I remembered that I had put her down when I ate a cookie the night before. She must have fallen into the box.

和訳

先週，私たちは引っ越しました。引っ越しの2週間ほど前から荷造りを始めました。引っ越しの日は，数名が荷物をトラックに積みに来ました。彼らはまず大きな家具を，それから箱を持って行きました。最後の箱がトラックに運ばれた時，家はとても空っぽな感じがしました。私がベッキーを忘れてきたことに気づいたのは，父の運転で新しい家に向かっている時でした。ベッキーは私が3歳の頃から持っているクマです。私にとってとても大切なものです。私は父にUターンして戻ってほしいと頼みました。父はしぶしぶながら戻ってくれ，私はあちこち探しました。残念なことにベッキーはどこにも見つけることができませんでした。きっと迷子になったのでしょう。新しい家に着いた時，すべての家具と箱が家の中にありました。自分の荷物の箱をいくつか見ましたが，まだベッキーを見つけることはできませんでした。その時母が私を呼ぶのが聞こえました。母はキッチンにいてケーキやクッキーが入った箱を開けていました。その箱のいちばん上にベッキーがいたのです。私は前の晩，クッキーを食べた時にベッキーを置いたことを思い出しました。ベッキーは箱の中に落ちたに違いありません。

引っ越しのエピソードが語られるので，話題が出てきた順にイラストを選んでいく。「引っ越しの日，家からトラックに荷物を運ぶ（②）」→（車で新しい家へ向かう途中，ベッキー（クマ）のことを思い出す）→「元の家に戻ってほしいと父に頼む（①）」→「元の家でベッキーを探す（④）」→（見つからない）（新しい家で自分の持ち物の中にも見当たらない）→（母に呼ばれる）→「クッキーが入った箱の上部にベッキーを発見する（③）」という順である。②→①→④→③が正解。

注
◇ precious「大切な；希少価値のある」

3

答え
(1)③　　(2)④　　(3)①　　(4)③　　(5)②

解説

🔊 get used to ～（～に慣れる）の used [juːst] は動詞 use の過去形 [juːzd] と異なり s の音は濁らないので注意。また used の d と次の t がつながり［ユースタ］のように聞こえる。さらに，get の t が脱落して get used to が［ゲッユースタ］となることもある。

スクリプト	和訳
Listen to this conversation between a student and the university accommodation office. Answer the questions below.	学生と学生寮事務室との会話を聞き，以下の質問に答えなさい。
M: Good morning. How can I help you today?	男性：おはようございます。今日はどのようなご用件ですか。
W: Good morning. I joined the university from overseas last week. I wanted to ask about my university accommodation.	女性：おはようございます。私は先週，外国から大学へ編入しました。大学寮についてお聞きしたいのですが。
M: Sure. Can I just have your name and accommodation details?	男性：わかりました。お名前と寮の詳細を教えてくれますか。
W: Of course. Here's my student ID. I'm staying in Langbrook Hall, room 201.	女性：はい。私の学生番号はこれです。ランブルック寮の 201 号室にいます。
M: Just a moment.... Okay, here you	男性：少々お待ちください。はい，確認できま

are. So, what can I do for you?

W: Well, to be honest, I was wondering if you had any other rooms available. The room itself is fine, quite comfortable in fact. But, it is located just over the main entrance and next to the student social area.

M: It's quite a convenient location, but I guess you are worried about the noise.

W: It's just a little difficult to get used to. People are coming into the building all day and there are sometimes parties or discos in the evening. I can study in the library, but it is difficult to sleep at night.

M: I'm sorry to hear that. We are quite tightly booked at the moment and I guess that room was the only one available. Just let me have a quick look through the system.

W: Thanks.

M: Okay. Actually, there are two rooms open at the moment. One is a double room in the same building, but on the other side. There is also a single room in Wentworth Hall.

W: A double?

M: Yes. Actually, there is nobody else there right now, but we can't make a guarantee that this won't change. The single has more space than the room you have now, so it comes out at an extra $20 per week.

W: I'm not really sure about sharing a room.... I guess I can pay the extra, so could you tell me the procedure?

M: You'd better check the room out first, just to make sure you like it. I'll

した。それでご用件は？

女性：ええ，正直なところ他に空いている部屋があるだろうかと思っているのです。部屋そのものはよくて実際とても快適なのですが，部屋の位置が中央玄関の真上で，学生の交流スペースの横なんです。

男性：とても便利な場所ですが，騒音が気になるのですね。

女性：慣れるのは少し難しいです。人々が建物に一日中入ってきますし，晩はパーティやディスコがあることもあります。図書館で勉強することはできますが，夜寝るのが大変です。

男性：それはお気の毒です。現在部屋がかなり埋まっているので，その部屋が唯一空いていた部屋だったのだと思います。すぐにシステムをチェックしますので，お待ちください。

女性：ありがとう。

男性：さて。実は現在，部屋は2つ空いています。1つは同じ建物ですが，反対側にある2人部屋です。ウェントワース寮に1人部屋もあります。

女性：2人部屋？

男性：ええ。実は，今現在は他に誰もそこにはいませんが，その状況が変わらないと保証することはできません。1人部屋の方は，今あなたがいる部屋よりも広いので，週に20ドル余分にかかります。

女性：部屋をシェアする自信はあまりありません。追加のお金は払えると思うので，手続きを教えてくれますか。

男性：まずはそこを気に入るかどうか確かめるために部屋を見る方がいいでしょう。先

call ahead and let the security at Wentworth know you are coming, and they'll show you around. I'll give you the form to take with you, and if you are happy with it, just fill in your personal details on this form, including your reasons for the request.

W: Thank you. When can I move in?

M: If you are okay with the room, I think it should be ready in a couple of days..., certainly by Friday.

W: Okay, well thank you for your understanding. Can I head over there now?

M: Sure! I'll call as soon as you go. I hope it works out.

に電話をしてウェントワースの警備にあなたが行くことを知らせておきますから，案内してくれるでしょう。持って行く書類をお渡しします。もし気に入ったらこの書類に，要望についての理由も含めてあなたのことを記入してください。

女性：ありがとうございます。いつ引っ越すことができますか。

男性：その部屋でよければ，2，3日中には…，金曜日までには確実に準備ができるはずだと思います。

女性：わかりました。ご理解いただきありがとうございます。今からそこへ向かってもいいですか。

男性：もちろんです。すぐに電話をします。うまくいくといいですね。

設問訳 選択肢訳

(1) 学生はなぜこの事務室に来ていますか。

① 彼女は大学で部屋を借りたいと思っている。
② 彼女は手付金を払う必要がある。
③ 彼女は部屋を変更したい。
④ 彼女はいくら払えばいいかわからない。

(2) 学生が経験している主な問題は何か。

① 夕方に勉強できない。
② 図書館でよい本を見つけることができない。
③ 図書館が部屋から少し遠い。
④ 夜，うるさすぎる。

(3) 現在の状況に対して事務室はどんな理由を挙げているか。

① 入居可能な部屋があまりなかった。
② その部屋は多くの設備の近くにある。
③ その部屋は便利で行きやすい。
④ 大学内で最も安い部屋だった。

Lesson 18

⑷ 事務室は 2 人部屋について何をほのめかしているか。

　①1 人部屋よりも安い。

　②現在別の学生もその部屋に滞在している。

　③部屋は空いているが，他の人がいつでも加わる可能性がある。

　④2 人部屋だが，他の誰もその部屋は使わないだろう。

⑸ その学生が最も選択しそうなものはどれか。

　①同じ建物の 2 人部屋を選ぶ。

　②別の建物の 1 人部屋を選ぶ。

　③現在のより安い部屋にとどまる。

　④他の安い部屋が空くまで待つ。

⑴　学生は 3 番目の発言で，any other rooms available（使用可能な別の部屋）があるかどうかをたずねている。その後，現在の部屋の環境に不満を述べているから，部屋を変更したいのだと判断できる。③が正解。すでに部屋を借りているので①は不正解。手付金や支払うべき金額についての言及はない。

⑵　現在の部屋に対する主な問題点が問われている。学生は 3 番目の発言で部屋の場所が玄関の真上で交流の場所に近いことを挙げ，4 番目の発言では騒音で夜は眠るのが難しいと訴えている。夜にうるさいのが問題なので④が正解。勉強は図書館でできると言っているので①は正しくない。よい本についてや図書館までの距離についてはふれていないので②，③も不正解。

⑶　事務員は 5 番目の発言内で，I guess that room was the only one available（その部屋が唯一の空き部屋だったのだと思う）と述べている。これは「入居可能な部屋があまりなかった」という①と一致する。便利な場所だと言ってはいるが，設備への近さや部屋への行きやすさ，その部屋が一番安いことが，女性が入居することになった理由だとは述べていないので②〜④は不正解。

⑷　学生の A double? という発言のあとに 2 人部屋の説明がある。現在は他の人はその部屋にいないこと，でもその状況が変わらないという保証はないと言っている。つまり，あとから他の人が加わる可能性もあるということである。③が正解。2 人部屋の部屋代については出てこないので①は不正解。

⑸　2 人部屋の説明のあと，もう 1 つの入居可能な部屋である 1 人部屋の説明がある。その部屋は現在の部屋より週に 20 ドル余分にかかる。学生は 2 人部屋は自信がなく，追加のお金を払う方，つまり 1 人部屋を選んでいる。1 人部屋は現在住んでいるランブルック寮ではなくウェントワース寮にあるから，②の内容と一致する。

注
◇ accommodation「宿泊施設」
◇ get used to 〜「〜に慣れる」※ to の後ろは名詞
◇ guarantee「確約；保証」
◇ come out at 〜「（費用が）〜になる」
◇ procedure「手続き；手順」

118

4

解答例

(1) They are at the park. The father and mother are watching the boy and the girl playing. The boy is pushing the girl on the swing and the girl is laughing.

(2) This is a train station. A train is coming up to the platform. Several people are waiting to get on the train.

(3) One of the men is standing and holding a cup of coffee. The other man is drinking his coffee at a table while he works on his computer.

(4) I'm very sorry. Are you okay? I didn't see you crossing the road. Shall I call an ambulance?

解説

(1)

スクリプト	和訳
How is this family spending their day?	この家族は 1 日をどのように過ごしていますか。

解答例

They are at the park. The father and mother are watching the boy and the girl playing. The boy is pushing the girl on the swing and the girl is laughing.

解答例の和訳

彼らは公園にいます。父親と母親が，男の子と女の子が遊んでいるのを見ています。男の子はブランコに乗っている女の子を押し，女の子は笑っています。

どこにいるか，何をしているか，どのような表情かなど，イラストからわかることを描写する。「ブランコに乗る」は ride on a swing。A girl is swinging. のように動詞として swing（ブランコをこぐ）を使ってもよい。

(2)

スクリプト	和訳
Look at this picture and describe what you see.	この絵を見て，見えるものを描写しなさい。

解答例

This is a train station. A train is coming up to the platform. Several people are waiting to get on the train.

解答例の和訳

これは電車の駅です。1 台の列車がホームへ来るところです。何人かの人が列車に乗るために待っています。

Lesson 18

何人かの人が列車を待っている様子なので，列車が駅に着くところだと推測できる。ホームの人々の様子などを描写してもよい。

(3)

スクリプト	和訳
Look at this picture. Describe the two men at the front.	この絵を見て，手前の2人の男性の様子を描写しなさい。

解答例

One of the men is standing and holding a cup of coffee. The other man is drinking his coffee at a table while he works on his computer.

解答例の和訳

男性のうちの1人は立っていて，コーヒーを持っています。もう1人の男性はコンピューターで仕事をしながらテーブルについてコーヒーを飲んでいます。

イラスト内にはさまざまな情報があるが，手前の2人の男性についてのみ描写する。2人のうちの1人は one，もう1人は the other で表せる。1人ずつの描写のほかに，They seem to know each other.（2人は知り合いのようだ）など，2人の関係性を説明してもよい。

(4)

スクリプト	和訳
Look at this picture. What do you think the driver might say?	この絵を見なさい。運転手は何を言うと思いますか。

解答例

I'm very sorry. Are you okay? I didn't see you crossing the road. Shall I call an ambulance?

解答例の和訳

すみません。大丈夫ですか。あなたが道を渡るのが見えませんでした。救急車を呼びましょうか。

本問はイラストの描写ではなく，運転手のセリフとして考えられるものを答える。手前の人物は車のせいでけがをしたと考えられるので，謝罪の言葉，相手の無事を確認する言葉，その後の対応の提案などが考えられる。

5

解答例

The lecture talks about evolution when animals are isolated on islands. According to Foster, bigger animals and even humans have become smaller when they are found on islands, and he called this type of evolution "island dwarfism". This is probably because

there is less food on islands and smaller animals need less food, so they can survive to pass their genes on to the next generation.　On the other hand, Foster also proposed another type of evolution called island gigantism, where smaller animals often become bigger.　This is because there are fewer predators on islands.
　One problem with island giants occurred when humans came to islands.　Many large animals were killed by humans or their animals and many have disappeared.

解説
英文訳

進化についての記事を読みなさい。では，始めてください。
制限時間：100 秒間

　進化について語る時，環境の変化は体の大きさといった側面において重要な役割を果たすことがあります。進化は多くの異なる方法で起こりますが，体の大きさという一面だけを見ることではっきりと思い浮かべたり想像したりすることがたやすくなります。
　一般的な一例は，島嶼部に住む動物の体の大きさです。島嶼部で少数の個体群が，多数派の本土の個体群から孤立します。これは少数の動物が何とか島へ飛ぶか泳ぐかした時に起こることがあります。けれども，鳥ではない動物や虫にとっては海面の上昇によって土地が切り離される時により一般的に起こります。
　これが起きると体の大きさは 2 つの方法で変化することがあります。これは科学者の J. ブリストル・フォスターが 1964 年にこの発見を説明してから，フォスターの法則と呼ばれています。
　フォスターは 116 種類の動物を比較しました。彼は島嶼矮化を発見しました。それは島のいくつかの動物は本土の動物よりも小さく進化するというものです。反対に，いくつかの動物が本土の同類の動物よりも大きくなると，フォスターは島嶼巨大化という名称を使いました。

スクリプト

Now listen to part of a lecture on evolutionary theory.

　Today I'd like to take a look at the theories which describe Foster's rule of island dwarfism and gigantism. The most commonly documented evolutionary change on an island is dwarfism.　This tends to occur with

和訳

では，進化論の講義の一部を聞きなさい。

　今日は島嶼矮化と島嶼巨大化のフォスターの法則を説明する理論を見ていきたいと思います。最も一般的に立証されている島における進化的変化は矮化です。これは大型の動物に起こる傾向にあり，恐竜から象の仲間まで，また島に住む初期の人類でも，多くのさまざまな集団

larger animals and has been found in many different groups, from dinosaurs to species of elephants and even island groups of early humans. The strongest theory for why large animal species evolve to become smaller concerns the smaller amount of food available on islands. Basically, smaller animals require less food and are therefore less likely to die from lack of food, meaning the genes for these smaller individuals are passed on to the next generation.

On the other hand, Foster's rule also describes a process called island gigantism. It is often more difficult for larger, carnivorous animals to reach islands, meaning that small animal species find themselves in a situation where there are few predators. Examples of island gigantism include the dodo, which evolved from a pigeon sized bird, up to the giant birds in New Zealand which were taller than a man. Many larger island species died out shortly after the arrival of humans to the islands. This is thought to be either because they were hunted directly by humans, or more commonly, were killed by predators brought along with the humans, such as dogs, cats and rats.

Give yourself 30 seconds to prepare your response to the following question. Then speak for 60 seconds.

Describe the process of island dwarfism and gigantism and the incidents that happened to many island giants.

で見られてきました。なぜ大型の動物が小さく進化するのかの最も説得力のある理論は，島で手に入れられる食料の少なさに関係があります。基本的に小型の動物は少ない食料で済み，したがって食料不足で死ぬ可能性が低くなります。このことはこれらのより小さい個体の遺伝子が次の世代に受け継がれるということを意味します。

一方，フォスターの法則では島嶼巨大化と呼ばれる過程も説明しています。大型で肉食の動物が島へ到達することは難しいことが多く，つまり小型の動物は気づいてみると，自分の天敵が少ない状況にいるということです。島嶼巨大化の例にはドードーが含まれています。ドードーは鳩くらいの大きさの鳥から進化し，ニュージーランドで人よりも背が高い大型の鳥になりました。多くの大型の島の種は，人間がその島へ来るとすぐに死に絶えました。これは人間によって直接狩猟されたか，もしくはより一般的には犬や猫，ねずみなど人間が持ち込んだ天敵によって殺されたかのどちらかのせいだと考えられています。

次の質問に答えるための準備時間が30秒間あります。次に答えを60秒間で話してください。

島嶼矮化と島嶼巨大化の過程と，多くの島の巨大動物に起こった出来事について説明しなさい。

解答例

The lecture talks about evolution when animals are isolated on islands. According to Foster, bigger animals and even humans have become smaller when they are found on islands, and he called this type of evolution "island dwarfism". This is probably because there is less food on islands and smaller animals need less food, so they can survive to pass their genes on to the next generation. On the other hand, Foster also proposed another type of evolution called island gigantism, where smaller animals often become bigger. This is because there are fewer predators on islands.

One problem with island giants occurred when humans came to islands. Many large animals were killed by humans or their animals and many have disappeared.

解答例の和訳

　講義では，動物が島に孤立した時の進化について述べています。フォスターによると，大きな動物，さらに人類も島で発見される時は小さくなっており，彼はこの手の進化を「島嶼矮化」と呼びました。これはおそらく，島には食料が少なく，小さい動物の方が少ない食料で済むので，生き残って次の世代に遺伝子を渡せたのが理由です。反対にフォスターは島嶼巨大化と呼ばれる別のタイプの進化，小さな動物がしばしば大きくなるという進化も提唱しました。これは島には天敵が少ないためです。

　島で巨大化した動物の問題は，人間が島へやってきた時に起こりました。多くの大型動物が人間や人間が飼っている動物に殺され，多くが姿を消しています。

island dwarfism（島嶼矮化）や island gigantism（島嶼巨大化）という専門用語を英語で（日本語でも）事前に知っていた人は少ないかもしれない。なじみのない語にうろたえず，読解の記事から新しい知識として用語とその内容を読み取れるかがポイント。読解記事では体の大きさという点から進化を見た時，島では体が小さくなるという進化（島嶼矮化）と，反対に体が大きくなる進化（島嶼巨大化）という２つのタイプがあるということを押さえておく。

　リスニングの講義では，２つの進化がそれぞれどのような動物に起こるかと，その理由として考えられることが説明されている。

注
◇ evolution「進化」
◇ visualize「～を思い浮かべる；視覚化する」
◇ isolate「～を孤立させる；分離する」
◇ dwarfism「矮化」　cf. dwarf「（童話などの）小人；（同種の普通サイズより）小型の動植物」
◇ gene「遺伝子」
◇ carnivorous「肉食性の」
◇ predator「捕食動物」

Lesson 18

Lesson 19
まとめの問題 3

問題冊子 p.120／
音声はこちらから➡

1

答え
(1)② (2)① (3)③ (4)④

解説
(1)②

スクリプト	和訳
M: Which of these laptops looks good to you? The white one is the cheapest. The blue one is the second cheapest.	男性：これらのノートパソコンのどれが君によさそうかな。白いのが一番安いよ。青いのは次に安い。
W: But they're heavier than the others, aren't they?	女性：でもそれらは他のパソコンよりも重いでしょう？
M: How about the red one? It's the lightest, but most expensive. <u>The silver one</u> seems to be in the middle, but <u>has the biggest memory</u>.	男性：赤いのはどう？ それが一番軽いけど一番値段は高いよ。銀色のはその間だけどメモリーは一番大きいね。
W: The red one is fine, but <u>memory is more important</u>.	女性：赤いのもいいけど，メモリーの方が重要よ。

設問訳 選択肢訳
女性はどのコンピューターを買う可能性が高いか。

① 白いノートパソコン。
② 銀色のノートパソコン。
③ 赤いノートパソコン。
④ 青いノートパソコン。

女性の最後の発言から，彼女は価格や重さよりもメモリーの大きさが重要だと考えていることがわかる。その前の男性の発言から，メモリーが最も大きいのは the silver one だから正解は②。

(2) ①

スクリプト	和訳
W: The Grand Hotel looks lovely. It has a pool and is near the beach. It's good for our holiday!	女性：グランドホテルがよさそうね。プールもあるし海岸にも近いし。私たちの休暇にぴったりよ。
M: It's not cheap, though. Look. The Hotel Superior is cheaper.	男性：でも安くはないね。見て。ホテルスーペリアの方が安いよ。
W: It's cheaper than the Grand, but doesn't have a pool. Or how about the Beachside Hotel or the Star Inn? They are near the beach, though they have no pool. Some of their rooms have a kitchen.	女性：グランドホテルより安いけどプールがないわ。ビーチサイドホテルかスターインはどう？ どちらもプールはないけど，海岸に近いよ。キッチン付きの部屋があるわよ。
M: Uh, I don't want to cook on holiday, anyway. I'd like to enjoy swimming in the pool even if it costs more.	男性：うーん，でも休日まで料理はしたくないな。たとえもっとお金がかかってもプールで泳ぐことを楽しみたいな。

設問訳 選択肢訳

最終的に男性は休暇にどこを提案しているか。

① グランドホテル。
② ホテルスーペリア。
③ ビーチサイドホテル。
④ スターイン。

最後の発言から，男性は値段が高くてもプールがあるホテルを希望していることがわかる。男性は初めの発言では「グランドホテルは安くない」と言い，ホテルスーペリアを提案しているが，最終的には値段よりもプールがあることを優先している。正解はプールがあるグランドホテル（①）。

(3) ③

🔊 order と「オーダー」，pizza と「ピザ」の発音の違いに注意。

スクリプト	和訳
W: I'm really looking forward to the new comedy at the movie theater today. And let's have dinner at that new restaurant.	女性：今日，映画館で見る新しいコメディが本当に楽しみだわ。そしてあの新しいレストランで夕食を食べましょう。
M: It might be hard to get a reservation today. How about calling some	男性：今日予約を取るのは難しいかもしれないよ。友だちを呼んで僕の家でピザを注文

friends and ordering pizza at my house?	するのはどう？
W: I think everyone will already have plans. If you don't want to go out for dinner, we could just order pizza.	女性：みんなもう予定があると思うよ。夕食を外で食べたくないのなら，ピザを頼むだけにしましょう。
M: Oh, sorry I promised we'd go out tonight. Let me call and see if they have a table.	男性：あ，ごめん，今晩は出かけようって僕は約束したんだったね。レストランに席があるか電話して確認してみるよ。

設問訳 選択肢訳

男性は何をしようとするか。

① 友人に電話する。
② 映画のチケットを予約する。
③ レストランの予約をする。
④ ピザを注文する。

> 夕食に関して女性と男性が交互に提案をし合っている。最終的には男性がレストランに席があるか電話をして確かめると言っているから正解は③。〈Let me ＋動詞の原形〉は「私に…させてほしい」と許可を取る表現だが，「自分が…しよう」と相手に提案する場合にも使われる。

(4) ④

スクリプト	和訳
M: Let's put the Christmas tree at the entrance this year. People will see it when they come to the door.	男性：今年はクリスマスツリーを玄関に置こう。誰かが玄関口へ来た時にツリーが見えるよ。
W: It might look nice, but the kids will want it in the living room. We need to put presents around it, remember.	女性：いいかもしれないわね。でも子供たちはリビングにツリーが欲しいと思うわ。私たちはツリーの周りにプレゼントを置く必要があるってことを忘れないで。
M: Okay, but not next to the TV again. Oh! How about getting another tree?	男性：わかった。でもまたテレビの横に置くのはやめよう。あ，もう１つ買うのはどう？
W: Let's just put one at the entrance, but get another small one for the living room, by the window.	女性：１つは玄関に置いて，リビング用に小さいのを買って窓辺に置きましょう。

設問訳 選択肢訳

彼らは何をしようとするか。

① クリスマスツリーを窓辺から移動させる。

② テレビの横にクリスマスツリーを置く。

③ クリスマスツリーをテレビから離して部屋の隅に置く。

④ 今年はツリーを2つ置く。

男性が2番目の発言で，クリスマスツリーをもう1つ買おうと提案している。女性はそれを受けて，今あるクリスマスツリーを玄関に置き，小さなツリーを買って窓辺に置こうと提案している。つまりツリーは2つになるから④が正解。

2

答え

(1) soccer　　(2) left, right　　(3) managers　　(4) concerts　　(5) gates

解説

◀€ カタカナ語は英語との発音の違いに注意。area「エリア」, manager「マネージャー」, lounge「ラウンジ」, gate「ゲート」など。

スクリプト	和訳
Welcome to the National Stadium tour. As you know, an international soccer game will be played here tomorrow, so you will see our staff preparing for that. We are now coming through the players' entrance and into the reception area. Most people never see the players until they run out onto the pitch, but they spend most of their time down here. This is the home team changing room on the left, with the visiting team's changing area on the right. Team managers and coaching staff use this lounge area and the room at the back is reserved for the TV and sound equipment. As you know, the stadium hosts several large concerts each year, as well as soccer games, so we need a lot of space for sound and lighting. Now, step this way. Imagine the cheers as you step through these famous gates and out onto the pitch.	ナショナル・スタジアムのツアーにようこそ。ご存知のように明日，ここでサッカーの国際試合が行われますので，スタッフがその準備をしているところをご覧いただきます。私たちは今，選手の入場口を通り抜け，受付に入ってきたところです。ほとんどの人は選手がピッチに走り出してくるまで選手を見ることはありませんが，選手たちはほとんどの時間を下のここで過ごします。こちら，左が地元チームの更衣室で，右が相手チームの更衣室です。チームのマネージャーとコーチがこのラウンジを使い，後ろの部屋はテレビと音響機器のために用意された部屋です。ご存知のようにこのスタジアムではサッカーの試合だけでなく，毎年何度か大きなコンサートも開催されます。ですから音響と照明のためにも広い場所が必要なのです。さて，こちらへどうぞ。この有名なゲートを通ってピッチへ出ていく時の歓声を想像してください。

Lesson 19

127

ナショナル・スタジアム・ツアーについて女性が話すのを聞いて，(1)〜(5) の空所を埋めて完成させなさい。

(1) 明日：国際的（　　　）の試合

(2) 更衣室：地元チーム（　　　）側，相手チーム（　　　）側

(3) ラウンジエリアはチームの（　　　）とコーチが使用する。

(4) スタジアムで行われるイベント：サッカーの試合と（　　　）

(5) 競技場への入り口：有名な（　　　）

スクリプトの下線部を参照のこと。

❸

解答

| Part A | (1)③ (2) a)① b)③ c)① d)③ e)② f)④ (3)③ |
| Part B | ① |

解説

Part A (1)③ (2) a)① b)③ c)① d)③ e)② f)④ (3)③

◀ 非制限用法の関係代名詞節の前にはコンマが置かれ，読む時には少し間を置くことが多い。この時関係代名詞節は先行詞に補足的な説明を加えているので，地の文よりも少し低い声で付け足すように読まれる。

スクリプト

Moore's first law, most commonly known just as Moore's law, was a theory created in 1965 by American Engineer Gordon Moore. The law talks about transistors, which are tiny switches in the circuits of certain electronic devices. It predicts that the number of transistors in a circuit should double every two years. What this means is that electronic chips, which contain transistors, should continue to shrink in size. It is easy to see that this has been the case when we look at the size of computers, or even simple calculators from the 1960s and 1970s. In fact, boosted by breakthroughs

和訳

単にムーアの法則として最も広く知られているムーアの第1法則は，1965年にアメリカのエンジニア，ゴードン・ムーアによって作り出された理論です。その法則はトランジスタに関するもので，トランジスタとは，電子機器の回路内の小さなスイッチです。その法則は，1つの回路内のトランジスタ数が2年ごとに2倍になると予測しています。これが意味していることは，電子チップは，これはトランジスタを含みますが，小さくなり続けるということです。1960年代，1970年代のコンピューターや単純な電卓の大きさを見れば，これが本当であることは容易にわかります。実際，科学や電子工学の飛躍的進歩にあと押しされ，ムーアの法則は2012年ごろまで通用し，回路内のトランジ

in science and electronics, <u>Moore's law held up until around 2012</u> and described not only the doubling of the number of transistors in a circuit, but also the number of pixels in digital cameras and the reduction in the cost of computer processors.

Moore's second law, also made in the 1960s and sometimes known as Rock's law, is a little different. Whereas <u>the first law predicts a decreasing of the cost of computer processors every two years,</u> <u>the second law predicts the cost of building a factory to produce new chips and processors will double every four years.</u>

As stated, Moore's law started to come apart after around 2012 as transistors got smaller and smaller. If it had continued in the same manner, transistors themselves would have gotten smaller than actual atoms by 2025. It seems that these two laws will clash at some time, <u>slowing the increase in processor speed as production costs rise too high.</u> At this point in time, a new form of technology will be needed if we hope to see ever-increasing computer speeds in the future.

スタの数が2倍になることだけでなく，デジタルカメラのピクセル数やコンピューター・プロセッサにかかる費用の減少についても説明していました。

ムーアの第2法則も1960年代に作られ，これは時にロックの法則としても知られており，第1法則とは少し異なります。第1法則がコンピューター・プロセッサの費用が2年ごとに減少することを予測していたのに対し，第2法則は新しいチップやプロセッサを生産する工場の建設費が4年ごとに倍になると予測しています。

すでに述べたように，ムーアの法則はトランジスタがますます小さくなるにつれ，2012年ごろから行き詰まり始めています。もし法則どおり続いていれば，トランジスタそのものは2025年までに実際の原子よりも小さくなることになっていました。これら2つの法則はいずれ対立し，生産コストが上がり過ぎていくにつれて，プロセッサの速度の上昇がゆっくりになるでしょう。この時点で，我々が将来，コンピューターの処理速度をさらに上げることを望むのなら，新しい技術の形が必要とされます。

選択肢訳

(1) ① 10　　② 35　　③ 47　　④ 60

(2) ① ムーアの第1法則　　② ムーアの第2法則
　　③ 2年　　　　　　　　④ 4年

(3) ① ムーアの2つの法則は1960年代以来，同じ速度で進歩してきている。
　　② 近い将来，原子より小さいトランジスタの生産が可能になるに違いない。
　　③ 将来プロセッサの速度が上がるペースは落ちることになるだろう。
　　④ デジタルカメラのピクセル数は4年ごとに2倍になるだろう。

○ワークシート

ムーアの第1法則：始まり（　　　）年　］　約 （A） 年間有効だった
　　　　　　　　　　終わり（　　　）年　］

	①ムーアの第1法則 ②第2法則		③2年 ④4年
単体のプロセッサ費用	a)	〜ごとに減る	b)
チップごとのトランジスタの数	c)	〜ごとに2倍になる	d)
プロセッサ/チップ工場の費用	e)		f)

(1)　第1段落冒頭に，ムーアの第1法則は「1965年に作られた理論」とある。また，第1段落最終文に「ムーアの法則は2012年ごろまで通用した」とある。2012 − 1965 = 47 だから，③が正解である。

(2)　単体のプロセッサ費用については第2段落第2文の第1法則と第2法則の比較の中で述べられている。コンピューター・プロセッサの費用の減少を予測しているのは「第1法則（①）」で，「2年ごと（③）」である。また，同文によると，工場の建設費は「第2法則（②）」で，「4年ごと（④）」である。チップごとのトランジスタの数の変化については第1段落で述べている「第1法則（①）」でふれられており，第3文に1回路内のトランジスタ数は「2年ごと（③）」に2倍になると説明されている。

(3)　①第3段落初めに，ムーアの第1法則は2012年ごろから行き詰まり始めているとあるので，同じ速度で進歩してきているという記述とは矛盾する。②原子については第3段落中ほどに出てくるが，これはトランジスタを原子レベルの大きさにすることの可能性の低さとして出されている例で，近い将来原子より小さくなるとは書かれていない。③最後から2文目の slowing the increase in processor speed 以降の内容と一致する。これが正解。④デジタルカメラのピクセル数は第1段落の最後に出てくる。これは第1法則の例なので倍になるのは2年ごとであり，4年ごとではない。

注
◇ circuit「（電気）回路；回線」
◇ shrink「縮む；小さくなる」
◇ boost「〜を押し上げる」
◇ hold up「持ちこたえる；（弁解などが）通用する」
◇ reduction「減少」

Part B ①

スクリプト	和訳
Pay attention to these two graphs. The first shows the growing cost for technology companies to keep up with	これら2つのグラフにご注目ください。1つ目のグラフはムーアの第1法則を維持するために技術系企業に必要な費用の増加を示していま

130

Moore's first law. The second shows the size of transistors over time. What can we conclude from a comparison of these two graphs?

す。2つ目のグラフはトランジスタの大きさを時間順に示したものです。これら2つのグラフを比較することでどんな結論が得られるでしょうか。

① 5ナノメートルより小さいナノチップは10ナノメートルのナノチップの倍以上のコストがかかる。

② ムーアの法則は2023年以降も続くと思われる。

③ 7nmの技術ノードは2020年までに生産されるだろう。

④ より小さいトランジスタを開発する時間は将来ますます長くなるだろう。

グラフA：次のレベルのチップ設計に進むためにかかる費用（100万USドル）

　　　古←集積回路の設計ノード→新

グラフB：トランジスタの大きさの予測（ナノメートル）

① グラフAから5ナノメートルの大きさのチップを開発するのには10ナノメートルの大きさのチップを開発する場合のコストの倍以上かかることがわかる。② トランジスタを小さくするスピードは行き詰まっているから，ムーアの法則は当てはまらなくなっている。③ グラフBより2021年の時点でトランジスタの大きさは10nmだから③とは矛盾する。④ グラフBよりトランジスタの大きさが小さくなる速度は2021年以降は頭打ちになることがわかる。一致しない。

4

解答例

(1) I live in Sumida. It's part of Tokyo. I've lived there for two years. It is famous for Tokyo Sky-tree.

(2) I like listening to music. I prefer classical music to rock or pop music. I also play the piano and the violin a little.

(3) 解答例1: Yes. I did a homestay in New Zealand when I was a junior high school student. I had a lot of fun there.

解答例2: No, I haven't. But I'd really like to go overseas. I like the ocean and nature so I want to visit Australia.

(4) I want to work in another country and learn about another culture. Now I speak only Japanese and English, but I'm going to learn some other languages so that I'll be able to communicate well with the local people.

(1)

スクリプト	和訳
Where do you live? Please tell me about your hometown.	あなたはどこに住んでいますか。あなたの地元について教えてください。

解答例

I live in Sumida. It's part of Tokyo. I've lived there for two years. It is famous for Tokyo Sky-tree.

解答例の和訳

わたしは墨田に住んでいます。東京にあります。そこに 2 年間住んでいます。東京スカイツリーで有名です。

問われているのは住んでいる場所。街や地域の地名を挙げるだけでなく，有名な場所の紹介など，その街の特徴なども説明する。

(2)

スクリプト	和訳
What do you do in your free time?	あなたは自由な時間に何をしますか。

解答例

I like listening to music. I prefer classical music to rock or pop music. I also play the piano and the violin a little.

解答例の和訳

わたしは音楽を聴くのが好きです。ロックやポップスよりもクラシック音楽が好きです。ピアノとバイオリンも少し演奏します。

問われているのは自由時間にすること。趣味などを答え，それをする理由なども述べるとよい。

(3)

スクリプト	和訳
Have you ever been overseas?	海外へ行ったことがありますか。

解答例 1

Yes. I did a homestay in New Zealand when I was a junior high school student. I had a lot of fun there.

解答例 2

No, I haven't. But I'd really like to go overseas. I like the ocean and nature so I want to visit Australia.

解答例 1 の和訳

はい。中学生の頃，ニュージーランドでホームステイをしました。とても楽しかったです。

解答例 2 の和訳

いいえ，行ったことはありません。けれども海外へとても行ってみたいです。海と自然が好きなのでオーストラリアを訪れたいです。

問われているのは海外へ行ったことがあるかどうか。まずは Yes か No で答える。Yes の場合はどこへ行ったか，そこでしたこと，考えたことなどを述べるとよい。No の場合は今後行きたい場所，または海外へ行かない理由などを述べるといいだろう。

(4)

◀ would you は「ウヂュー」のようにつながって聞こえる。

スクリプト	和訳
What would you most like to do in the future?	将来いちばんやりたいことは何ですか。

解答例

I want to work in another country and learn about another culture. Now I speak only Japanese and English, but I'm going to learn some other languages so that I'll be able to communicate well with the local people.

解答例の和訳

別の国で働き，別の文化について学びたいです。今は日本語と英語しか話せませんが，現地の人たちとコミュニケーションがうまくとれるように別の言語もいくつか学ぶつもりです。

質問は，would you like to ...「…したい」に most「いちばん」が挿入されている。I'd like to ... または I want to ... に続けて将来やりたいことを述べる。理由や将来のために現在やっていること，これからやろうと思っていることなどを添えるとよい。

5

解答例

The man is upset that the dance and theater groups will be using the second floor of the student center. The usual building for dance and theater groups was damaged and so they need to share the space. The man says it is already hard for his band to reserve time for the rehearsals. He suggests other places for the dance and theater rehearsals. Also, he thinks his band may need to look for another place to rehearse.

Lesson 19

大学が学生センターの使用に変更を加えようとしています。変更に関する注意書きを読んでください。制限時間は 45 秒です。

学生センター利用方法の変更について

多くの学生がすでにお気づきのように，先日のハリケーンでロビンソンビルが被害を受けました。そこにはダンススタジオとリハーサル室があります。大学では建物の修理を行わせているところですが，それには最長で 12 カ月かかるかもしれないことをご承知おきください。このため，現在音楽部やバンドの練習に使用されている学生センター 2 階の使用に制限を設ける予定です。ダンス部と演劇部の部員は土曜日と日曜日の午後 2 時から 2 階の使用が認められ，別の時間帯も予約すれば利用できます。2 階はすでに常時使用されていることは承知していますが，ロビンソンビルに必要な修理を行っている間，どうぞご理解いただけるようお願いします。

🔊 what you mean は「ワッチュミーン」のようにつながって聞こえ，you の音は非常に弱い。

スクリプト	和訳
Now listen to two students discussing the notice.	では，この注意書きについて 2 人の学生が話し合うのを聞きなさい。
M：Have you seen this? Totally unbelievable!	男性：これを見た？ まったく信じられないよ！
W：What is it? Just give me a second to read it.	女性：何のこと？ ちょっと読んでみるわね。
M：I mean, I heard that there was some damage to the Robinson building, but they can't just take over the student center like this. We already find it hard to book time for our band rehearsals.	男性：ロビンソンビルに被害があったってことは聞いたけど，こんなふうに学生センターを乗っとるなんてありえない。僕らのバンドの練習を予約するのは今でも大変なのに。
W：Why? How often do you rehearse?	女性：どうして？ どのくらい練習をしているの？
M：We try to book two sessions a week, but we usually only get one. If the dance club uses the second	男性：週に 2 回予約しようとしているんだけど，たいてい 1 回しか取れないよ。もしダンス部が 2 階を使うとしたら，予約がもっ

floor, it will become harder to make reservations.

W : You haven't looked at it properly, have you? The hurricane blew half the roof off. A lot of equipment got destroyed, too. It's going to take a while to fix that, and probably cost a lot, too.

M : Even so, they need to have a better plan in place. There are other places around campus which the theater students could use, surely. How about the cafeteria? It's not used except for lunch and dinner.

W : I think they need a proper studio space. The student center has sound proofing, and also lights and recording equipment. The dance groups will need that. I don't think a cafeteria would be suitable.

M : Yeah, I see what you mean. I just wish there were some way for them to balance this out better. Weekend afternoons are when everyone is free. We may need to look off campus, and that's going to cost us a lot.

Give yourself 30 seconds to prepare your response to the following question. Then speak for 60 seconds.

The man expresses his opinion regarding the university's notice. State his opinion and the reasons for the opinion.

と難しくなるだろう。

女性：あなたはこのことをきちんと見ていないんじゃない？　ハリケーンが屋根の半分を吹き飛ばしたのよ。多くの設備も壊れたでしょ。それを直すには時間がかかるだろうし費用もずいぶんかかるでしょう。

男性：そうだとしても，大学側はもっといい案をちゃんと出すべきだよ。演劇部が使えそうな場所は大学の周りの他にもきっとあるよ。カフェテリアはどうかな。あそこはランチとディナー以外には使われてないよ。

女性：彼らにはちゃんとしたスタジオが必要だと思うよ。学生センターは防音だしライトや録画設備もあるし。ダンス部にはそれが必要でしょう。カフェテリアはふさわしい場所じゃないと思うな。

男性：君の言いたいことはわかるよ。僕はただ，もっとうまくバランスをとるやり方があればなと思って。週末の午後はみんなが空いている時間なんだ。僕らは大学の外にも目を向けないといけないかもしれない。それってずいぶんお金がかかるだろうな。

次の質問に答えるための準備時間が30秒あります。次に答えを60秒間で話してください。

男性は大学の注意書きについて自分の意見を言っています。彼の意見とそのような意見を持った理由を説明しなさい。

解答例

The man is upset that the dance and theater groups will be using the second floor of the student center. The usual building for dance and theater groups was damaged and so they need to share the space. The man says it is already hard for his band to reserve time for the rehearsals. He suggests other places for the dance and theater rehearsals. Also, he thinks his band may need to look for another place to rehearse.

解答例の和訳

男性はダンス部と演劇部が大学センターの2階を使うということに気分を害しています。ダンスや演劇に普段使う建物が被害を受けたため，彼らは場所を共有する必要があります。男性は，バンドの練習の時間を予約するのは今でも大変だと言っています。彼はダンスや演劇の練習には他の場所を提案しています。また男性は自分のバンドは練習のために他の場所を探す必要があるかもしれないと考えています。

大学の掲示は，ダンス部と演劇部が使用している建物がハリケーンで被害を受けたため，代わりに学生センターの2階を使用するという内容である。それに対する男性の意見と，男性がそう考える理由が求められている。男性は大学の決定に不満を持っている。理由は彼がバンドの練習で学生センターを利用しており，今でも予約が難しいからである。大学の決定に対する彼の提案や対策として，彼はダンス部や演劇部が他の場所で練習することや，自分たちが大学外で練習することを挙げている。

注

◇ rehearsal「（劇，演奏などの）稽古，練習，リハーサル」
◇ restriction「制限；規制」
◇ currently「現在は；今のところ」
◇ sound proofing「防音」

問題冊子 p.124 ／
音声はこちらから➡

1

解答
②

解説

 sign up も clean up も n と u の音がつながって「サイナップ」，「クリナップ」の
ように発音される。

スクリプト	和訳
① Older people are often isolated and feel lonely, especially if they cannot leave their homes. Companion Club is free to sign up on a day-to-day basis to meet, chat and become friends with senior citizens in our city.	① 老人は孤立し，孤独を感じることがよくあります。家から出られない場合はなおさらです。コンパニオン・クラブでは，1日単位で自由に登録し，市内のお年寄りと出会い，おしゃべりし，友だちになることができます。
② Enjoy our city clean-up, held every Saturday morning with the Our City group. Join whenever you can to clean up a different part of the city each week. With over 100 members, you're bound to meet new people every time.	② 毎週土曜日の朝に行われている街の清掃活動を，アワー・シティーグループと一緒に楽しみましょう。毎週市内のさまざまな場所を清掃するので，いつでもご都合のいい時にご参加ください。100名以上の会員がおり，毎回，きっと新しい出会いがあるはずです。
③ Friends is a joint campus and city project, which brings children with severe learning difficulties to join games and a fun atmosphere in the university sports hall. Held every Sunday from 3 to 5, we need active, friendly people to help run the events.	③ フレンズは大学と市の共同プロジェクトです。学習に大きな困難を抱えている子供たちを大学の体育館でゲームに参加させ，楽しい雰囲気を作ります。毎週日曜日の3時から5時に行われ，イベントの運営を手伝ってくれる活動的で親しみやすい人を求めています。

④ Green Earth is a volunteer project that plants trees in and around the local area. While it is free to join, training is necessary, so we ask volunteers to sign up for three-month projects. Meet people and make friends while saving the planet!

④ グリーン・アースは地元とその周辺に木を植えるボランティアプロジェクトです。参加は自由ですが，訓練が必要なので，ボランティアの方には３カ月のプロジェクトへの登録をお願いしています。地球を救いながら，人々と出会い，友だちになりましょう！

① コンパニオン・クラブ　　　② アワー・シティー
③ フレンズ　　　　　　　　　④ グリーン・アース

	a) 柔軟性	b) 環境に配慮，自然保護	c) 友だち作り
①コンパニオン・クラブ	○１日単位	×	○ お年寄りと
②アワー・シティー	○ 都合のいい土曜日の朝	○ 清掃	○ 会員 100 名以上
③フレンズ	× 毎週日曜	×	△言及なし
④グリーン・アース	×３カ月登録	○ 植樹	○

「柔軟性」の点で条件を満たしているのは，１日ごとに参加できるコンパニオン・クラブと自分が都合のよい土曜日の朝に参加できるアワー・シティー。「環境・自然保護」の活動をしているのは，清掃活動をしているアワー・シティーと植樹を行っているグリーン・アース。両方の条件を満たしているのはアワー・シティーで，最後の条件「友だち作り」についても 100 名以上の会員がおり，毎回新しい人と出会うことができるだろうと言っている。すべての条件を満たしているので②のアワー・シティーが正解。

注
◇ sign up「（署名して）登録する；参加する」
◇ be bound to *do*「必ず…する；きっと…するはずだ」

2

解答
(1)③　　(2)②　　(3)④　　(4)①　　(5)②

解説

◀━ Pre-Socratic schools，Classical schools は初めて出てくる用語で，しかも対比されているので，明確にゆっくりと発音される。専門用語が初めて出てくる時には，or や which で始まる語句で言い換えが行われることも多く，その場合も最初に提示される用語はゆっくりめに発音される。

スクリプト

In this introduction to Western Philosophy, I'd like to begin today by discussing some of the ancient philosophers.

For the sake of keeping things simple at this stage, I would like to divide today's talk into pre-Socratic schools and classical schools, which began with Socrates in the 5th century BC.

Pre-Socratic philosophers tended to focus on metaphysics, which means they were interested in the world around them and how things existed. They looked for ways to explain nature without using the stories of gods or supernatural beings. Many of these philosophers thought about the substance or matter that the universe was made of. They first believed that everything was made up of just one kind of matter, such as fire, air or water. Another concept the pre-Socratic schools focused on was the reason for change. Why did things change from one state to another? How did fire burn or ice melt? Some thought everything around us was constantly changing, while others argued that there was no change, that everything was fixed. These arguments moved forward to create the concept of logic and basic scientific thought.

Ancient Philosophy moves on to the three most influential classical philosophers, Socrates, Plato and Aristotle in the 5th and 4th centuries BC. In this era, there was a jump from

和訳

この西洋哲学入門の授業で、今日は何人かの古代哲学者について論じることから始めたいと思います。

この段階ではわかりやすくするために、今日の話をソクラテス以前の学派と古典学派に分けたいと思います。古典学派は紀元前5世紀にソクラテスとともに始まります。

ソクラテス以前の哲学者は形而上学に重点を置きがちでした。つまり、身の回りの世界と物事がどのように存在するかに関心をもっていました。彼らは神や超自然的な存在の物語を使わずに自然を説明する方法を探しました。これらの哲学者の多くは、宇宙を構成する実体や物質について考えました。彼らはまず、万物は火や空気や水といった唯一の物質だけからできていると考えました。ソクラテス以前の学派が重点を置いたもう1つの概念は、変化の理由でした。なぜ事物は1つの状態から別の状態へ変化するのか。どのように火は燃え、氷は溶けるのか。ある者は我々の周囲の万物は常に変化し続けると考え、またある者は変化などなく、すべては不変だと主張しました。これらの議論は、論理の概念と基本的な科学的思考を生み出すことへ進んでいきました。

古代哲学は、紀元前4、5世紀の最も影響力のある3人の古典哲学者、ソクラテス、プラトン、アリストテレスへとつながります。この時代には、現在我々が科学と呼んでいる自然哲学から、人類と人類社会がどう振舞うべきかへの

natural philosophy, which we now call science, to how humans and human societies should behave.

Actually, there is no direct written record of what Socrates taught: what we know comes from the writings of his student, Plato. According to these writings, Socrates was concerned with ethics, or how people should act towards one another and know right from wrong. What we know as the Socratic Method, was a way of asking questions using logic to break down a problem into possible solutions. This method is the origin of many concepts of modern society from debate to science to teaching. For example, if you questioned a statement by asking "Why do you say that?", or "Is there another opinion?" you would be using the Socratic Method.

Plato expanded on the Ethics of Socrates to incorporate politics and the study of knowledge into philosophy. He believed that humans should use their knowledge of good and evil to work towards happiness. His most important work, written around 380 BC was a Socratic Dialogue known as "Republic". This dialogue discusses concepts of justice to describe a city-state populated by three kinds of people: producers such as farmers and craftsmen, soldiers, and rulers, and has influenced human thought and politics ever since.

The final major classical philosopher was Aristotle, whose influence on later schools of thought was probably the

飛躍がありました。

実は，ソクラテスの教えを直接書き記した記録はありません。我々が知っていることは，彼の弟子であるプラトンの著作によるものです。これらの書物によると，ソクラテスは倫理学，言い換えれば，人々はお互いにどう振舞うべきか，善悪の判断をどう知るべきか，に関心がありました。私たちがソクラテス式問答法として知っているものは，問題を解決可能なものにまでかみ砕くために，論法を用いて質問をする方法でした。この方法は，討論から科学，教育まで，現代社会の多くの概念の元となっています。例えば，「なぜあなたはそう言うのですか。」とか「別の意見はありますか。」とたずねることにより，とある発言に疑問を投げかけたとすると，それはあなたがソクラテス式問答法を使っていることになります。

プラトンは政治学と知識研究を哲学に取り入れるために，ソクラテスの倫理学について詳細に説明しました。彼は，人々は幸福を目指すために善悪の知識を使うべきだと信じていました。彼の最も重要な著作は，紀元前380年ころに書かれ，「国家」として知られているソクラテス式対話です。この対話では正義の概念を論じ，3種類の人間が住む都市国家を描写します。3種類の人間とは，農民や職人などの生産者，兵士，統治者です。それ以来，この対話は人間の思考や政治に影響を与えてきました。

古典哲学の最後の重要人物はアリストテレスです。後の学派への彼の影響はおそらくすべての古代哲学者の中で最も大きいでしょう。プラ

greatest of all the Ancient philosophers. A student of Plato, Aristotle expanded philosophy to cover a wider range of topics, such as science, metaphysics and art. One example of Aristotle's influence on the modern world comes from a form of deductive logic, whereby a conclusion, or synthesis, is reached from two other truths. This is called a syllogism and has been a central method of philosophy up to the modern period. A classic example of the syllogism can be understood in the following example.

First, a truth or premise is stated. Look at the sentence here: All mammals are warm-blooded. This is known as the major premise. A minor premise is then stated, such as the example here: All humans are mammals. Finally, we have the conclusion: All humans, therefore, are warm-blooded.

Aristotle also believed humans could work towards happiness, in a similar way to Plato, but knew that we could not always control our environments to create an ideal situation. He suggested the recipe for happiness is to find the middle way between too much and too little. This example of the middle way also extended to his thoughts on politics and has influenced political theory as a more humane concept when compared to Plato's republic.

There were a number of other important Classical Philosophers, which are covered in the handout. Please make sure to read about these before we move on to the next stage.

トンの弟子であるアリストテレスは哲学を発展させ，科学や形而上学，芸術といった広い範囲の話題を扱いました。現代へのアリストテレスの影響の一例は，演繹法の一形態が元になっています。そこでは結論，あるいは演繹的推理が，2つの異なる真実から導き出されます。これは三段論法と呼ばれ，現代にいたるまで，哲学の中心的な方法です。三段論法の古典的な例は，次のような例で理解できるでしょう。

まず，真実または前提が言明されます。この文を見てください。「すべての哺乳類は温血である。」これは大前提として知られています。次に小前提が示されます。このようなものです。「すべての人類は哺乳類である。」最後に結論に達します。「したがって，すべての人類は温血である。」

アリストテレスもプラトンと同じように，人類は幸せを目指していると信じていましたが，我々が常に理想的な状況を作り出すために環境をコントロールできるわけではないということを知っていました。彼は，幸せの秘訣は超過と不足の間の中庸を見つけることだと提案しました。この中庸の考え方の例も彼の政治への考え方まで及び，プラトンの国家論に比べてより人間的な概念として政治理論に影響を与えてきました。

他にもたくさんの重要な古典哲学者がいました。それはプリントで扱っています。次の段階に進む前に，必ずそれについて目を通しておいてください。

Lesson 20

(1) この講義の主なテーマは何か。

① 古典哲学者のソクラテス以前の哲学者よりも大きな重要性。

② アリストテレスが他の哲学者の業績からどう学びそれを発展させたか。

③ 古代期の最も重要な考えと哲学者についての概要。

④ 古代哲学者の何人かが現代社会に及ぼす影響。

(2) 教授によれば、ソクラテス以前の哲学者に関する次の文のうち正しくないものはどれか。

① 彼らは神の物語を用いずに世界を理解しようとした。

② 彼らは自然界を説明するために宗教的な信仰を用いた。

③ 初期の哲学者は、万物は 1 つの物質で作られていると考えた。

④ 彼らのうち何人かは物がどのように燃えたり氷が溶けたりするのだろうと考えた。

(3) 講義によれば、次のうちソクラテスの影響について正しい文はどれか。

① ソクラテスの仕事は物質と変化の科学に影響を与えてきた。

② 後の哲学者はソクラテスの書物を読んで知見を得た。

③ ソクラテスは善悪を区別する方法がわからなかった。

④ ソクラテス式問答法は社会が発展する助けとなった。

(4) 講義では、プラトンの「国家」は〜として説明されている。

① 3 種類の人間がいる都市の記述。

② 人間が幸せを得るための手引き。

③ 社会での人々の役割を決める方法。

④ 善対悪の説明。

(5) 教授によると、アリストテレスの幸福の考えはどのようなものか。

① アリストテレスは、人々は真実に基づく結論に達する必要があると示した。

② アリストテレスは、人々は中庸の道を探す努力をするべきだと認識した。

③ プラトンは 3 種類の人間しかいないと考えた。

④ アリストテレスは、人々は幸せになるために環境を変えなければならないと知っていた。

長く専門的な内容なので、集中力が必要。あらかじめ問いに目を通し、聞き取るべきポイントをチェックしてから取り組もう。

(1) 講義冒頭では the ancient philosophers（古代哲学者）について論じると言っており、続いてソクラテス以前の哲学者、そしてソクラテス、プラトン、アリストテレスを順に解説している。古代哲学と哲学者について全体の流れを追っているから、③の outline（概要）が適している。ソクラテス以前の哲学者と古典哲学者を比較してどちらが重要かということは述べていないから①は不正解。②、④の内容は講義の一部でふれているが、全体を通した主なテーマではない。

(2) 教授の講義の内容と一致しないものを選ぶ問題。第 3 段落に注目する。①は第 2 文の「神の物語を使わずに自然を説明する方法を探した」と一致する。同じ文の最後にある「超自然的な存在」は宗教に通じるものであり、それも使わずに自然界を説明しようとしていたのだから、②はこれとは一致しない。第 4 文に彼らが「万物は唯一の物質だけからできてい

ると考えた」とあり，これは③と一致する。第6～7文にある「どのように火は燃え，氷は溶けたのか。」という問題は，ソクラテス以前の学派が考察した内容であり，④は講義の内容と一致する。以上より教授の講義と照らし合わせて正しくないのは②である。

(3)　第5段落第4文の This method は Socratic Method（ソクラテス式問答法）を指しており，これが現代社会の多くの概念の元となっていると説明している。これは④に通じる。①の物質と変化についての考察はソクラテス以前の哲学者が考えたこと。第5段落初めにソクラテスが直接書いた書物はないとあるので②も不正解。第5段落第2文で，ソクラテスはどのように人々が善悪を知るかに関心があったとあるが，善悪を理解していなかったという説明はないので③も不正解。

(4)　プラトンの Republic（国家）については，第6段落で説明されている。「この対話では正義の概念を話し合い，3種類の人間が住む都市国家を描写」とあるから，①が講義の内容と一致する。第6段落第2文に「人々は幸福を目指すために善悪の知識を使うべきだ」というプラトンの考えが示されているが，これは「国家」の説明ではないので，②，④は不正解。③の内容も触れられていない。

(5)　アリストテレスの幸福の考え方は第7～9段落で扱われており，第9段落第2文で「幸せの秘訣は超過と不足の間の中庸を見つけること」と提案しているから②が正解。①，③は幸福についての考えとは関係がない。④について，講義では「環境をコントロールできるわけではないと知っていた」とあるので不正解。ちなみに，プラトンは幸福を目指すためには善悪の知識を使うべきだと考えていた。

注
◇ philosophy「哲学」
◇ metaphysics「形而上学」
◇ substance「物質」
◇ influential「大きな影響を及ぼす」
◇ ethics「倫理学」
◇ incorporate A into B「A を B に組み入れる；合体させる」
◇ justice「正義」
◇ deductive logic「演繹法」
◇ synthesis「演繹的推理」
◇ syllogism「三段論法」
◇ premise「前提；根拠」

3

解答例
(1) A) What kind of book do you like to read?（SF ／空想科学小説）
　　 B) Which book do you think has influenced you the most?（猿の惑星）
　　 C) What book would you like to read next?（もっと多くの古典的な本）
(2) A) What do you usually do on your day off?（家族と過ごす）
　　 B) What time do you usually begin and finish work?（9時に始めて6時に終える）
　　 C) What do you usually eat for lunch when you are at work?（弁当を持ってくる）

Lesson 20

(3) A) Do you remember the first electronic device you used?（両親が買ってくれた携帯電話）

B) What kinds of device do you use most often in your life?（スマートフォン）

C) What do you think are the worst aspects of using technology?（仕事から離れるのが難しいこと）

(4) A) How long have you been working in your current job?（（編集の仕事を）10年）

B) What kind of work would you choose?（現在の〔編集の〕仕事）

C) What is the most enjoyable aspect of your current job?（まったく新しい本を企画すること）

解説

(1) A) What kind of book do you like to read?（SF／空想科学小説）

B) Which book do you think has influenced you the most?（猿の惑星）

C) What book would you like to read next?（もっと多くの古典的な本）

スクリプト	和訳
M: Hello, may I ask you some questions?	男性：こんにちは，いくつか質問をしてもいいですか。
W: Sure.	女性：もちろん。
M: What kind of book do you like to read?	男性：どんな種類の本を読むのが好きですか。
W: I love science fiction. It's exciting to imagine what our life would be like with robots and other new kinds of technology in the future.	女性：SF が好きです。未来にロボットや他の新技術で私たちの生活がどのようになるか，想像するのはわくわくします。
M: Which book do you think has influenced you the most?	男性：あなたに最も影響を与えたのはどの本だと思いますか。
W: It's "Planet of the Apes". I saw the movie first and then read the original. The story is so suggestive and it's hard to believe it was written before I was born.	女性：『猿の惑星』です。映画を最初に見て，それから原作を読みました。話がとても示唆的で，私が生まれる前に書かれたなんて信じがたいです。
M: What book would you like to read next?	男性：次に読みたいのはどの本ですか。
W: I haven't decided yet, but as "Planet of the Apes" was impressive, I want to read many more classics.	女性：まだ決めていないですが，『猿の惑星』が素晴らしかったので，もっとたくさん古典的なものを読みたいと思っています。

(2) A) What do you usually do on your day off?（家族と過ごす）

　　B) What time do you usually begin and finish work?（9時に始めて6時に終える）

　　C) What do you usually eat for lunch when you are at work?（弁当を持ってくる）

スクリプト	和訳
M: Hello, may I ask you some questions?	男性：こんにちは, いくつか質問をしてもいいですか。
W: Sure.	女性：もちろん。
M: <u>What do you usually do on your day off?</u>	男性：休みの日はいつも何をしますか。
W: I usually spend time with my family. When it's sunny, I take my children to a park and play catch with them.	女性：いつも家族と過ごします。晴れていれば, 子どもを公園に連れて行き, 一緒にキャッチボールをします。
M: <u>What time do you usually begin and finish work?</u>	男性：いつも何時に仕事を始め, 何時に仕事を終えますか。
W: I usually work from nine to six, but I leave a bit earlier on Thursdays to take my kids to English school.	女性：いつも9時から6時まで働きますが, 毎週木曜日は少し早く帰って, 英会話スクールに子どもを連れて行きます。
M: <u>What do you usually eat for lunch when you are at work?</u>	男性：仕事をしている時, いつもお昼に何を食べますか。
W: I usually bring lunch, but sometimes buy chocolate for dessert at the shop across from the station.	女性：いつもはお弁当を持って来ますが, ときどきデザートに駅前のお店でチョコレートを買います。

Lesson 20

(3) A) Do you remember the first electronic device you used?（両親が買ってくれた携帯電話）

B) What kinds of device do you use most often in your life?（スマートフォン）

C) What do you think are the worst aspects of using technology?（仕事から離れるのが難しいこと）

スクリプト	和訳
M: Hello, may I ask you some questions?	男性：こんにちは，いくつか質問をしてもいいですか。
W: Sure.	女性：もちろん。
M: <u>Do you remember the first electronic device you used?</u>	男性：初めて使った電子機器を覚えていますか。
W: I remember clearly the day my parents finally bought me a cell phone when I was a junior high school student. I'd been wanting to get one for a long time because many of my friends already had one in elementary school.	女性：私が中学生の時に，両親がついに携帯電話を買ってくれた時のことを，私ははっきりと覚えています。私の友だちの多くは小学校ですでに携帯電話を持っていたので，私は長い間，携帯電話が欲しいと思っていたのです。
M: <u>What kind of device do you use most often in your life?</u>	男性：あなたの生活で最もよく使う種類の電子機器は何ですか。
W: I use the smartphone most. I used to use computers a lot, but now I mainly use the smartphone even at work.	女性：スマートフォンを最もよく使います。コンピューターをよく使っていましたが，今は仕事でも主にスマートフォンを使います。
M: <u>What do you think are the worst aspects of using technology?</u>	男性：テクノロジーを使うことについて最もよくない側面は何だと思いますか。
W: I feel it's becoming more and more difficult to get away from work. I can see emails from the customers at home, and sometimes I write them back from home when it seems urgent.	女性：仕事から離れる時間を持つのがより難しくなって来ていると感じます。家でもお客様からのメールを見ることができ，緊急に見えるものについてはときどき家から返信しています。

A) first experience of technology（テクノロジーの最初の経験）は first electronic device you used（あなたが使った最初の電子機器）と言い換えてたずねることができる。

B) regularly＝「定期的に；頻繁に」。普段使うデバイスをたずねる。インタビューでは use most often と言っている。

C) negative（否定的な）だから，テクノロジーの悪い面についての相手の見解をたずねる。more and more difficult と言ってよくない面について述べている。

146

(4) A) How long have you been working in your current job? ((編集の仕事を) 10 年)

B) What kind of work would you choose? (現在の〔編集の〕仕事)

C) What is the most enjoyable aspect of your current job? (まったく新しい本を企画すること)

スクリプト	和訳
M: Hello, may I ask you some questions?	男性：こんにちは，いくつか質問をしてもいいですか。
W: Sure.	女性：もちろん。
M: How long have you been working in your current job?	男性：今の仕事をしてどのくらいですか。
W: I've been working as an editor for about ten years.	女性：編集の仕事を 10 年くらいしています。
M: If you could apply for any job, what kind of work would you choose?	男性：もしどんな仕事にでも応募できるとしたら，どんな仕事を選びますか。
W: I would rather stay in my current position. I really love my work here.	女性：むしろ現在の仕事にとどまるでしょう。本当に今のこの仕事が大好きなのです。
M: What is the most enjoyable aspect of your current job?	男性：あなたの今の仕事で最も楽しい側面は何ですか。
W: I love it most when we're planning a brand-new book. It requires a lot of time and effort, but it's so exciting to create something new.	女性：最も好きなのは，まったく新しい本を企画している時です。たくさんの時間と手間がかかりますが，何か新しいものを作り出すことはとてもわくわくします。

A) the time のあとが現在完了だから，勤務時間ではなく，現在の仕事を始めてから今までの働いている期間を問う。current「現在の」を使えるとよい。

B) would like は want の丁寧な表現。stay in my current position とあるので，「編集の仕事にとどまること」と答える。

C) インタビューでは the best thing を the most enjoyable aspect で表している。答えでは brand-new という語を用いている。

4

解答例

The Great Schism of 1054 happened between the Eastern and Western Christian Churches. Although the whole of the Roman Empire had become Christian, the empire was split into East and West in 395 AD. These sides spoke different languages and had different rulers, so differences also appeared in the churches. There were problems over land, belief and who was in charge, and so in 1054, after much tension, the Great Schism happened and the Christian Church split.

Lesson 20

歴史とキリスト教についての文章を読みなさい。では，始めてください。
制限時間：100秒間

　キリスト教の歴史の中で最も重要な出来事の1つは1054年の大分裂です。分裂は，ある人々の集団が意見や信条の違いのせいで2つの集団に分かれる時に起こります。大分裂はキリスト教会を西ヨーロッパのローマカトリック教会と，主に東ヨーロッパ，ギリシャ，ロシアの東方正教会に分け，そのため，東西分裂としても知られています。

　分裂の起源はその何世紀も前のローマ帝国の成長と拡大にありました。そのように巨大な帝国を管理するために，紀元245年にローマ帝国はローマを中心とした西ローマ帝国と，現在はトルコにありイスタンブールとして知られるビザンティウムを中心とした東ローマ帝国または名をビザンツ帝国に分けられました。

　キリスト教は紀元4世紀にコンスタンティヌス大帝のもと，ローマ帝国の全体で採用されました。けれども，395年にローマ帝国は支配者，つまり皇帝が2人になりました。片方はローマにいて，そこではほとんどの人がラテン語を話し，もう片方はビザンティウム（当時はコンスタンティノープルと呼ばれていた）にいて，そこではギリシャ語が主要な言語でした。これは2つの地域に緊張が起こる状況を作ることとなり，何世紀も後に大分裂へと結びつきました。

スクリプト	和訳
Now listen to part of a history lecture.	では，歴史の講義の一部を聞きなさい。
Last week we covered the events that led up to the split in the Roman Empire between east and west. As you can imagine, this split between land, emperors and languages created differences and misunderstandings in the Christian church as well. As these tensions continued, the Christian beliefs in the two areas also began to differ.	先週，私たちはローマ帝国が東西に分かれることにつながった出来事を扱いました。ご想像どおり，この，土地と皇帝と言語の分裂は，キリスト教会にも意見の相違と不和を生み出しました。これらの緊張が続くにつれて，2つの地域のキリスト教信仰も違うものになり始めました。
Possibly the major difference was that the Western Church changed the text of an important statement of belief. This statement was given by the church during church services and the Eastern	おそらく主な違いは西方教会が重要な信条の文言を書き換えたことでしょう。この信条は礼拝の間に教会から与えられるもので，東方教会は新しい西方教会の信条の言葉に反対しました。

Church disagreed with the words of the new Western statement.

In addition to disagreements over what they believed, there were also political tensions. Both churches claimed the Balkan area of Europe was their territory, and so disagreed about their boundaries.

信じるものが異なっている上に，政治的な緊張もありました。どちらの教会もヨーロッパのバルカン地域は自分たちの領土だと主張し，双方の境界についての意見が一致しませんでした。

Finally, the Western Church felt that their leader, the Pope, who was based in Rome, should be leader of the whole Christian Church. The Eastern Church disagreed and felt the leader of their church in Constantinople was equal to the Pope.

最終的には，西方教会は自分たちの長でありローマを拠点とするローマ教皇がキリスト教会全体の長となるべきだと考えました。東方教会は反対し，コンスタンティノープルにある彼らの教会の長はローマ教皇に匹敵すると考えました。

This disagreement reached a peak in 1054 when the Eastern Church refused the demands of the Western Church and the schism became official.

この不一致が 1054 年にピークに達したのは，東方教会が西方教会の要求を拒否した時で，分裂が公のものとなりました。

Communication did continue between the churches, but they were more or less separate organizations, a situation which continues to this day.

教会間で連絡を取り合うことは続きましたが，彼らはほとんど別の組織で，その状況は現在も続いています。

Give yourself 30 seconds to prepare your response to the following question. Then speak for 60 seconds.

次の質問に答えるための準備時間が 30 秒間あります。次に 60 秒間で話しなさい。

Explain the background history and possible reasons for the Great Schism of 1054 between the Eastern and Western Christian churches.

1054 年の東西キリスト教会の大分裂の背景となる歴史と，原因として考えられるものを説明しなさい。

The Great Schism of 1054 happened between the Eastern and Western Christian Churches. Although the whole of the Roman Empire had become Christian, the empire was split into East and West in 395 AD. These sides spoke different languages and had different rulers, so differences also appeared in the churches. There were problems over land, belief and who was in charge, and so in 1054, after much tension, the Great Schism happened and the Christian Church split.

解答例の和訳

1054 年の大分裂は東西のキリスト教会の間で起こりました。ローマ帝国全体はキリスト教徒になっていましたが，帝国は紀元 395 年に東西に分けられました。東西は異なる言語を話し，異なる支配者がいたので，教会にも隔たりが現れました。土地，信仰，誰が治めるかの問題があり，多くの緊張が続いたあと 1054 年に大分裂が起こり，キリスト教会は分裂しました。

大分裂が起こるまでの歴史的な背景と，なぜ大分裂に至ったかという原因を説明する。1054 年に大分裂が起こる以前に，ローマ帝国が東西に分かれたこと，それぞれ言語や支配者が異なり，政治的な緊張も続いていたことなどを取り上げる。the Great Schism（大分裂），Christian church（キリスト教会），the Roman Empire（ローマ帝国）などの用語は，読解資料の中に出てくるのでスピーキングにも利用しよう。

注

◇ split into「～に分裂する」
◇ expansion「拡大」
◇ dominant「支配的な；有力な」
◇ set the scene for ～「～が起こる状況を作る」
◇ tension「緊張，緊迫状態」
◇ territory「領土」
◇ boundary「境界」